DIFFERENT
WHITE PEOPLE

DIFFERENT WHITE PEOPLE

RADICAL ACTIVISM FOR ABORIGINAL RIGHTS 1946–1972

DEBORAH WILSON

UWAP
UWA PUBLISHING

First published in 2015 by
UWA Publishing
Crawley, Western Australia 6009
www.uwap.uwa.edu.au

THE UNIVERSITY OF
WESTERN
AUSTRALIA

National Library of Australia Cataloguing-in-Publication entry
Wilson, Deborah M., author.
Different white people: radical activism for Aboriginal rights 1946–1972 / Deborah Wilson.
ISBN: 978 1 742586 65 6 (paperback)
Aboriginal Australians—Legal status, laws, etc.
Aboriginal Australians—Civil rights—History.
323.119915

Typeset in Bembo by Lasertype
Printed by Lightning Source

For my children Sarah and Brandon
and in memory of Bob Wilson

FOREWORD

Different White People is an important addition to the literature on
the enduring fight for Aboriginal rights. But it also adds to the wider
national story of political activism and the role of left wing unions
and the Communist Party in particular. This is an aspect of Australian
politics which has largely been forgotten and which sharply distinguishes
the years during and after the Second World War from the succeeding
period leading up to the end of the twentieth century. So significant
and distinctive was the politics of this era that Deborah Wilson's account
provides an essential component for a coherent understanding of the
troubled history of relations between indigenous and settler Australians.
And that story runs through the experience of every generation since 1788.

There have been different white people from the start, and they can
be found in every generation and in all parts of the continent. They
were distinguished by their adoption of racial attitudes which often
varied widely from common views of their contemporaries. They
were often more sympathetic towards the Aborigines and were, as
a result, sometime critics of the whole colonial project. Their often
outspoken advocacy did not win friends and they were shunned and
abused. But they could not be ignored. There was too much to trouble
even the toughest conscience. Violence along the frontiers of settlement
accompanied Australian life for 140 years. Aboriginal despair and
deprivation was all too apparent and enduring.

The different white people were often loners and eccentrics, but they usually drew inspiration from quite respectable intellectual traditions and from currents of opinion prominent overseas and particularly in Britain. Religion was the most common source of dissent. Christian missionaries from the great European mission societies played prominent roles in all the colonies establishing institutions and providing succour as well as the promise of salvation. Christian doctrine was important because it contained the message of racial equality and the belief that all of humankind was of one blood and, all alike, capable of salvation. During the nineteenth century the friends of the Aborigines, as they were often known, drew strength from what they saw as the central tradition of the English common law, which suggested that all the subjects of the Crown should be considered as equal regardless of racial difference. Britain too became the leading opponent of global slavery after the Empire-wide abolition of the institution in 1833. To many colonial dissidents, the Aborigines were treated in ways indistinguishable from slavery.

But for all the earnest advocacy of the different white people, the dispossession of the tribes proceeded without a pause. Frontier violence continued into the first third of the twentieth century and the colonial, and state, governments established systems of control and protection which removed all legal rights from Aboriginal communities. But new generations of dissidents emerged, drawing inspiration as their forebears had done from Christianity. And new ideas were added to the mix. The League of Nations introduced the idea of trusteeship and took strong stands against slavery and forced labour. But the greatest force for change came from the development of human rights during the years between the two world wars, culminating in the establishment of the United Nations in 1945 and the drafting of the Universal Declaration of Human Rights in 1948. Running parallel with these developments was the sudden surge in decolonisation in the 1940s and 1950s. These were all developments which inevitably influenced Australian attitudes and policies and provided inspiration for the new generation of activists. The total collapse after 1945 of the idea of racial difference and hierarchy (following the revelation of the Holocaust) forced a complete transformation of Australian thinking long premised on ideas of Aboriginal inferiority and primitiveness.

Much of the activism so well related by Deborah Wilson came from the left of the political stage. By the early twentieth century there were assorted socialist clubs and societies, members of which challenged contemporary ideas about race and Aboriginality. But the most powerful new force came from the men and women inspired by Marxism with its message of liberation from Imperial domination and, above all, by the way in which it overturned the prevailing ideas about race and hierarchy. Whereas racial doctrine pictured the world as divided vertically and hierarchically by race, Marxists saw the great divisions as horizontal; distinguishing class from class. Oppression and domination arose not from biology but from politics and economics, and therefore open to challenge and change.

It was not surprising, then, that Australian communists took up the Aboriginal cause in the 1920s and 1930s, and even more effectively in the 1940s while the party retained some of the authority and prestige gained as a result of the great and victorious alliance between the Soviet Union and the Western Powers. And this is the story which fills the colourful, dramatic pages of *Different White People*. It will bring back an almost forgotten era for older Australians, and introduce younger readers to a time of dynamic political development which makes contemporary politics look dull and conformist. For there is no doubt that Australian political life benefitted from the presence of a well-organised radical left wing party with a professional cadre dedicated to change. The Cold War dramatically affected the role and status of the Communist Party, and eventually removed it far beyond the political mainstream. The dream of a socialist Australia faded away. In that sense, the communists failed completely. But their activism for Aboriginal advancement had lasting benefits. Australia was a much better place as a result.

So this is a story of significance although it concentrates on one issue during a single generation. But the central theme remains highly relevant today. Australians still give earnest attention to the question of reconciliation, and we are currently engaged in a national debate about the constitutional recognition of Aborigines and Torres Strait Islanders. Most of the activists in this engaging study have passed away or have retired from active political engagement, but their legacy lives on. They have found in Deborah Wilson a judicious and worthy chronicler of their crusade.

Henry Reynolds
June 2015.

CONTENTS

CONTENTS

NORTHERN TERRITORY Wave Hill Walk-Off:

ACKNOWLEDGEMENTS

The research for this book was completed while I was a PhD candidate at the University of Tasmania. Its content is drawn in large part from that thesis. Over the four years of my PhD journey, I was privileged to be supervised by Professor Henry Reynolds. I express sincere appreciation to Henry. Without his support and encouragement through difficult times, this project may not have been completed. I thank Henry for being my teacher and friend.

I was most fortunate to be awarded the Alma Stackhouse Scholarship, which significantly assisted me while researching and writing. Other support by the University of Tasmania is also acknowledged. I particularly thank Dr Hamish Maxwell-Stewart for his encouragement and assistance in the production of this book. I am also grateful to Dr Tom Dunning (head of History at the University of Tasmania until his recent retirement). Tom's wise guidance, especially towards the end of my candidature, was invaluable. Assistance provided by Dr Mitchell Rolls (University of Tasmania's Aboriginal Studies program) is also appreciated.

I thank staff members in archives, libraries, organisations and institutions across Australia for their diligent assistance with any queries, requests or visits. I particularly acknowledge New Theatre's permission to allow copies of *Rocket Range* (including programs and publicity material for the play) to be sourced from the New Theatre Collection at Mitchell Library. I also thank the Australian Institute of Aboriginal and Torres Strait Islander Studies (AIATSIS) for providing me with a copy of *The Warburton Film*.

Many people have contributed their time, input and thoughts to this book. I am particularly grateful to Brian Manning, Jan Richardson, Philip Nitschke, John and Gwen Bucknall, Lenore Bassan, Mark Aarons and Max Bound for sharing their memories and personal perspectives with me. It is with sadness that I note the passing of Max Bound and Brian Manning before this publication was completed.

It is most important that the wonderful support of all at UWAP be acknowledged, particularly that given by Terri-ann White. Many thanks also to UWAP's Katie Connolly for her fastidious editing of my manuscript.

When I embarked on this project of research and writing in 2009, the most enthusiastic supporter was my father. Whilst on his annual visit from Coffs Harbour to Tasmania a year later to visit me and my kids, he became gravely ill. Emergency surgery in Launceston revealed advanced bowel cancer. Six weeks later, I took a frail but doggedly determined man back up to New South Wales. He died four months later, aged eighty-one. I hope I have done him proud. Vale Bob Wilson.

The past five years or so have been incredibly challenging in many ways. I love and thank my children Sarah and Brandon for trying to understand just how tough it has been.

I hope I have inspired them to reach for the stars.

ABBREVIATIONS

AAL	Aboriginal Advancement League
ABSCHOL	Aboriginal Scholarship Society
ACTU	Australian Council of Trade Unions
AEU	Amalgamated Engineering Union
AIATSIS	Australian Institute of Aboriginal and Torres Strait Islander Studies
AMIEU	Australasian Meat Industry Employees' Union
APC	Australian Peace Council
ASIO	Australian Security Intelligence Organisation
AWU	Australian Workers' Union
BWIU	Building Workers' Industrial Union of Australia
CAR	Council for Aboriginal Rights
CDNR	Committee for the Defence of Native Rights
CIS	Commonwealth Investigation Service
CPA	Communist Party of Australia
FCAATSI	Federal Council for the Advancement of Aborigines and Torres Strait Islanders
FMWU	Federated Miscellaneous Workers' Union

ABBREVIATIONS

ILO	International Labour Organization
MHR	Member of the House of Representatives
MLA	Member of the Legislative Assembly
NAWU	North Australian Workers' Union
NTCAR	Northern Territory Council for Aboriginal Rights
T&LC	Trades and Labor Council
UDHR	Universal Declaration of Human Rights
UN	United Nations
WILPF	Women's International League for Peace and Freedom
WRE	Weapons Research Establishment
WWF	Waterside Workers' Federation

Introduction

Between the end of World War II and the early 1970s, two emergent and distinct movements coincided as white activists fought important campaigns for Aboriginal rights. This book presents an account of that activism. Radical involvement is examined in a trilogy of case studies about significant campaigns in the Pilbara, Central Australia and the Northern Territory.

The period under scrutiny was quite exceptional in terms of Aboriginal rights advancement and radical left-wing popularity. Communist Party membership was at its highest in Australia during the 1940s and the (often communist-controlled) union movement was extremely powerful. Communists and unionists rallied to support Aboriginal people living in remote Australian regions. Stirred passions and interests inspired these 'different white people' (often from eastern seaboard cities) to action. Left-wing activists became significant contributors to the Aboriginal rights movement, supporting tribal or semi-tribal peoples with lifestyles far removed from the experience of their predominantly urban-dwelling memberships.

It is important to bear in mind that this period was also one of dramatic international advancement for human rights. As the world community recovered from World War II, emergent powers were keen to establish a new global order. Establishment of the United Nations (UN) epitomised this desire to eliminate possibilities of wars between countries, and to create a platform for dialogue between member states. The pursuit of human rights led to creation of general documents, particularly the Universal Declaration of Human Rights (UDHR). With graphic understanding of the Holocaust came total discrediting of any racial thinking at UN level and thus, absolute rejection of racism. It was also at this pivotal time that the process of decolonisation accelerated at remarkable speed, as numerous countries (for example, India, Ceylon and the Philippines) gained their independence from colonial rule. International policies needed to accommodate this changing environment, and the rights of indigenous populations became a matter of global importance.

This book evolved over a period of six years. My original idea – to write a story of union activism for Aboriginal rights – was sparked in 2008 while writing an honours thesis.[1] Research on that project about white Australian musicians supporting Aboriginal rights uncovered occasional references to left-wing supporters of rights campaigns. One particularly interesting source I located was a little book published by a formidable union. The *Builders' Labourers' Song Book* presented fascinating musical depictions of victory over oppression in Australia.[2] Lyrics celebrated bush struggles, Eureka miners, worker rebellions and Aboriginal rights campaigns. I found a passionate musical call for Gurindji land rights in the Northern Territory intriguing: why were these union members in south eastern Australia so committed to the rights of Aboriginal people in the far north? And how did they know so much about their plight?

As I now know, unions were deeply involved with Gurindji workers and their families from the day they walked away from Wave Hill cattle station in 1966 (indeed, well before that event). Their long-running commitment was significant. It is not surprising that my new knowledge about worker organisations supporting Aboriginal rights culminated with a decision to focus my doctoral thesis on this topic. It made sense that I should write about something I understood, and past experience working for a union bolstered my confidence to break down the jargon and delineate the policies. This is not to say that the study was a union history, nor was it a labour history. My research focus was upon left-wing contributions to Aboriginal rights campaigns.

This book is drawn in large part from that PhD thesis.[3] And like that earlier work, in this account the actions of left-wing participants are contextualised within broader activist movements and changing political environments. One thing I had not anticipated at the outset of my doctoral study was the prominent role that communists would play in the narrative. My original (albeit naive) intention had been to simply investigate how union members supported Aboriginal peoples in their struggles for rights and land. The unexpected prominence of communists in the activism often occurred due to their close involvement and affiliation with the unions I had originally intended to study. Thus, Australian communists were soon to assume a substantial role in the narrative I was slowly piecing together.

I decided to concentrate on three Aboriginal rights campaigns in remote regional Australia, with overlapping timeframes. In this way, the nuanced study became longitudinal. My narrative begins in Western Australia in 1946. It then progresses through the 1940s and 1950s in Central Australia, and then into the 1960s and 1970s in the Northern Territory. Whilst left-wing activism during the postwar period had appeared within wider discussions about Aboriginal rights, in-depth study about the topic at hand was lacking. In my PhD thesis (and now this book), contributions of left-wing activists are the primary focus. This strategy promotes thorough investigation of left-wing activism during three campaigns and prominently highlights these important and positive examples of the support of these 'different white people' for Aboriginal rights.

Using a broad-based approach, I have been able to examine a raft of social, political, economic and industrial issues within each campaign. This means that my narrative has become much more than a political or social history. The activists are the central characters. Investigation of their activism has allowed a much better understanding of the campaigns themselves (and this point is particularly relevant with regard to the effects of the weapons testing programs on desert Aboriginal peoples). In this way, aspects of Aboriginal rights campaigns assume far greater complexity.

The writing of Aboriginal history has changed significantly over past decades. I believe that this book is a modern interpretation of extremely important contributions to the Aboriginal rights movement. It is crafted as an engaging analysis of change during a pivotal period of transition. The three case studies identify strong linkages and support networks involving not only the marginal left-wing activists but also numerous moderate groups, and even extremely conservative bodies. These often incongruous affiliations produced three formidable campaigns for Aboriginal rights, and the important roles of unionists and communists within this wider movement are closely scrutinised. Those associations between radical activists and others are explored as the Aboriginal rights movement moved towards a model of self-determination.

There are ten chapters. Chapter One contextualises material that follows in the three case studies. An overview of humanitarianism during the nineteenth and twentieth centuries is presented, pertaining particularly to Aboriginal rights. Changing national and international attitudes to indigenous and broader human rights are outlined, followed by an introductory discussion of union involvement with Aboriginal rights. The chapter concludes with description of communist attitudes and policies regarding indigenous rights, at local and international levels.

Chapters Two and Three deal with the Pilbara walk-offs. Of these, the first describes Western Australia's historical responses to Aboriginal rights and pastoral industry conditions in the Pilbara region. A key left-wing supporter of the movement is introduced, and with the start of the walk-offs comes particular emphasis upon communist press coverage. Chapter Three provides detailed analysis of the contributions by left-wing activists over the first three years of the Pilbara campaign.

Chapter Four introduces the case study examining the weapons testing programs in Central Australia, along with comprehensive description of the background and establishment of the tests. The issues surrounding the dangers to desert Aboriginal peoples are outlined. Left-wing activists who took up this cause are introduced and contextualised within the wider protest movement. Attention then moves to a discussion about the nuclear tests, focusing upon their impacts upon nomadic peoples who were inconveniently in the way. Chapter Five explores left-wing responses to the establishment and conduct of weapons testing in Central Australia. Several representations of artistic protest by communists vividly display contemporary views. Radical activism is also discussed within the wider peace movement, with numerous examples of this activism examined. In Chapter Six, activism during the nuclear testing program is explored. Communist activities are prominent and this section also includes a discussion about communist front organisations. Also included is discussion about protests against the establishment of a controversial weather station and an analysis of left-wing reaction to a startling government report and associated film exposing the shocking situation for desert Aboriginal people living within the testing zone.

The final four chapters concern what is commonly known as the 'Gurindji walk-off' in the Northern Territory. Chapter Seven presents the background to this dispute, including industrial actions attempted by Aboriginal pastoral workers over previous decades. The walk-off is contextualised within the evolving national Aboriginal rights movement and broader international developments. The important precursor Award case which sparked the unrest is also examined. In Chapter Eight, focus turns to events as the Gurindji walk-off campaign commences and its support network establishes. Left-wing press coverage of events is conspicuous as the industrial campaign erupts into a struggle over land. In Chapter Nine, the nature of the campaign and its ultimate objectives are the focus. Left-wing support for the walk-off across the country is highlighted. The actions are contextualised alongside wider rights campaigns and governmental responses, before a number of prominent participants in the activism are closely scrutinised in Chapter Ten.

In the following chapter, discussion begins with a historical overview. This includes an introduction to Australia's Aboriginal rights movement, the unions relevant to this study, the Communist Party, and other pertinent national and international factors in the period leading up to 1946 (when the Pilbara walk-off commences).

Chapter One

Background

When land inhabited by indigenous peoples is colonised by others, monumental and irreversible change happens. From 1788, many groups of nomadic hunter-gatherer peoples living across the Australian continent were brutally confronted when uninvited European visitors assumed permanent residence. Anthropologist Hugh Brody described this process as prosecuted by 'white men with many powers and purposes'. The newcomers' pervading notion was that unevolved natives should be civilised and controlled. So, with colonialism came conflict, then social and economic interdependence, as indigenous peoples necessarily adapted to new ways. This drastic cultural shock permeated hunter-gatherer societies across the globe where ancient cultural norms promoting egalitarianism, mutual respect, sharing and eco-logical responsibility had guided societies for many thousands of years. Sophisticated languages and music communicating complex indigenous laws (governing moral obligations and responsibilities of territory) were replaced by the rigours of British law. These new European ways were perceived as alien and bizarre.[1]

Aboriginal peoples on the Australian continent tried, and failed, to recover the territory that Britain claimed. Traditional hunter-gather lifestyles and rituals, medicines, ceremonies and Dreamings were largely wiped out by advancing white settlers with guns, fences and profit margins. Any ethical duty of care binding a colonising country was conveniently disregarded as British, then Australian, governments appropriated lands and relocated peoples. The nature, extent and duration of conflict varied across regions and tribal areas. Common triggers were disputes over land, water and women; and exacerbated by the mutual non-knowing or understanding of the other's culture.[2]

Humanitarianism in the nineteenth century

Not all Australian colonial residents embraced the extreme consequences of invasion. Evidence of early humanitarian concern for dispossessed Aboriginal people has been identified by numerous scholars. For example, Brian Plomley comprehensively researched colonial missionary and administrator George Augustus Robinson's activities. He transcribed and then published Robinson's descriptions of the 'humane' removal and resettlement of Aboriginal peoples from Van Diemen's Land to Flinders Island between 1829 and 1834. Plomley also examined benevolent and compassionate actions towards Aboriginal peoples by explorer Jorgen Jorgensen in that colony at around the same time.[3] In a broader example, Henry Reynolds examined the activities of colonial humanitarians actively supporting Aboriginal rights in *This Whispering In Our Hearts*.[4] At a time when colonial Australia was so rapidly and profitably overwhelming Aboriginal peoples and lands, the actions of these benevolent Europeans deserve a closer look. What influenced the actions of these humanitarians? And why were these colonial residents willing to assist Aboriginal people so recently dispossessed by their own powerful new society?

To address these questions, a brief examination of what was influencing colonial Australian thinking is timely. Attitudes to the continent's original inhabitants were affected by a variety of global ideas and events, and it is important to contextualise ethical conundrums and this rise in humanitarianism accordingly. Indeed, this flow of 'trans-national' knowledge heavily influenced Australia's colonial racial thinking and legislative controls over non-white people.[5]

Relationships between Aboriginal peoples and Europeans evolved at a time when religion and Social Darwinism competed for popular belief and endorsement. Contemporary Christian thought buoyed humanitarian beliefs that all people were created by God (in his image) and that their souls were immortal. Aboriginal people needed saving. Monogenesists employed religion to battle the tenets of scientific racism which were sometimes used by administrators to justify injustice perpetrated upon indigenous peoples with little or no agency. Indeed, racism had become the rationale for many colonists to justify suppressing the natives' resistance. Australia's colonial mentality often reflected how slave-centric West Indies and southern American states viewed black people. That is, as a different race, Aboriginal peoples needed different treatment and management. Some Europeans became deeply influenced by what they witnessed on the frontier that was affecting peoples they were beginning to know and understand. Their strange cultures were becoming better understood and appreciated. In this way, perceived injustices and violence became catalysts for European support by a small but vocal group for the rights of those whose lifestyles and cultures were so manifestly different.[6]

Colonial thinking was built upon accepted philosophical positions of many theorists, and two are particularly pertinent here. Two centuries earlier, John Locke had devised a framework justifying property ownership. One famous premise identified that once a man worked the soil the land was his, and this philosophy continued to underpin British laws of property ownership or right. This naturally denied ownership rights for Aboriginal hunter-gatherers, as their culture did not incorporate agricultural practices combining labour and land. One particular argument by Jean-Jacques Rousseau complemented Locke's theory. He held that primitive native peoples would be swept along a path of civilisation as civil societies evolved. Moral codes and laws would then be instituted as a social contract to administer property accumulation and division of labour. Colonial thinking incorporated both of these theories to help justify land acquisition and natural dominance over indigenous peoples.

Underlying British procurement of any lands from indigenous peoples was the idea of *terra nullius*. This doctrine decreed that as Aboriginal people merely wandered over the land rather than resided in a manner that British society understood, that formal occupancy and ownership of the Australian continent was up for grabs. And grab they did, justifying their actions with a powerful combination of English and international laws. At the same time, the British claimed to have acquired sovereignty, and the relationship assumed traditional form as the omnipotent Crown ruled white and black subjects.

Some colonists began questioning the ethical underpinnings of a society which (so abruptly) displaced indigenous peoples from their lands. Previously accepted philosophical theories were failing to justify unfolding events. Growing social consciousness suggested that dispossession of indigenous lands inferred moral obligation to safeguard the welfare of the dispossessed and compensate for appropriated lands. A British House of Commons

Select Committee investigated the rights of indigenous peoples in colonised countries in 1837. Repercussions of the British Anti-Slavery Society's hard-won successes were filtering through colonies, and attitudes were changing. In 1833 slavery throughout the British Empire and its colonies was finally abolished, in what Reynolds identified as 'one of the most popular [humanitarian] crusades of the 19th century'. Anti-slavery crusaders then channelled their considerable energies and attention towards the rights of indigenous peoples around the globe. Australia's 'first land rights movement' evolved during the 1830s when British and colonial advocates lobbied for Aboriginal claims to land, culminating with formation of the British and Foreign Aborigines Protection Society. Contrasts between the cruelties of slavery and those perpetuated as a result of colonisation fuelled heated and emotional debates in Britain and Australia.[7]

Benevolent Christian beliefs about racial equality drove a wave of missionaries across the globe to locate, and then save, colonised indigenous peoples. Aboriginal protectors were increasingly appointed to safeguard rights and provide protection from white abuse. But battling the benevolent Christians and humanitarian British reformers were scientists driving racial treatment of indigenous peoples, based on the tenet that white and black were unique and separate species. Phrenologists measured skulls, extrapolating from these anatomical findings to declare that difference in shapes and sizes of heads meant reduced intellectual capacity in black people. From the late 1800s a powerful new scientific approach to race known as eugenics emerged, along with concomitant beliefs of racial superiority and even more dangerous ideals of preserving racial purities. Coupled with this was an almost obsessive fear of colour, and a need to protect white Australia by limiting the rights and numbers of anyone coloured differently.[8]

Moving into the 1900s

Enthusiastic humanitarianism of the early nineteenth century waned. From around 1860 until the 1920s most Europeans chose to look the other way, and the Aboriginal plight was overwhelmingly ignored. A defensive mindset reinforced the concept that Australia was a 'white man's country', weighed down by the incapability of black men. Social Darwinism provided a moral ideological platform for progress and prosperity, endorsing mentalities of other colonised nations dealing with their own questions of what to do with their indigenous populations. In short, Darwinians believed that Aboriginal peoples would eventually die out, as the evolutionary process positioned the fitter white race as survivors. People of mixed descent had been herded onto reserves, in colonial responses to dilemmas about what to do with the large 'half-caste' populations depending upon white authorities for welfare services and protection.[9]

With Federation in 1901 came an immediate racial declaration, as the major political parties united to support and create a 'White Australia' policy. 'White Australia' legislation drew a 'colour line' around the country, in a loud announcement that 'whiteness' epitomised national identity. Australia's architects of federation drew upon trans-national ideas (particularly from the United States) to design laws that would keep their country as white as possible. The collective power of the *Immigration Restriction Act 1901* and *Pacific Islander Labourers Act 1901* was immense. Non-white workers were expelled, as Australia rushed to preserve and protect the nation's racial integrity. Whilst support for this legislative protection of the white race was widely applauded, other people representing a broad cross-section of the community did oppose it. They included left- and right-wing activists, church congregations, and most understandably, immigrants and international workers.[10]

In Australia, supportive organisations such as the Aborigines' Protection League and Victorian Aboriginal Group began to appear. Members of these groups were white. Importantly, activist organisations driven by Aboriginal people were also established at this time, and the Australian Aboriginal Progressive Association was a trailblazer for the indigenous political rights movement during the 1920s. The Australian Aborigines' League, led by activist William Cooper, and the NSW Aborigines Progressive Association also became prominent among Aboriginal-run organisations. This energetic Aboriginal activism was famously punctuated by the sad proclamation of Australia's national 'Day of Mourning' on 26 January 1938, while most white Australians were out and about celebrating the 150th anniversary of invasion.[11]

Knowledge of Aboriginal peoples grew as anthropological investigations revealed societies rich with intricate cultures and deep understanding about land and relationships to it. Australian studies received formal recognition with the establishment of the first Chair of Anthropology at Sydney University in 1925. This appointment of A. R. Radcliffe-Brown was prompted, in large part, by Australia's 'acquisition' of New Guinea following World War I. The peoples of Australian-administered Papua and New Guinea were considered far more bound by cultural traditions than Australia's culture-contacted mainland indigenous population, hence the creation of this new anthropological opportunity to study groups perceived to be less impacted by Western civilisation.[12]

In 1933, A. P. Elkin became the new Chair of Anthropology (a position he held for nearly twenty-four years). Anthropologists Ronald and Catherine Berndt described this as a halcyon period when 'field research flourished'.[13] This enthusiastic drive for anthropological knowledge was, however, a double-edged sword at a time when eugenicists worried about racial mixture and its potentially unfortunate results. Donald Thomson was one anthropologist who did not embrace this element of scientific thought. His writings about Arnhem Land reflected deep

respect and friendship with people with whom he lived and photographed during the 1930s and 1940s. Thomson learnt customs,
language and hunting skills, as local people welcomed him into
their country.[14] He actively advocated Aboriginal messages and
needs to governments and universities, and his valiant attempts to
oppose the weapons tests during the 1940s and 1950s are noted in
later chapters.

Scientific exploration of Aboriginal culture was matched by
growing artistic interest. Writers, actors, musicians and artists
created conduits for Aboriginal stories into mainstream Australia
by weaving people, places and cultural practices into their work.
The Jindyworobak movement exemplified these connections
to Aboriginal culture by white writers and poets. This group
formed during the late 1930s, its name coined from an Aboriginal
word meaning to join or annex. Powerful literary pieces publicised and vindicated Aboriginal connections with their land.
Jindyworobakism matched musical output between 1940 and
1960, as both artistic genres reflected the white Australian need to
embrace and understand Aboriginal culture.[15]

League of Nations and the International Labour Organization

Australia was a foundation member of the League of Nations,
which was established at the 1919 Paris Peace Conference. This
intergovernmental body formed part of a broader strategy to
create a peaceful world community and avoid another brutal
world war. Of relevance here, the League introduced a notion of
sacred trusteeship, whereby civilised countries assumed control
and protection over uncivilised societies. As a consequence, at
the conclusion of World War I, Australia became the mandated
administrator and 'protector of natives' of New Guinea, reporting
its activities to the League.

A controversial race card was played early by a prominent League member country. In 1919 Japan's attempt to incorporate a racial equality provision into the preamble of the League's Covenant was defeated, meaning that some member nations of the new global affiliation immediately became more equal than others. This result also epitomised more broadly the perceptions of fear towards non-white races by Australia, Britain and the USA at that time. Japan's suggestion was debated at length. The USA (which never joined the League) was influential in discussions. It feared that racial equality threatened US ability to legislate in its own interests: the yellow and black folk were just fine when controllable by discriminatory laws. Britain also discounted this idea of racial equality as unrealistic thinking, as blacks would never be the equals of whites. The British Empire position was, of course, highly influenced by member countries such as Australia and South Africa (which were dealing with their own racial problems). Australia's view was uncompromising. Prime Minister Hughes flatly opposed any statement of racial equality in the Covenant compromising his country's tight rein on its non-white people and demographic composition. Hughes' influence on the British position was significant. When that country voiced opposition to the Japanese racial equality clause, the initiative immediately negated as a unanimous vote in favour became unachievable.[16]

To address a wide range of international problems, the League established agencies to tackle matters such as disarmament, health, justice, slavery and refugees. One such agency aimed to improve conditions for workers by setting international labour standards. International Labour Organization (ILO) membership included delegates from the League's member countries, plus representatives of employer and employee organisations. In 1930 the ILO formulated the important Forced Labour Convention (aimed at suppressing the use of compulsory labour by involuntary workers).

During the latter half of that decade, several other conventions specifically addressed recruitment, contract and employment conditions of indigenous workers.[17]

Unions and Aboriginal workers

Union attitudes regarding Aboriginal workers varied during the first half of the twentieth century. Examples pertaining to two unions with large pastoral worker memberships illustrate that diversity of thought. When the North Australian Workers' Union (NAWU) formed in 1926, it denied membership to all 'coloured' workers, except those people who were Maori, 'American Negroes' or who had a European parent. Thus, people deemed 'full-blood' Aboriginal were prohibited. Communists called (to no avail) for the NAWU to protect exploited Aboriginal workers and abolish racial barriers.[18]

The Australian Workers' Union (AWU) held a different position. In 1927 its rules changed, allowing Aboriginal people and the 'offspring' of marriage between people of Aboriginal and European descent to become members. AWU support of Award wages and conditions for Aboriginal workers was, however, often compromised by the need to represent the majority of their membership (the white workers), whose demand in pastoral settings may have been diminished by the availability of a cheap Aboriginal workforce if Award provisions were equal. Societal views inhibited struggles for Award inclusion. Common among these were beliefs that Aboriginal culture clashed with European productivity requirements within employment settings, and that Aboriginal workers were simply unable to work at the rate and quality of white workers.[19]

Growing union interest in the rights of Aboriginal people was evidenced in the publication of an influential pamphlet. *New Deal for the Aborigines* was written by the federal president of the Sheet Metal Workers' Union in 1939.[20] Tom Wright, leader of the union, was also vice-president of the NSW Trades and Labor Council (T&LC) and importantly, it was this body which endorsed publication of the comprehensive thirty-two-page booklet. Wright had worked in the bush, and his views about Aboriginal rights were influenced through correspondence with anthropologist Olive Pink.[21] *New Deal for the Aborigines* was widely circulated and some of its recommendations about 'full-blooded Aborigines' were endorsed at the All-Australian Congress of Trade Unions in 1940. Wright (also a communist) demanded that tribes with more than twenty-five members be granted an 'inviolable reserve', with full rights to minerals, water and timber. He believed that this would ensure survival of Australia's 'contented and prosperous Aboriginal native people'.[22] Wright also endorsed the anthropological findings of Donald Thomson, who had been commissioned by the Commonwealth Government during the late 1930s to survey Aboriginal people in Arnhem Land. Several of Thomson's recommendations were included in Wright's *New Deal*, including a proposal for 'special courts' to deal with 'native offences', the abolition of police constables acting in dual roles as 'protectors', and establishment of a Native Affairs department.[23]

Relationships between unions and the Communist Party were to seesaw from the 1920s until the 1970s. Antagonisms between some unions and the Party were often evident, with the AWU (closely aligned to the Labor Party) a particularly ardent opponent during the early Cold War period. Its hostility also extended to the Australian Council of Trade Unions (ACTU), which AWU officials viewed as communist-controlled during the late 1940s and early 1950s.[24] But in a positive example of collaboration, Queensland's Aboriginal workers were staunchly supported by communists and more militant unions during the 1950s. Workers (particularly in northern Queensland) became politically aware, as regular influxes of southern workers with 'sophisticated' communist and unionist knowledge boosted strong union membership and industrial power.[25] But regional differences were also evident. Northern Australian unionists markedly shifted their position, from connection with international communist policies, to localised motivation by members to help Aboriginal people they had personal relationships with and were committed to help. In this example, racism was lessening as the needs of Aboriginal people were increasingly included in NAWU policies, and they consequently earned greater respect as good workers and community members.[26]

Communism and Aboriginal rights

Australian communists wasted no time in establishing a firm position of support for Aboriginal rights that was never to waver. When Australia's Communist Party was established in 1920, its members connected to global politics in a new and exciting way. This marked their important break with colonial 'linkages' to a more mature relationship with the outside world. Australian communists were influenced by knowledge that fellow socialists around the world were organising to protect their civil and political rights. The Party presented opportunities to engage with diverse issues such as Aboriginal and women's rights. Communists attended study classes and groups, wrote literature, created art, and presented struggles in dramatic and musical form.[27] In this way, communism offered worldly sophistication to this newly organised group of activists seeking to overthrow the oppression inflicted by capitalist society.

As membership numbers grew, support intensified. There were as few as 300 members in 1928, but with the looming Depression and militant opposition to threatened industrial rights came a sharp increase in sign-ups. Workers identified the potential of this radical new political party. Disillusioned unionists turned to the

Communist Party for industrial and political protection against the oppressive capitalist class. Membership grew from nearly 500 in 1930 to over 2,000 by the end of 1931, as communism attracted a large number of unemployed men. The Party also widened its interests, establishing an agrarian section in 1930 to capture imaginations in the bush. In a pivotal move, a communist was elected as leader of the powerful Miners' Federation in 1934. Comrades then moved into positions of power in the Railways' Union too, as the labour movement attempted to counteract inroads that European fascism might make into Australia.[28]

Party numbers increased to nearly 3,000 by the end of 1935 (including growing female and rural membership). Communist influence in unions also advanced, with members assuming leadership positions in the Federated Ironworkers' Association, and Sheet Metal Workers', Waterside Workers' and Seamen's unions. Communists developed less aggressive (and more planned) strategies. They used the arbitration system to their advantage, improved their public relations with lots of membership meetings, effectively publicised their campaigns, and utilised mainstream media to good effect. By the end of the decade, members totalled 4,500.[29]

In 1921, the Australian Communist Party had been admitted to the Moscow-based 'Third Internationale' (known also as the Comintern, or Communist International). But, although Australian communists toed the international Party line, they also brought to the table very distinctive local idiosyncrasies and vivid recent local experiences of industrial upheaval.[30] Member organisations adhered to twenty-one conditions of this peak international body, and Condition Eight is particularly pertinent here: it demanded support by communist parties worldwide for 'emancipation in the colonies' of their 'oppressed nationalities'.[31]

Australian communists also embraced Soviet 'national minorities' policies. The Soviet position on indigenous rights was framed within strategies developed by Joseph Stalin during the 1920s and

1930s to accommodate the needs of national minorities. In 1921 Stalin announced that responses to the 'national question' would protect these groups, while liberating colonial peoples from imperialist oppression. He believed that this strategy broke down 'the wall between whites and blacks'.[32] In his 1924 *The National Question* lecture, Stalin expressed appreciation for Vladimir Lenin's contribution to solving the national problem. He believed in Lenin's view that 'oppressed peoples' in all colonies should achieve self-determination and secede into independent states. According to Stalin, revolution held the key and 'dominant' nations needed to support this end.[33]

Australia's Communist Party published its first national newspaper commentary about Aboriginal rights in a succinct and powerfully written front-page article on 26 January 1923. On this poignant anniversary of British colonisation, readers learned dark communist truths about Aboriginal workers in the Northern Territory. These pastoral 'slaves' performed their duties under duress, were not paid, lived in shocking conditions, and were not allowed to leave.[34] Communist newspapers continued to publish numerous articles highlighting oppression, police brutality and pastoral worker treatment throughout the 1920s. They also called for trade unions to actively support Aboriginal worker rights.[35]

An important front-page article appeared in *Workers' Weekly* in 1928. Stark repercussions of colonisation were depicted in vivid communist prose. The following excerpts demonstrate the emotionally driven power of the words:

> The annals of Australian pioneering history are smudged with the blood of natives, slaughtered, not because they resisted the white intruder, but mainly because they were in the way of the big squatter, and when forced under economic pressure to spear a sheep or bullock, were invariably rounded up and a few shot to show the rest that the white man's property must be respected...

...the bleached bones of hundreds of natives bear testimony to the ruthlessness of "our brave pioneers" against a people whose only crime was to take back what had been taken from them.

And only last week...seventeen natives in the Northern Territory were shot down in cold blood by the police – old men, women and children...forced to come to a certain watering place on account of the dry season and because the squatter's cattle watered there, the natives had to be shot out of the way.[36]

∞

Legacies of colonisation were also addressed at a global level. In 1927 a Pan-Pacific regional group of the Comintern was established. This network was a 'space to openly contest the racism and chauvinism of Australia's history of settlement', with communists 'the first transnational activists to see colonialism as a necessarily racist and destructive experience for indigenous people'.[37]

Communist focus upon Aboriginal rights was maintained during the early 1930s. This ardent approach is somewhat surprising. The country was floundering within the Great Depression and social issues surrounding high unemployment and decreased real wages impacted severely upon most Australians. But (as identified above), Party membership figures indicate that few people were clearly doing a lot of work.

A comprehensive *Draft Policy of Struggle Against Slavery* was released by the Australian Party in 1931. From that time onwards, communist writings in their Australian newspapers and policy documents almost always capitalised 'Aborigines'. This demonstrated respectful acknowledgement of Aboriginal peoples as members of a valid discrete nationality or broad cultural group. The *Draft Policy* demanded full economic, political and social rights for Aboriginal people. A lengthy preamble damned the 'inhuman exploitation' and 'campaign of mass physical extermination...the murder drive'. Communists exposed colonial legacies as cold, hard facts:

> Such gentle British colonising devices as "Abo shooting hunts", poisoning of the only water holes in the desert country, cyanide in the meat, and strychnine in the flour, police shooting parties, burning the bush over their heads, segregating sexes, kidnapping the children – particularly females – and putting them to work hundreds of miles away from their race and parents, killing off the game...thus starving them to death, arresting without any warrant or for that matter, any cause whatever, the most virile men in the tribes (after killing off the aged and infirm) and forcing the arrested to work with chains around their necks on Government roads and for station owners, issuing licences to any capitalist desiring to employ "unlimited numbers of natives without pay for an indefinite period", setting up organisations of crawlers and kidnappers, known as "Aborigines Protection Boards" to enslave the remaining members of the tribes, and "Mission Stations", under dope-peddlers to muster the youth so that they can be sold into slavery – such truly British methods were used, and are still being used to enslave the Australian Aborigines and to totally exterminate the races so that the crimes of British and Australian imperialists may be covered up.[38]

⚮

Communists were passionately conveying their truths about Aboriginal Australia. They wanted the world to know. Raw writing style matched brutal content. The 1931 policy presented fourteen innovative demands for Aboriginal rights. These included: the right to property, education, employment opportunity, cultural protection, industrial equity, equality before the law, women's and children's rights and safety, abolition of all missions and Aboriginal

Protection Boards, and 'absolute political freedom' (including full citizenship). Yet again, union campaign support was urged to 'win back...part of their native country and common rights as human beings'. The final demand was radically innovative:

> The handing over...of large tracts of watered and fertile country, with towns, seaports, railways, roads, etc., to become one or more independent aboriginal [sic] states or republics. The handing back... of all Central, Northern, and North West Australia to enable [Aborigines] to develop their native pursuits. These aboriginal [sic] republics to be independent of Australian and other foreign powers. To have the right to make treaties with foreign powers, including Australia, establish their own army, governments, industries, and in every way be independent of imperialism.[39]

These demands exemplify the aggressive communist approach to Aboriginal rights. This policy was no lukewarm lip-service response to Stalin's national question. Australian communists called upon 'workers, intellectuals, humanitarians, scientists [and] anti-imperialists' to join this vigorous campaign.[40] Party support for Aboriginal rights demonstrated enormous commitment and solidarity.

Australian communists placed great credence on what they believed to be happening in the Soviet Union. A 1932 *Workers' Weekly* article slammed the scientific approach to race prevalent at that time, and praised the Soviet Union as a state 'where ALL races and people have economic and social equality and all "national" states within the Union have complete control of their own affairs'.[41] Australian communists were urged to believe that Soviet treatment of its national minorities (such as Jewish or Roma peoples) and indigenous peoples (including numerous Siberian ethnic and language groups and Arctic Sami peoples) exemplified how Australia should frame its policies for indigenous peoples. *Workers' Weekly* reported Soviet indigenous workers 'being given control of the land for cultivation…equal status with all other sections of the population'. It identified 'no punitive expeditions to drive them from the land, no wholesale slaughter, no social injustices; but the opportunity to develop themselves, encouragement and assistance to work out their own destiny'.[42] The Soviet Union sounded utopic, and Australia's humanitarian comrades were probably impressed.

In a blatant propaganda exercise, *Workers' Weekly* contrasted the Soviet treatment of Roma people with Australia's abuses of Aboriginal people:

> In Moscow alone there are five cooperative gipsy [sic] artels [worker groups operating as cooperatives] for the manufacture of foodstuffs, metal containers and chemicals. Many gipsies [sic] are now working in the giant undertakings of Socialist construction, in collective farms, as school teachers, as singers, in the opera houses, as engineers and architects. In fact, every avenue before open only to the dominant Russians is now open to the gipsies [sic] – and they are hastening along those avenues with the energy and enthusiasm of greyhounds long held in leash.[43]

The article predicted communist elimination of the imperialist and capitalist invention of racial superiority, and replacement by cultural equality and opportunity. Four years later, *Workers' Weekly* revealed the Soviet recipe that Australia could duplicate: 'The Soviet government has solved all the problems of the minority peoples by its policy of providing them with financial, technical, educational and economic assistance'.[44]

⚮

What was really happening in the Soviet Union was unthinkable for most Australian communists. Stalin's purges began in

1934, with his attempts to purify Party and State. Soviet officials questioning or opposing Stalinism were removed with progressively more gusto as Stalin's power soared. The period from 1934 involved 'systematic terrorizing...no one was safe; everyone was suspect...Arbitrary arrest and summary execution became the norm...Stalin had become the Party'.[45] Stalin's national minority sentiments were later found to be subterfuge. His contempt for Soviet peoples such as Ukrainians, Muslims, Jews and Georgians (of whom he was one) was eventually revealed.[46] But as far as most Australian communists were concerned, Stalin's policies were as ethical as the high moral code they believed him to possess.

As we now know, such idealism disguised little actual knowledge. But, as brief examples illustrate here, two prominent Australians were acutely aware of what was actually going on. Communist poet Dorothy Hewett visited the Soviet Union in 1952. Sixteen years later, she reflected upon that trip in *The Hidden Journey*. Her poem included images of starvation, devastation and 'paper faces' of political prisoners seen through 'blinkers on her eyes' and creeping doubts. She contrasted 'commissars [pulling] pale fur coats to their ears' with 'ragged' children begging and a Siberian man half-naked in the sleet. Doors were banged late in the night, microphones were hidden, and people unexplainably disappeared. Hewett walked through streets hearing 'marvellous lies'. In her poem, hindsight was no excuse:

> *We are all guilty, ignorance was as inexcusable*
> *As the blissful cataracts that closed on our white eyes*[47]

Another Australian communist visited the Soviet Union in 1951. And like Hewett, writer Frank Hardy harboured silent (but grave) concerns about the implementation of communism there. Hardy later wrote of his trip in a cathartic, perhaps purgative, article published in the *Bulletin* and London's *Sunday Times* during 1968.[48]

A blissful ignorance had prevailed in Australia's early postwar years as communists worked for 'peaceful transition' to the 'ordered and just society' supposedly operating in the Soviet Union.[49] Comrades Hewett and Hardy apparently knew otherwise at that time, but had chosen not to disclose. Hardy wrote of his 1951 Moscow trip, 'I saw what I wanted to see'. He described his writings at that time as disguising his disillusionment, and born of his loyal idealism within 'the web of Stalinism'.[50]

∞

Truths of Stalinist Soviet policy and activity were officially exposed by Soviet First Secretary Nikita Khrushchev in 1956. Stalin's reign of terror had ended with his death in 1953. Khrushchev had been an ardent and loyal supporter of his predecessor, but in his famous 1956 speech, he dramatically changed tack to denounce Stalin's policies. Khrushchev not only exposed horrendous tolls of the purges and mass executions, but also attacked Stalin's foreign policies, strategic incompetence and narcissistic rule by terror. This period also marked the rise of communism in China, as that country and the Soviets vied for acknowledgement as communist world leader.[51]

Australia's Communist Party post–World War II

Passionate comrades worked tirelessly for the Party and within unions. Communist membership surged from 4,000 in 1940 to its peak of 23,000 in 1944, when radical politics became much more appealing to a wider socio-economic base, including intellectuals. But by 1952, this number dropped dramatically to 6,000. Several factors influenced this sharp decline. In 1949 Party leader Lance Sharkey was jailed for uttering and publishing seditious comments. A campaign of fear ensued, with more arrests for dubious offences.

Members left in droves. Decreasing numbers occurred due to damage inflicted by the Cold War, ongoing revelations about the Soviet Union, and the rise of anti-communist organisations. B. A. (Bob) Santamaria's 'Catholic Social Studies Movement' is a notable example of such a fear campaign. It aimed to protect unions and the Labor Party from communist influence and control. This group received financial backing from the powerful Catholic Church, following Santamaria's negotiations with Victoria's influential Archbishop Mannix.[52]

A powerful anti-communist party also emerged. In a bitter 1955 factional split, a Catholic Action splinter group broke away from the Labor Party to form the Democratic Labor Party (DLP). This Party intended to wipe out communist influence in unions and the Australian Labor Party (ALP), and DLP preferences enabled conservative governments to maintain power until 1972. Cold War fears of communism were palpable. In 1950 conservative commentator Norman Cowper warned of 'key industries' vulnerable to 'sabotage' by communist-controlled unions.[53] Antagonists described communists as 'human vermin', 'ratbags', 'poor stooges' or 'poisonous'. Indeed, Mannix called them 'the scourge of Satan'.[54]

Robert Menzies and his government attempted to ban the Communist Party in 1950 and 1951. The infamous 'Petrov' espionage case initiated a fresh smear campaign upon anyone connected with communism. Many members resigned as sectarian debate raged about whether the Party should maintain Soviet line, or operate under a moderate Australian socialistic model based more traditionally within roots of the working-class movement. Following the 1956 Khrushchev speech, a mass-exodus of Party intellectuals occurred. By 1960 the international communist movement split, with loyalties pledged to the Soviet Union or China. Australian communists also divided, as allegiances to Stalinism competed with less tarnished Maoist philosophies. A small group splintered away to form a small version of the Communist

Party subtitled 'Marxist-Leninist', and members embraced writings by Marx, Lenin, Stalin and Mao.[55]

Global context

Following establishment of the United Nations (superseding the League of Nations), international attention turned to human rights. UN support for decolonisation was declared in its Charter, and countries were moving away from colonial control to self-government and determination. India is a notable example where the rise of nationalism and peaceful resistance culminated with independence in 1947.[56] Within this rapidly changing environment of international relations, an important UN declaration presented new challenges for countries with indigenous populations. Australia's Minister for External Affairs H. V. 'Doc' Evatt presided over General Assembly adoption of the Universal Declaration of Human Rights (UDHR) in 1948. Australia and forty-seven other countries unanimously supported it.

But supporting the UDHR and agreeing to work within its guidelines were very different things, and Australia's contrary position is important to note. The UDHR contained thirty Articles declaring equality of all before the law, freedom of movement within and in/out of countries, the right to marry and own property, voting rights, and equitable pay and employment conditions. In 1949 Australia's Department of the Interior identified localised problems with at least five of its Articles. It was considered that the Declaration would compromise the way Australia treated Aboriginal people and its power to remove children under the 'half-caste' policy. Other government powers under threat were: the ability to restrict movements in the NT, to permit marriages between Aboriginal and non-Aboriginal persons, to deny voting rights, and to control the right (at that time banned) of Aboriginal people to work in licensed premises or the mining industry.

Australia's governing officials hoped the country's indigenous population would be exempt from UDHR Article powers, as Aboriginal peoples were considered to be uncivilised and unable to protect or provide for themselves. The Australian government position was that its kind and benevolent approach was for the good of people unable to cope with freedoms and potentials embodied within the Declaration.[57]

Australia's position was further stated a few years later. At the tenth UN General Assembly in 1955, it announced that two covenants being drafted would not be applied to the Aboriginal population: the International Covenant on Economic, Social and Cultural Rights, and on Civil and Political Rights. Australia again argued protective rather than discriminatory motives, with indigenous people requiring guardianship until successfully assimilated into Australia's mainstream white society.[58]

Conclusion

By 1946 – as the year when the first case study presented here began – Aboriginal rights in Australia were being considered by political and non-political bodies, both domestically and overseas. Calls by emergent Aboriginal rights support organisations were now powerfully reinforced by key international covenants promoting the rights of indigenous peoples. Australian communists (guided by the Soviet position) already had a strong tradition of supporting Aboriginal rights. Prior to 1946, union support for Aboriginal rights varied, but (as the next two chapters identify) their solidarity for the Pilbara walk-off would manifest as strong and resolute.

≪≫

In the following chapter the first of three case studies presented here commences with an overview of the Pilbara walk-offs.

WESTERN AUSTRALIA
Pilbara Walk-Offs

Chapter Two

There were Aboriginal guards all round as we met McLeod. We came to an open space and he said, "We'll sit here and wait". Suddenly they were all around us. One was Clancy McKenna, one of the main strikers. They were incredibly friendly towards us. They said we were "different white people".[1]

This was Dorothy Hewett's recollection of her first encounter with Pilbara Aboriginal people in December 1946. The 24-year-old communist novelist, journalist and poet had travelled over 1300 kilometres from Perth with her husband Lloyd Davies, a fellow communist and lawyer. They arrived in Port Hedland, a small isolated town situated approximately halfway up the Western Australian coast. Hewett's mission was to write articles about an Aboriginal walk-off for Western Australia's communist newspaper *Workers Star*, but those stories were never written. Twenty years later, she explained her writers' block: '...after a month in Hedland, I realised that the kind of background and knowledge necessary was not something learned on a brief visit, but lived over a long period'.[2]

Hewett's description of her clandestine assignation with Aboriginal workers tells so much in so few words. Pilbara Aboriginal workers had walked away from pastoral bosses. With help from many white friends they were able to sustain a lengthy industrial campaign in the middle of nowhere. This was possible despite relentless pressure from powerful pastoralists and the inhibitive shackles of Western Australia's 'protective' legislation. People met secretly, plans were covertly hatched, and Aboriginal activists fought in strength and solidarity, supported by others who were definitely 'different white people'.

∞

On International Labour Day in 1946 an extraordinary thing began happening in the Pilbara. From the first of May onwards, Aboriginal station workers and their families stopped work on more than twenty pastoral properties across a huge area of over half a million square kilometres. Some of those stations are identified in the map following. More than 800 people walked away from oppressive and abusive work settings at the beginning of the economically crucial shearing season, and many never returned.

Somehow, Aboriginal workers from many different tribes and language groups on numerous white-owned stations managed to coordinate industrial action on a grand scale.[3] They successfully collaborated across an enormous area of rugged country to walk away from white bosses and crude sheep station homes. And, poignantly, in most cases those homes were on the workers' own traditional lands. Aboriginal people had walked away from much more than just oppressive working conditions.

Two chapters in this book about the Pilbara walk-offs describe communist and unionist support for Aboriginal rights. Attention focuses upon the first three years of the dispute (1946 to 1949), and substantial detail is identified via invaluable communist newspaper reports. This collection of articles is particularly important, because many records of WA's Communist Party were destroyed in a fire and the largest repository of the state's Party at Battye Library is (consequently) patchy.[4] Communists and unionists across the country rallied to support the Aboriginal workers and their families. Pastoralists and the state government reacted fiercely against them. Communist newspapers conveyed the Pilbara story to members and interested onlookers across the country. With publicity came support that was substantial and ongoing.

Aspects of the Pilbara walk-offs have been recounted by participants, observers and academics in books, theses, even poems.[5] Here, focus is upon communist and unionist support for Aboriginal rights, and their organisations' pivotal support roles. In 1946 anything happening in the remote Pilbara region was barely

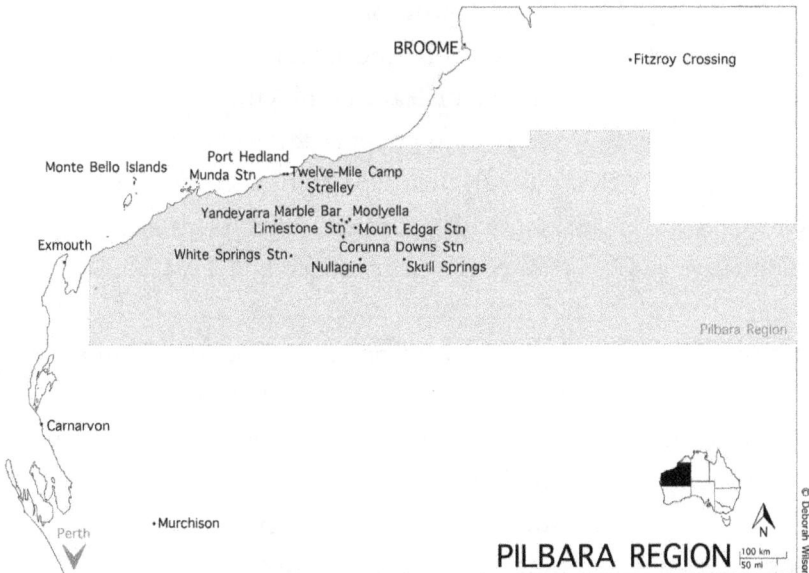

PILBARA REGION

35

newsworthy in Perth, let alone in distant eastern states. But it was not long before people across Australia knew of (and were supporting) Aboriginal workers in a place few had probably even heard of.

Background to the walk-offs

Aboriginal people in WA lived under colonial, then state government, control following establishment of the Aboriginal 'Protection' system in the mid-1880s. The north-west was opened up for European pastoral settlement in 1863, and land grants were handed out to eager frontiersmen. There was no convict labour in the Pilbara, and so the abundant Aboriginal people became a most convenient, cheap workforce. With traditional hunting grounds overrun by grazing animals, these workers became increasingly dependent upon white bosses. Indeed, in 1890 Aboriginal peoples were actually banned from hunting in their own territorial grounds. Local area 'protectors' (usually policemen) were responsible for monitoring the movements and activities of their scattered Aboriginal populations.[6]

Protection involved control. Aboriginal people required protector permission to marry or leave employment, there were no regulations or minimum requirements for payment of workers, and children were routinely removed from their families by the Chief Protector, as their 'legal guardian'. After a ten-year amnesty, the 'native passes' system was reintroduced to Port Hedland in 1944. This meant that Aboriginal travel between districts without permission from protectors was forbidden. The 'three-mile' rule denied permission for 'mixed descent' people to be within three miles (5 kilometres) of that port town. Aboriginal people were, consequently, a vigorously controlled, and readily available, cheap labour force. And pastoralists and governments were most keen to continue this tradition.[7]

During the first half of the twentieth century, Aboriginal people gravitated to pastoral stations as land available for them to live and hunt upon decreased and their needs grew. A co-dependent relationship emerged, as Aboriginal people became inexpensive and indispensable labour for white bosses. Black workers learned to survive within a system of rigid authority and control comprising 'labour, rations and dependency'.[8] During the interwar period, smaller family-owned stations were sold to big investment companies – the 'absentee landlords'. In this changed environment, station managers with guns and keys to ration sheds held omnipotent power. Robert Fellowes Lukis was lessee of White Springs Station in 1946. He witnessed ramifications of the 'wool boom' following World War II that enabled prosperous station owners to move south, leaving trusted managers to run their lucrative remote businesses.[9]

When WA Labor Senator Dorothy Tangney travelled through the Pilbara in late June 1946, she reported meeting 'only one res-ident owner of a property'. She also discovered 'big landowning companies and absentee owners' exploiting Aboriginal people, and failing to supply basic things such as proper wages, sanitation and accommodation.[10] Large British-based conglomerate Vestey (and associate company Australian Investment Agency Pty Ltd) owned seven WA stations, with estimated total land ownings of up to 4,045 square kilometres.[11] Their pastoral labour force was almost entirely comprised of Aboriginal workers. An ex-Vestey employee described the typical station scene:

> The usual stock camp consists of about 15 boys (Aborigines) and their wives [and] children and the aged and infirm...None of the natives is paid...Bashings are very frequent. If a native decides he doesn't like working at any particular place he is usually given quite a thrashing to change his mind and quite often he is chained up. There are no kitchens, washing facilities,

bathrooms, latrines, or sick bays for Aborigines. Housing usually consists of any old piece of tin the native can lay his hands on... Whites force their attentions on lubras [slang term used during that period – refers to Aboriginal women and girls] and nothing is said or done by owners...[12]

Noel Hartley worked as a nurse in the southern Pilbara Murchison region in 1947. She also joined the Communist Party at around that time. Hartley vividly recalled the treatment of Aboriginal workers:

At shearing time...the Protector of Natives, the local sergeant of police, would say to the people camped in the creek beds and humpies "Be on the first mail truck back to the station or you're in gaol".[13]

Noel's sobering experiences influenced lifelong commitment to Aboriginal rights. She joined the Aboriginal Advancement Council and established strong relationships with Aboriginal women, encouraging several to actively pursue positions in activist organisations.

∞

Escaping the cruelty and deprivations of Pilbara stations would take strength and solidarity. As the war concluded, Aboriginal workers confronted their predicaments with new knowledge of potential for change and improvement. With that brutal international conflict came a more level playing field that was soon identified by Aboriginal participants.

Legacies of war

World War II left indelible footprints upon the Pilbara region and many Aboriginal people were directly or indirectly affected by its presence. Unprecedented employment opportunities arose in districts desperately attempting to recover. The 'Thirty Years Drought', yo-yoing wool prices, blowfly infestations and two severe cyclones in 1939 and 1941, had ravaged the Pilbara's pastoral economy. Fears of invasion drove white families away from the coast. An exodus of fit young men to the armed services left the Port Hedland area without its usual pool of workers.[14] In December 1941 a state government document 'instructed police officers to ensure that as many Aborigines as possible were employed' to fill the gaps. Any who refused were to be removed to 'native settlements', and 'disciplined until placed in employment'.[15]

During the war Australia's army established training and defence facilities, roads, airstrips and other infrastructure in the north-west. To do this it employed a large workforce of Aboriginal labourers on construction sites as waged employees. For probably the first time in their lives, Aboriginal workers began to receive proper wages. They discovered their industrial monetary worth to be the same as white workers. Their work was being valued accordingly and productivity rewarded commensurately. A similar situation occurred in the NT, where Aboriginal people employed by the military also realised that 'slave-like conditions of the past' were not to be tolerated or endured.[16]

A related scenario played out on the wharves of the region's main wool port at Port Hedland. Aboriginal men were employed to replace white wharfies who joined up during the war. Workers suddenly receiving standard Award wages and conditions on the wharves were soon asking questions. If they could be paid fairly and reasonably at one worksite, why couldn't station owners also pay Aboriginal workers the same as their white counterparts?[17]

As far as the government was concerned, the less awareness Aboriginal workers had, the better things would be. New restrictions on physical access to Port Hedland by Aboriginal people were implemented. In 1942 the state Labor government declared the town a 'prohibited area' for Aboriginal people. It cited this action a response to an Army request for 'security purposes', but there was a more likely explanation. Following an influx of nearly 100 white soldiers, the government deemed Aboriginal women too promiscuous to be allowed to remain. Indeed, a commanding officer communicated his fear about 'soldier-mad' women to Premier Bray. While the government seemingly considered the libido of the Aboriginal women dangerous, it appears that the possibility that young soldiers might liaise sexually was not entertained. The controls were a simple way for 'white interests' to better manage Aboriginal workers they considered to be subversively influenced by the rhetoric of communist activists. Hence, a pass system was implemented and only very necessary Aboriginal employees were allowed special dispensation to enter the area.[18] But the exigencies of war had transformed some Aboriginal people into high-value workers. Both black and white workers had parity, maybe equality, for a short and exciting time.

Although pertaining to stations in the NT, comments by anthropologists Ronald and Catherine Berndt are relevant to this discussion about the Pilbara. They described the conclusion of war as

> an end pregnant with foreboding...[with] far-reaching implications for change in the future, for upsetting the *status quo* [their italics] which existed on so many pastoral stations, a *status quo* imposed by Europeans and assiduously upheld by them.

The Berndts viewed legacies of war as exciting catalysts for change: a time for passivity to transform into active resistance.[19] Aboriginal army employees had been introduced to hygienic living conditions, healthy diet and proper wages – the precedent had been set, and possibilities of parity with white employees had become realities for some.

Aboriginal pastoral worker conditions of employment were not prescribed by any Award in WA. In 1943 the AWU had attempted to instigate new arrangements protecting those slipping through safety nets of state or federal awards. The AWU were forced to capitulate to the insistent Department of Native Affairs, and inserted a clause which was in essence a 'slow-worker' provision. This meant that Aboriginal workers would be treated as incapable of work at the same rate or quality as a white worker, and their recompense (that is, pay and conditions) not regulated or controlled. The local protector and Commissioner for Native Affairs had full discretion in individual cases, and so the situation remained one where Aboriginal workers worked within a lucky-dip system of employment. Some stations paid more and provided better conditions, but the majority did not.[20]

∞

Legacy of the halcyon war years lingered, as new knowledge of possibilities spread. Bargaining power became a useful new concept for Aboriginal workers. The transient workforce dispersed, and many moved back to the stations where wool prices were rising sharply. Word spread about the possibility that working for the white man might actually be beneficial for black men and women too. Equal wages, nutritional rations and habitable, sanitary living quarters became increasingly desirable notions. The bar had been set high during the war, and now it was the turn of station owners and managers to treat fairly their invaluable pool of Aboriginal workers. Lack of any award protection meant that the highly prized industrial safety nets of arbitration and conciliation were unavailable for this significant pool of employees.[21] Aboriginal workers needed to establish their own version of union solidarity.

We can speculate about the impact of knowledge and insight that war ironically brought to these Pilbara people. Would the Aboriginal workers have banded together in defiance of white bosses without the experience and courage that civilian war service gave them? The Pilbara situation was unique: the region was so geographically remote from law makers and enforcers in Perth. This meant that Pilbara Aboriginal people were able to 'get away' with activities such as owning firearms, or living in illegal de facto relationships, or raising children who would more likely have been stolen away in towns further south. This 'local pragmatism' encouraged some independence within the white system of control.[22]

What we do know of the impact of war is that fair army wages and conditions became catalysts bolstering Aboriginal workers to make a bold and defiant stand. We also know that this courageous venture was staunchly supported by the Communist Party and trade unions. As historian Peter Biskup identified, 'the war had created extremely favourable conditions for the party's activities… Aboriginal station hands were "getting ideas"'. Workers in the Pilbara region had already devised strategies whereby industrial dissatisfaction converted into mini-rebellions or stubborn resistance. For example, 'they could always walk out on the pastoralists and yandy [pan] for alluvial tin around Marble Bar'.[23] The war had enlightened Aboriginal workers about the European way of life, and once the walk-off began, unions identified with them as 'fellow workers'.[24] The solidarity of Aboriginal workers was to be reinforced by organised white activists. One such unionist and communist was particularly active, and his role in the walk-offs is introduced next.

Communist and unionist Don McLeod

Donald William McLeod was a rough and tough white Pilbara man. Unusually, he was also fiercely committed to Aboriginal rights. Just the sort of bloke pastoralists and government officials didn't want anywhere near their strategically protected Aboriginal workforce. McLeod was a jack of many trades – wharfie, fencer, gold-fossicker, well-borer, mechanic and miner – in his Pilbara stomping ground. At times he was a wharf unionist. He was also, for a time, a communist. McLeod's exploits with Aboriginal activists during the Pilbara walk-offs combined all the elements of a rollicking good yarn – adventures in the outback, trips into and out of dusty jails, cunning plans, gutsy fights for basic human rights. His support and advocacy for Pilbara Aboriginal people was, as will be shown, relentless.

McLeod's association with the Communist Party probably began in 1944. In a letter to a union official, McLeod declared himself 'a Party member undisclosed', working with Aboriginal people as his 'party task'.[25] In 1945 Perth-based communist Anne Ridgeway corresponded with McLeod about his activism for Aboriginal rights. These letters are located in a Commonwealth Investigation Service (CIS) file. In August Ridgeway forwarded McLeod Party information and an application card for distribution. She undertook to 'send more later'. A week later Ridgeway again wrote, advising of difficulties locating a communist willing to become Port Hedland's Party organiser. Her passion was clear:

> I feel so strongly about the situation in the Nor-West that if you feel it would be of use, I am prepared to throw up my job as Country Organiser, and take a job up there in Port Hedland, to establish the C.P. in that centre. I feel with you that this matter is of vital importance.

Ridgeway instructed McLeod how to recruit. Here we learn how communists signed up new comrades:

> You [have] not to my knowledge brought in a single recruit or started a branch...You know that you are entitled to enroll [sic] people whom you think are suitable to join the party filling card as per instructions and your name as proposer. I will second any proposal, then application card must be submitted to State Committee for acceptance, [and] enquiries are made.[26]

∞

Party membership for McLeod continued in 1946. Lloyd Davies (who met with McLeod when he and wife Dorothy Hewett visited the Pilbara that year) was certain of his status: 'at that time [he] was a member of the Communist Party'.[27] In an interview with writer (and ex-communist) Max Brown in 1953, McLeod declared his membership in the Party during the years of the walk-off and initial aftermath.[28] Anthropologist John Wilson identified a three-year membership of the Party. He believed McLeod's communism was motivated by the need to cultivate a power base of support for the walk-offs.[29] When McLeod left the Party is unclear, but according to ex-communist Geoff McDonald, he was still a comrade in 1948. He cited a national Party report that year praising the work of 'a Communist, Don McLeod'.[30] WA communist newspaper *Workers Star* editor Graham Alcorn recalled McLeod leaving the Party in 'about 1950'. He believed that McLeod became disillusioned with a lack of support from a Party which, at the time, was focused upon national coal strikes and federal political attacks.[31]

McLeod's role in the Pilbara walk-offs has been debated at length. He has been variously touted as the paternalistic leader of Aboriginal industrial actions, as benevolent supporter of

Aboriginal people, or as a conniving communist who recruited vulnerable and dispossessed people to the cause. The evidence suggests that McLeod's intentions were genuine and that he was driven primarily by his affection and respect for Aboriginal workers and their families. These were the people he called 'this unassuming, dignified group of stoics'.[32] McLeod's humanitarian characteristics were repeatedly identified by Brown, and Mandle ascribed a fierce loyalty and sense of decency to McLeod, while acknowledging potential 'paternalism' in his relationship with Aboriginal people.[33] Lloyd Davies (the Perth communist lawyer) described McLeod as a 'passionately altruistic man'.[34] Donald Stuart's first-hand account of the walk-offs (written in fiction-alised style) portrayed McLeod as a man with great compassion and a keen sense of social justice.[35] McLeod's understanding of the destruction of Aboriginal culture was conveyed in his own simple prose:

> Their life, controlled by legal and spiritual rule of accepted law, is a pattern of unselfish dedication of the young and vigorous in undemanding service to the old and the very young...we have unthinkingly ground them down into the dust of their beloved homeland, merely because they refused to part with the spiritual links with their cultural heroes and be harnessed to make a pile of spending money for the gratification of certain privileged families.[36]

When interviewed in 1978, McLeod's words still radiated fire in the belly fuelling his fight for Aboriginal justice:

> What we got here is stolen property. We've stolen the black fellow's land, we've given him no compensation. We set out to destroy him. It's a matter of genocide, deliberately organised genocide, but the black fellows are too tough...they didn't die away.[37]

Literature examining the Pilbara walk-offs places McLeod centrally within the story. But, although he was indeed an important figure in these events, McLeod was not the leader of the walk-offs. As will be identified, leadership was shared among key Aboriginal participants but McLeod's role was, nevertheless, extremely important. His actions are examined within the wider narrative of communist and unionist support for the remarkable stand by Aboriginal people of the Pilbara.

McLeod's activities featured prominently in the walk-offs, hence this lengthy introduction to his role in these events. A question thus arises: how did a white man achieve such an influential position in remote area Aboriginal affairs? McLeod's attendance at an important Aboriginal law meeting four years prior to the walk-offs provides part of the answer. According to Brown, the overriding objective of the meeting was 'to revitalise ceremonial life, and if possible, find a means to halt the continuing decimation of the desert people as they moved into contact areas'. At that gathering, McLeod's role was officially sanctioned via conferred status in the wider Aboriginal community. His industrial advocacy for oppressed Aboriginal workers became official: he was appointed by lawmen and elders as their delegate and representative. Participation in the six-week-long law meeting at Skull Springs (far-eastern Pilbara) in 1942 cemented McLeod's formal acceptance into the Aboriginal community.[38]

For McLeod, the Skull Springs meeting was like a 'Black Eureka' and 'some sort of small United Nations' where many Aboriginal lawmen came from far and wide to meet and to organise for rebellion.[39] The meeting was attended by around 200 traditional lawmen of twenty-three language groups, from as far as 1,600 kilometres away. McLeod was the only white man present. They conferred on McLeod the 'authority to take decisions in this area as problems arose', referring also to the proposed 'strike' action planned at that meeting.[40] Thus, the 1946 walk-off was already being planned in 1942. McLeod's important role in the community was also confirmed at the meeting:

> ...in order that I could meet and discuss problems with the State as a man of status, I was given title to one hundred and fifty square miles of country surrounding the town of Nullagine.[41]

Knowledge and understanding of the white systems of law and administration were crucial attributes. McLeod had these, and Pilbara Aboriginal people needed to acquire them. His own extensive research into WA's post-1880s legislation convinced McLeod that squatter-controlled governments had conspired to continue their 'divine right [to] the unpaid labour of the indigenous Aboriginal population'. He determined to fight to change the 'protection' laws and their 'brutal and dehumanising' characteristics.[42] McLeod described Aboriginal workers as 'slaves...tied to their pastoral masters' by the provisions of the *Aborigines Act 1905*, giving 'squatters and the police...absolute control in the north'.[43] Following the Skull Springs Law meeting, McLeod became 'a recognized trouble-maker in official eyes', as he 'annoyingly argued' with government officials about basic human rights and entitlements for Aboriginal workers.[44] In 1942 he helped organise protests and strikes in Port Hedland against the 'imperious and paternalistic' permit system introduced by the Bray government (as detailed previously). Two years later Bray was to describe McLeod's activities to his Minister for the North West as a 'communist intrusion into Aboriginal affairs', and opening doors for the recruitment of Aboriginal people to the dark forces of communism.[45]

In his appointed role as representative and negotiator, McLeod proceeded to agitate for improved conditions for Aboriginal people in WA. At a month-long Communist Party 'School' in 1945 he elucidated plans for the walk-offs to Perth members. Dorothy Hewett recalled this event:

I was in the Marxist study group conducted by J. B. Miles...
when bearded Don McLeod arrived from the north in his ill-
fitting blue suit, to astound us all with his arguments and grasp
of Marxist theory...we listened spellbound...The hardline [sic]
Communists already had begun to call his vision utopian.[46]

Support by the Party and trade unions was promised. McLeod
established his communication strategy with *Workers Star* editor
Graham Alcorn.[47] *Workers Star* was a six-page Perth weekly tabloid
Communist Party newspaper. The CIS estimated 1945 circulation
at 3,900 copies per week.[48] Communists valued McLeod as their
key strategic representative in the north. His natural affinity with
Aboriginal people meant he was the ideal 'organiser': the man who
could encourage industrial and political activity among Aboriginal workers.[49] In what was to become a reciprocal relationship,
McLeod educated Perth communists about Pilbara Aboriginal life.
He addressed the twelfth State Conference of the Party in mid-
March 1946, describing the plight of workers in simple terms and
highlighting the isolating permit system preventing Aboriginal
people's education about possibilities of equity and Award wages.
This event was a crucial opportunity for McLeod to recruit communist supporters to the Aboriginal cause.[50]

By the time he left Perth to return to the Pilbara, McLeod had
put enormous energy into agitating for the cause with as many
people as possible – government officials, the Communist Party,
unions, the press, anyone he could engage on this issue. He was
determined that when the walk-offs began, Aboriginal workers
and families would have maximum exposure and support in the
potentially sympathetic heartland 'down south'.[51] McLeod later
argued that the 'general public' was unaware of the conditions
and rules for Aboriginal people, and laws restricting interaction of
white and black ensured that this culture of ignorance continued.
He explained that 'the Aborigines had been kept deliberately

illiterate, underprivileged, and largely unpaid, underfed and unsheltered'. McLeod argued that the white community had been successfully fed the government and mission line that Aborigines were 'unworthy people only fit for such treatment'. He believed the destruction of Aboriginal culture to be an intentional program aimed at subduing these indigenous peoples into powerless, but extremely lucrative, workers.[52]

In early 1946, McLeod was ready for action. During the previous year he was nominated by the Aboriginal community as an honorary inspector who could enter stations to monitor and report on Aboriginal conditions (and enforce provisions of the *Aborigines Act 1905*). This endorsement was ignored by the WA government. That denial of McLeod's official advocacy role became catalyst for large-scale industrial mayhem. Indeed, McLeod's snub, and rejection of the workers' right to organise by the government, could well have been the 'central [political and industrial] issue of the strike'.[53]

Government correspondence during the previous year comprehensively illustrates McLeod's predicament. Two Pilbara station owners had written to Bill Hegney (Member of the Legislative Assembly representing the Pilbara region), complaining about McLeod's disruptive influence upon their Aboriginal workers. Hegney referred the matter to the Commissioner for Native Affairs, who promptly informed the MLA that McLeod's application as honorary inspector would be denied. The Commissioner's quiet contempt for McLeod is clear in a further letter that same day to the Inspector of Natives in Broome, where he wrote 'McLeod is a man of doubtful political antecedents'.[54]

But McLeod had the last word before the walk-offs began. On 30 April 1946 he wrote to Labor Premier Wise, advising him of the impending action. McLeod informed Wise of his previous attempts a year earlier to negotiate his honorary inspectorship with Commissioner for Native Affairs Francis Bray. He pointedly suggested that Wise act with haste to 'correct the backwardness' of the Aboriginal situation, before the opposition parties exposed the ineptitude and complicity of the Department of Native Affairs, thereby discrediting and defeating the government at the forthcoming polls.[55]

On the same day McLeod communicated with Wise, he also wrote to Sheet Metal Working Agricultural Implement & Stove Making Industrial Union of Australia (hereafter known as 'Sheet-metal Workers' Union') leader Tom Wright. McLeod attached a copy of his correspondence to the Premier, and appealed for 'solid practical support' for striking workers. McLeod also advocated union 'resolutions to WA Premier Wise [calling for] the granting of an honorary inspector of Native Affairs of their own choosing'. And he asked for 'resolutions of solidarity sent to myself', so that he could show the Aboriginal workers that they were 'not alone in their courageous struggle'.[56]

McLeod had been groomed by the Pilbara Aboriginal community to become the conduit between the power of the State and the powerlessness of the Stateless. Hope that he could legally advocate on behalf of impoverished, abused workers had been comprehensively dashed by a government refusing to recognise his role as official representative. This rejection was the last straw and Aboriginal people were about to take matters into their own hands.

The Pilbara walk-offs begin

McLeod's report in *Workers Star* on 3 May 1946 alerted readers that Aboriginal workers had withdrawn labour from many Pilbara stations two days earlier. A week later the Party's Sydney-based *Tribune* published a similar article, thus ensuring national coverage of the events.[57] The *Tribune* stories about the walk-off were mainly sourced from *Workers Star*. Of note, McLeod's reportage here incorrectly identified the Pilbara walk-offs as 'probably the first' of their kind. Aboriginal workers and their families had, for example, walked away from Cumeragunja in 1939.

Several years of secret meetings and covert planning sessions had translated into real action by aggrieved workers and dependant families. So how did this carefully designed event unfold? And, how were the actions of such a large number of workers and families from different stations across this vast area coordinated and supported?

Widespread industrial action was conducted with remarkable efficiency. McLeod was emphatic that the instigation of the walk-offs should be attributed to the people of the Pilbara: 'Through persistent and secret communication on the part of Aboriginal organisers such as Dooley Bin Bin and Clancy McKenna, the strike began'.[58] He was adamant: 'I didn't coordinate the strike. The Lawmen had a good tight grip on the whole business. It was left to the blackfellas and I worked through them'.[59] Indeed, fifty years later McLeod was still adamant that Aboriginal organisation drove the walk-offs.[60]

Organisation of this campaign was structured and strategic. Aboriginal organiser Dooley Bin Bin, the 'travelling Lawman', advocated for and with the desert people. Another, Clancy McKenna, represented people in 'settled areas'. McLeod joined this 'executive group' as the third main player, with leadership from 'others delegated by the strikers from time to time'.[61] Dooley Bin Bin (hereafter, 'Dooley') and McKenna had been appointed to their roles by the wider Aboriginal movement: elders and lawmen at the Skull Springs meeting in 1942 had formally chosen those men to represent and lead Aboriginal people from stations in the desert and 'civilised' settings.[62] McKenna's life experiences were mixed. Though a pastoral worker in the white world, he also lived traditionally as an initiated man. He moved around to a number of stations, thus developing relationships with a large number of Aboriginal people across the region.[63] This probably

increased his awareness of grievances and concerns at many stations, making him a very useful industrial organiser.

Organising Aboriginal workers across a large geographical area
to walk-off on the same day necessitated a clever tactic to overcome the illiteracy of the participants. Inventively, McLeod and
Dooley made up thirty sets of 'calendars'. These were ruled-up
sheets with fifty squares to be crossed off each day, down to the
final day (first of May) marked in red. This highly efficient coordination of the walk-offs was 'a brilliant piece of organisation'.[64]
McLeod's calendar, as his crude whitefella version of a message
stick, was the clever and critical tactical tool which station workers understood and utilised. The near clock-work precision of the
walk-offs is all the more remarkable given the nature of pastoral
work in the Pilbara. The political organisation of workers in a
large industrial workplace such as a factory, for example, would be
relatively straightforward when compared with the coordination
of so many workers at so many workplaces dotted across such a
vast region of outback Australia.[65]

Any meetings between McLeod and Aboriginal organisers
definitely needed to be kept secret. Until 1949, Section 36 of
the *Aborigines Act 1905* stipulated that no white man could be
within five chains (about 100 metres) of a congregation of natives.
McLeod recalled that 'all our meetings were conducted in a
clandestine manner'.[66] Indeed, when the Department of Native
Affairs got wind of the walk-offs, their immediate response was
to pursue McLeod, armed with that very Section. An 'Urgent
Telegram' from Commissioner Bray to departmental Inspector
O'Neill at Fitzroy Crossing indicated anxious urgency:

Proceed first plane Port Hedland native labour situation now
very disturbed and strikes taking place because of McLeods
[sic] insidious anti fascist communistic activities Cooperate with
police in any possible firm action against McLeod but may now

> be possible obtain evidence breach Section 39 for being on place
> where natives congregated Press for full term imprisonment...[67]

McLeod's meetings with Aboriginal people were, indeed, illegal and dangerous. McLeod later recounted that he and Dooley were forced to creep through mangroves outside Port Hedland during the early days of the walk-offs. He remembered police 'perched' on banks above them, shining torches at random across the area. McLeod, Dooley and their Aboriginal co-conspirators lay 'on their bellies' to avoid detection while conducting their meeting. Similar scenarios were to play out for the next two years.[68] It was, as McLeod later described, 'wild west country in those days...the local squatter and police [ran] the town'.[69]

Rumours abounded three months after the first walk-offs that station owners and managers wanted to take matters into their own hands. Plans for 'basher gangs' to teach non-compliant Aboriginal workers a lesson were reported in the *Tribune*.[70] Squatters were later alleged to have spread further rumours that 'Mr. Don McLeod...has been jailed for 20 years, and that the police will soon arrive to shoot up the Aboriginal strikers'.[71] The attitudes of station owners mirrored those of the Country Party, which advocated on behalf of rural industries at national level. During 1946 the Country Party issued a 'Federal Election Policy Statement'. Its barbed rhetoric identified the 'Australian Communist in the same category as a venomous snake – to be killed before it kills'.[72] McLeod was most likely similarly viewed: as a dangerous subversive best dispatched from the situation as quickly and efficiently as possible. Ironically though, McLeod was actually more scathing of the ALP and the AWU than of his more obvious right-wing political adversary:

> Although it is the Country Party which traditionally capitalised
> on the unpaid blackfellow, it wasn't they who did the dirty on

the blackfellow – this was the role of the Labour Party through the influence of the Australian Workers' Union.[73]

This comment deserves a closer look. During the latter half of the 1940s, the AWU held an anti-communist position. The union view was that communist stirrers were responsible for industrial unrest among shearers, and members distanced themselves from strikes staged in the eastern states during 1945. The AWU was also refusing to affiliate with the peak body of Australian unionism, citing communist control of the ACTU. During the Chifley Labor Government years (1945–1949) the AWU closely aligned themselves to the Labor Party's anti-communist line.[74] Industrial unrest among disgruntled shearers also spread to WA sheds, where wages were lower than the eastern states. It is conceivable that Aboriginal pastoral workers may have listened with great interest, as shearers shared their knowledge of the potential for industrial action to get you what you deserve. The AWU had washed their hands of shearer strikes in the eastern states – they deemed those independent actions to be driven by communist ratbags. McLeod's attitude to the AWU and the Labor Party was likely strongly flavoured by his membership of the Communist Party and the anti-Labor Party stance that communists held at that time.

The Department of Native Affairs had actually been more than aware of the impending walk-offs. Months earlier they had received reports from a Port Hedland policeman, identifying visits from Aboriginal organisers to stations around the region. Workers had been told of the plans for industrial action, and the officer was very aware that McLeod was a central figure in organising the event.[75] We can only speculate that the state government had chosen not to act upon this early advice, instead deciding to watch and wait as proceedings unfolded.

Pilbara realities

Solidarity in any industrial action is imperative. When Pilbara workers and their families walked away from their pastoral station homes, they needed security of knowledge that they were part of a larger coordinated action achieving what it had set out to do. In the vast areas of the Pilbara, news needed to travel fast, and a solid support network underpinned this rebellion. People travelled to two camps. The Twelve-Mile Camp (near Port Hedland) and inland Moolyella Camp (near Marble Bar) became the central activity points throughout the walk-offs.[76] Coordination of action then spread from these camps to remote areas via an extremely efficient network of Aboriginal activists.

Getting to the camps was not a simple process. Molly Williams was an Aboriginal worker who abandoned her station mistress. She related that people walking away carried their belongings to the nearest railway siding, and then waited for a train to transport them to one of the camps.[77] This process was not as simple as it sounded, because the distances up north are huge. In 1946 the Pilbara rail experience involved an eight-hour trip from Port Hedland to Marble Bar, passing near to a number of stations. The 'Spinifex Express...friendliest train in Australia' ran once per week. Sidings, where it stopped to collect passengers or transfer freight, mail and stores, were often nothing more than a shed or lean-to pub. Timetables for travel were necessarily flexible, as trains were always reliably late. Common delays included waiting for the Flying Doctor Service to arrive, or cuppas at siding stops when the guard 'boiled the billy' for passengers. One driver liked to stop his train to pick Sturt's desert peas, while another regularly imbibed to excess at Marble Bar before passing out in the guard's van during the return trip to Port Hedland.[78] It is not hard to imagine scenes of Aboriginal families with piles of possessions waiting patiently at sidings for trains they knew would eventually come.

Perth author Bert Vickers wrote an important novel about Aboriginal attempts to escape Pilbara misery. *The Mirage* presented a narrative version of his play *Stained Pieces* that confronted audiences at Perth's radical New Theatre in the late 1940s. Vickers was not a communist, but known travelling companion with other Realist Writer Group members (and communists) Katharine Susannah Prichard and Joan Williams.[79] *The Mirage* is an extremely confronting book. It poignantly describes young Aboriginal characters attempting to leave Pilbara squalor and poverty during the period of the walk-offs. Vickers had lived and worked in Pilbara shearing sheds for ten years. His disturbing prose reflected the 'pitiful fate', 'prejudice and discrimination' and 'destruction' of Aboriginal people 'brought up to live the white man's life but finding no place in it'.[80]

∽

By the time that Aboriginal workers and families walked away from Pilbara sheep stations in May 1946, the infrastructure that would support them over the next months and years had been established. In the next chapter, a closer examination of swift and vigorous left-wing support for Pilbara Aboriginal people is presented. Enid Conochie recounted examples of that support in action, at a conference in 2005. During the Pilbara campaign her two sisters had made the long trip north to 'help' at a camp, in response to publicity about the walk-offs in *Workers Star*. University student (and communist) Enid remained in Perth, 'helping, marching and raising funds...for the pastoral workers who were in trouble, in gaol at that time'.[81] Ample coverage of unfolding events in the Pilbara inspired communists like Enid and her sisters to swing into action. The 'different white people' were ready to go. And one of the most important things they could do was to publicise the story.

Chapter Three

Things will never be the same in the Pilbara[1]

Communists had publicised harsh realities of Aboriginal Australia in their newspapers and journals since forming their Party in 1920. Articles about Australia's great shame increased exponentially as the century progressed. These publications present a wealth of information about Australia's treatment of Aboriginal people and response to their suffering and abuse. Commencing in 1920, communist newspapers published a vast number of items exposing (often as 'scoops') the plight of Aboriginal people in rural and urban settings. Many of these articles contained progressive and respectful rhetoric mirroring, with remarkable similarity, modern-day commentary about Aboriginal rights and needs.[2]

The Party published its first national newspaper story about Aboriginal people in WA during 1927. The *Workers' Weekly* documented Royal Commission findings of police brutality, recounted by the head of Forest River Mission in the East Kimberley. Reverend E. Gribble told of sixteen Aboriginal people, 'burned in three lots of one, six and nine. Only fragments of bone, not larger than one inch, remain'. These killings were thought to have avenged the Aboriginal killing of a station owner. The story also detailed police brutality against white men, thus balancing reportage regardless of the victim's race. Later articles in 1933 and 1934 described other aspects of Kimberley life, such as Aborigines 'reeking with disease', including leprosy and venereal diseases. Chief Protector Neville reportedly 'protected' the 'offending squatters', while women were raped and infected.[3]

Less than two decades later, communist reportage was describing a very different situation in the remote north-west. This time there was no spilling of blood in the black versus white conflict. Rather, these articles were about a new kind of Aboriginal rebellion. Pilbara people were standing up to station bosses in a non-violent reaction to cruelty and oppression. This time the nature of the conflict was passive, and the weapons were much simpler and more effective...feet.

Getting the story out

Mainstream media attention to the bold Aboriginal action was minimal. Communist coverage became the crucial conduit enabling white Australia to learn about events in the Pilbara. Indeed, the *Tribune* informed readers that 'to date (May 17), there has been a daily press blackout due to the big influence of the pastoralists in W.A. Newspapers Ltd.'. This 'censorship blackout...imposed by metropolitan papers' was also emphasised in the next edition.[4] The people wielding this influence (the pastoralists and government) were later described by Don McLeod as 'our rich and powerful friends' – the squattocracy of the north-west.[5]

Perth-based *Workers Star* journalist Joan Williams recalled that her communist newspaper was the only state publication covering the Pilbara events.[6] Editor Graham Alcorn recalled silent or distorted mainstream press coverage, and considered that *Workers Star* prompted 'support [that] was wide and immediate'.[7] McLeod's recollection of media coverage vindicated these claims. Indeed, he castigated WA newspapers that 'deliberately suppressed [information] by the monopoly-controlled media'.[8] Communist lawyer Lloyd Davies endorsed this view of an 'almost total blackout' of coverage about the walk-offs in mainstream papers. He believed that 'the dailies in other states were forced to rely upon [communist newspapers]…and often quoted from articles in reporting the strikes'.[9] Indeed, the state's leading newspaper, the *West Australian*, did not provide adequate reportage of the situation for the next three years.[10] Armstrong cited the *West Australian*'s 'selective and distorted coverage of the strikes', which reported that only six, and not twenty, stations were affected by the walk-offs.[11]

The communist press had initiated and then become the key publicist as events unfolded in the Pilbara. WA communist Noel Hartley highlighted the impact of these newspapers upon her personal activism: 'I decided to join [the Party in 1948] because [it] cut across class, economic status, religion etc., had a world outlook and was a pioneer in promoting self-determination and equal rights for Aborigines through their press'.[12]

Initial repercussions of the walk-offs

Government response to the walk-offs was swift and potent. McLeod and other 'troublemakers' were thrown into jails across the Port Hedland district and news quickly spread to *Tribune* readers. A prominent front-page story reported unions bristling with 'bitter indignation' following the arrest of McLeod, Clancy McKenna and Dooley Bin Bin. They were charged with contravening Section 15 of the *Aborigines Act 1905*, for 'enticing Aboriginals from service'.[13] McKenna was quickly sentenced to three months' hard labour, while white protagonist McLeod was released on bail. McLeod argued that the arrest of Clancy was 'kept secret from me...The trial was over before I heard of it, or I would have defended Clancy [who was] "defended" by an inspector'.[14] Dooley was also sentenced to three months' hard labour. He recounted that imprisonment process to participants at the 1963 Federal Council for Aboriginal Advancement conference. He had been taken to Marble Bar jail and chained by the neck for six days. He was then chained to the back of a truck for transfer to his Port Hedland trial.[15] By the time Dooley had been incarcerated, the *Tribune* reported that 'eight hundred workers, chiefly station employees' had walked away from workplaces. While some had achieved higher wages and better conditions as a result of their actions, all were still calling for McLeod to be acknowledged as their white representative.[16]

Union support was soon evident. Joan Williams recalled that the Seamen's Union 'immediately came out in support' by banning the handling of wool in Port Hedland:

> We realised that the main thing we could do was alert all the unions where we had influence at the time...When other unions followed this lead and supported the Aboriginal workers, this gave a lead to the population generally.[17]

The Coastal Docks, Rivers and Harbour Workers' Union instigated a strike levy of sixpence per week upon its members.[18] *Workers Star* and the *Tribune* reported that the Port Hedland AWU branch unanimously passed a resolution of support (as did the Amalgamated Engineering Union, or AEU), and that the carpenters' and boot-makers' unions, AEU and Women's Charter Committee had written letters of support to Labor Premier Frank Wise.[19] This was an attempt to urge government rectification of Aboriginal conditions.

The government, however, was already more than aware of conditions on stations. The *Tribune* reported that during the trial of McKenna and Dooley, Inspector O'Neill admitted 'that squatters were permitted to employ natives without regard to provision of accommodation, sanitation, bedding, ground sheets or other amenities'.[20] The government not only knew of, but also condoned, pastoral employee conditions via its neglect to provide legislative or industrial safety nets.

For McLeod, any publicity was useful. Looking back in later life, he recalled his arrest and brief jailing as strategically driven by government and pastoralists to get him out of the way: 'While I was free I was a danger. I was a communist. I was subversive and I was in danger of halting the progress of the north'.[21] When interviewed by the *Tribune*, McLeod had outlined his strategy:

If I am immobilised now the campaign may die out without publicity. My retention in custody would weaken the campaign...
If publicity comes, good, I don't mind, as this will only be one more arrest for the Government to explain'.[22]

McLeod's theory was correct. Following his release on bail, support broadened nationally. The *Tribune* reported the Aborigines' League in NSW congratulating McLeod and McKenna for their brave stance, and praising unions that supported the Pilbara campaign. According to the League, this display of broad union support was living proof that all Aborigines should collaborate with unions, to achieve 'justice and...a new deal'.[23]

By early June national union support was broad. Queensland's T&LC and Victorian Unions (including the Carpenters, Meatworkers, Ironworkers and Building Trades Federation) pledged support to Pilbara workers.[24] At a Redfern Trades Hall public meeting, Sydney unionists and Aboriginal people passed a resolution of support and protest that was forwarded to Prime Minister

Chifley.[25] In Launceston, an Australian Railways Union resolution congratulated Pindan Aboriginal workers, and condemned the jailing of McKenna, Dooley and McLeod.[26] Clearly the plight of fellow workers had struck a nerve with unionists across Australia. That two of the organisers were Aboriginal was perhaps not the main issue for union supporters, but rather that of the necessity for Pilbara workers to negotiate a fair deal.

Workers Star and the *Tribune* published a letter written in jail by McLeod to Peter Hodge (known at that time as 'Padre'). This ex-army clergyman was soon travelling to the Pilbara actively supporting the Aboriginal workers.[27] Hodge had recently been appointed honorary secretary of the Committee for the Defence of Native Rights (CDNR). This Perth-based lobby group had been speedily established on 28 May to support Pilbara people and appeal to unions and humanitarian groups. It was initially coordinated by the two communists, writer Katharine Susannah Prichard and medical doctor Alex Jolly, along with *Workers Star* editor, Graham Alcorn. McLeod was vice-president. The CDNR conducted public meetings and raised funds, circulating 20,000 leaflets about the Pilbara walk-offs. Membership was largely comprised of communists.[28] Alcorn recollected that 'it was a thumping success'.[29]

Katharine Susannah Prichard's commitment to Aboriginal rights had begun much earlier. In 1928 her novel *Coonardoo: the Well in the Shadow* created outrage with its graphic descriptions of sexual exploitation by white station men upon Aboriginal women.[30] Her 1932 short story *The Cooboo* featured a violent narrative describing harsh station life. Prichard's writing sprang from firsthand experience, after staying on a northern WA property with Aboriginal women and stockmen. She wrote *Happiness* the same year. Again the setting was a station, where offal was a special treat for the workers. Aboriginal people were, nonetheless, depicted as proud, strong and resilient.[31] In the short stories *N'goola* and *Flight*, Prichard explored cruel stories of children stolen away because they had white fathers. Her son Ric Throssell explained that the central characters in her Aboriginal stories were always women – she felt comfortable talking with them and identified with their plight.[32] Prichard was a member of the Communist Party for fifty years. She remained loyal to the Soviet Union and was (Throssell noted) buried under the 'Red flag' in 1969.[33]

Alex Jolly's involvement with Aboriginal rights campaigns was similarly extensive. Membership of the Party meant that he was watched with interest by CIS during the 1940s. In November 1946 Jolly stood (and was elected) as a communist candidate in his Perth local government area, and an article about this political activity in *Workers Star* was added to his security file. Jolly had joined the Party in 1933, and collaborated with another suspected communist (Fred Rose) to write a thesis about Aboriginal ethnology in 1942.[34] A CIS dossier reveals that Jolly came to WA in 1940 as resident medical officer at Broome, where he also studied anthropology. In 1942 he moved to Perth and became president of the Eureka Youth League (deemed a communist training organisation) in 1944. CIS first connected Jolly with the Pilbara movement on 23 May 1946. He was identified as convenor of a meeting protesting the arrest of 'communist Don MCLEOD', and was reported conducting another at Perth Town Hall on 31 May. By 30 August, the CIS described him as CDNR chairman. In January 1947 Jolly's political aspirations climbed higher, when he was endorsed as communist candidate in the federal election.[35]

McLeod's letter to Hodge thanked the CDNR for securing 'legal assistance to fight my case', and urged establishment of a wider lobby group to fight for the rights of all WA Aboriginal people. His statement of hope was articulate:

...by moral and other assistance they [Aborigines] may regain their simple human dignity and we can hope that...they may take their place beside us as equal citizens and with us, help to build, to our mutual advantage, the future state in Australia, free from want, fear, aggression and intellectual domination.[36]

The 'legal assistance' referred to was by Fred Curran, a Perth-based lawyer who often represented McLeod and Aboriginal workers charged with a range of offences.

McLeod was clearly a busy correspondent during the first weeks of the walk-off. He wrote to union leader Tom Wright on 17 June, telling of the 'many letters [of] support' he had received, and responding to a number of questions Wright had posed in a letter on 10 May. McLeod informed Wright of the 'four point programme set up by the strikers themselves':

> The right to organise and appoint reps
> Minimum cash wage of 30/– weekly
> Sympathetic interpretation of Reg 81 concerning housing and food
> Rights for elected reps to have access to all workplaces to enforce act.

To these McLeod added, 'coupled of course with demands for the release of the native leaders'. Wright and McLeod both expressed the same desire to force constitutional change, so that Aboriginal affairs fell within Commonwealth jurisdiction. In this way, McLeod envisaged a national system of training and rehabilitation, plus allocation of 'inviolable reserves for those who have any form of tribal organisation left'.[37]

Padre Hodge also wrote to Wright in mid-June. He thanked Wright for his union's 'generous financial help' for CDNR, and enclosed a list of organisations 'supporting North-West natives'. These included WA branches of unions (the AWU; hospital employees; railways; tramways; metals; harbour workers;

boot-makers; engineers; painters; bricklayers; carpenters; nurses) and the ALP, and university and women's organisations. Inter-state support included Queensland's T&LC, NSW and Victorian unions, and the SA Council for Advancement of Aboriginal Women.[38] Such significant support from so many organisations across a wide geographic area (evident only three weeks after CDNR commenced operations) exemplifies the energetic activity of its members. A week later Hodge (with President Alex Jolly) again wrote to Wright, informing him of CDNR's appeals to the World Federation of Trade Unions, UN, ACTU and federal ministers. Wright was urged to throw his support behind this 'urgent matter', and to lobby the peak world union body and the UN.[39]

By late June communist newspapers reported successful protests by unions and other supporters securing the release of McKenna and Dooley from jail. At McLeod's trial, counsel Fred Curran argued the *Aborigines Act 1905* was a form of slavery that ignored the 1833 British Slavery Abolition Act, and was likely unconstitutional. He announced CDNR's intention to appeal McLeod's substantial fine of £96/16/6.[40] Curran reportedly described the Aboriginal workers as '...serfs, tied to the land-owner as securely as any feudal serf in the middle ages'.[41]

Aboriginal rights activist Mary Bennett (then living in London) articulated similar rhetoric in a letter to Tom Wright: 'I do earnestly hope that the communist party will take up the subject of pay and conditions for the natives who suffer a serfdom...that is indistinguishable from slavery'.[42] Bennett's correspondence also usefully identified the broadening of international interest in Australia's Aboriginal rights situation. She included a description of a *Reynolds' News* (London newspaper) article on 2 June that detailed the walk-off and vividly described impoverished Aboriginal conditions for its British readers.

McLeod and the law

In early August McLeod was again arrested while running afoul of a different section of the *Aborigines Act 1905*. This time his alleged crime was to meet with a group of Aboriginal people.[43]

McLeod's latest transgression occurred while attempting to negotiate on behalf of Aboriginal advisers. In a 1987 film documentary Aboriginal worker Sam Coppin explained that he had twice asked police to recover ration coupons for Aboriginal people from stations which were illegitimately withholding them. These coupons were distributed by the government to stations for distribution among workers. Coppin asked their white representative to intervene, because he possessed the most critical negotiating skill. That is, McLeod spoke language the government used.[44]

When McLeod approached police (the protectors) to obtain more coupons, it was immediately obvious that he had broken the law: he had to have met with Aborigines in order to ascertain their needs. McLeod even cheekily arrived at the police station with an Aboriginal deputation.[45] Following his arrest McLeod sent a telegram and letter to the Rationing Commission in Perth, outlining his attempt to negotiate and subsequent detention.[46] Deputy Commissioner Anderson then wrote to Commissioner for Native Affairs Bray, asking him to clarify the position in the Pilbara and distancing his Office from any withholding of rations.[47] The *Tribune* reported that the government and station owners' withholding of coupons was an attempt to 'starve them [Pilbara Aborigines] into submission'. The Aboriginal response to this harsh new tactic was decisive: they initiated another damaging wave of walk-offs. Union support again emerged. The AWU wrote to Minister for Native Affairs Coverley, requesting that food and clothing coupons be granted to the large group of Aboriginal people now attempting to establish their own enterprises, free from station life and hardships.[48]

McLeod was arrested and jailed seven times between 1946 and 1949. He later listed his crimes:

...three times for being within five chains of a congregation of natives, three times for inciting natives to leave their lawful employment, and once for forgery! The last case serves to illustrate the depths to which the authorities would sink in order to get me out of the way...[49]

His commitment to the Pilbara Aboriginal movement is powerfully illustrated by those statistics. McLeod's dedication to the cause was authentic and relentless. His battles with the law were also indicative of broader anti-communist feeling within governmental ranks. Right-wing unions exerted considerable influence upon the ruling Labor Party government and its journal *(Westralian Worker)*, and there was no state-based peak union body (a trades and labour council or similar) to offer a voice to left-wing organisations. It was therefore expected that workers (hence unions) would merge into the ALP and toe the Party line. Communists were not liked or tolerated, and were not even allowed to attend District Council forums, thus 'excluded from important industrial deliberations'. Indeed, the ALP pledge clearly identified its position on communists:

I hereby pledge myself to adhere to and uphold and support the principles of the ALP and support candidates selected by the ALP for public offices and I also decree I am not a member of any other political party (including the Communist Party).[50]

McLeod's actions (as Party member) came at a time when antagonism between government and the communist organisation was extremely high.

Government officials were not the only people irritating McLeod. On 16 August *Workers Star* reported that CDNR had communicated a threat on McLeod's life to the Minister for Justice and Native Affairs.[51] Station owners and managers were extremely hostile towards McLeod. He was viewed as a subversive whose presence among Aboriginal people was destabilising and dangerous. *Workers Star* detailed McLeod's dilemma, and the story read like an excerpt from a Wild West novel. Dick Lee (publican of Port Hedland's Pier Hotel) was described as a 'fanatical hater of communism' being used as the squatter's 'stooge'. The article's writer described fears that a 'local Ku Klux Klan' of 'basher gangs' was being established to attack Aboriginal people and their supporters. In the presence of a police officer Lee allegedly threatened to 'blow McLeod's head off' if he did not leave by the next morning.[52] This communist rhetoric was strong, clearly designed to paint a picture of victimisation and anti-left paranoia against McLeod. *Workers Star* editor Alcorn recalled that his newspaper 'issued a leaflet naming [Dick Lee]', which was widely distributed around the Port Hedland region by communists.[53] This example exemplified communist solidarity for McLeod, and unity with the Wild West from supporters in the south.

Workers Star and the *Tribune* also reported the arrest of another white man. CDNR secretary Hodge had arrived in the Pilbara on 13 August intending to protest McLeod's arrest and take up the cudgel for Aboriginal rights. But from the moment he set foot on Pilbara soil at Nedlands Aerodrome, Hodge was covertly pursued by police. McLeod transported him to a remote location close to Twelve-Mile Camp, where he intended to meet with about 100 Aboriginal pastoral workers. But as Hodge began to speak, he and McLeod were immediately arrested by intrepid officers and carted off to jail. Hodge's charge was (ironically) that which he had intended to protest on behalf of McLeod. He was charged with 'meeting with natives without the protector's permission'.[54] As well as reporting the dilemma of the padre and McLeod, the *Tribune* grasped the opportunity to share with national readership the intricacies of the West's 'Protection' model. As the *Tribune's* writer explained, 'protector' and the 'police' were one and the same:

'[They] arrest a charged native, bring him into Court and then "protect" his interests at the trial'.[55] This harsh reality of Aboriginal life had been clearly and explicitly conveyed. There was no room for misunderstanding.

Support for Pilbara Aboriginal workers and their families continued to grow. An open letter by Hodge appealing for CDNR support called upon unions to levy members 'to assist their black fellow workers'.[56] Communist journalist Williams covered the walk-offs until her Perth newspaper *Workers Star* ceased publication in 1950. She believed that Hodge's arrest was perfectly timed, and 'increased the sense of outrage. Support widened'.[57] Port Hedland's AWU branch resolved to assist the Pilbara people, and this support became vitally important as industrial disputation escalated over the next year.[58]

Tribune readers also learnt that support for Pilbara Aboriginal people had gained international recognition. In London the Anti-Slavery Society, League of Coloured Peoples and National Council for Civil Liberties all pledged support and protest. As identified earlier, *Reynolds News* (described in the *Tribune* as a 'co-operative newspaper') reported the 'Pindan' situation.[59] An Anti-Slavery Society publication described the walk-offs to British supporters as 'Natives Forced Back to Serfdom'.[60] *Workers Star* journalist Williams recalled that the Society's interest in the walk-offs was aroused when she sent a photo of Pilbara Aboriginal people in neck chains and accompanying story to its office in England. She related that the Anti-Slavery Society 'then took up the cause'.[61]

National support for Pilbara workers

Peak union bodies in other states added formal support to the Pilbara workers. *Workers Star* reported Queensland and South Australian T&LC's 'giving enthusiastic backing'.[62] The Queensland T&LC asked all of its state 'provincial' councils and individual unions to assist the Aboriginal workers.[63] Three WA unions (painters, boot-makers and the Fremantle carpenters' branch) all pledged support for charges against McLeod and Hodge to be quashed. Similar protests were also formally lodged in late September by the Mt Isa T&LC in Queensland, the Building Workers' Industrial Union of Australia (BWIU) national body, and Bendigo Trades Hall Council.[64] Thus, only four months after the walk-offs had begun, the country's union movement had mobilised and was proactively supporting workers in the Pilbara.

By late September the reality of the situation was becoming grimmer for activist Aboriginal workers and their families. McKenna wrote to the CDNR, asking for help. Describing low food supplies and minimal cash at Twelve-Mile Camp, he requested money be 'wired', to allow purchase of 'flour, tea and sugar from Marble Bar'.[65] Fortunately, however, the ration coupon situation had improved. 'Striking' workers had initially been refused coupons by the Department of Native Affairs – a measure described in the *Tribune* as punishment for daring to leave what the government considered as benevolent settings hosted by kindly station owners. According to the newspaper, CDNR protests had prompted reinstatement of these basic requirements. McKenna reported some promising progress as Twelve-Mile Camp residents established a vegetable garden. Indeed, the *Tribune*'s description of life there was glowing: 'Democratic organisation, planning and discipline characterise the camp of the natives'.[66] Here, comments by two observers are interesting. Max Brown identified that vegetable gardens and crops such as peanuts and beans were largely the responsibility of Don Stuart, a 'special category officer' with the Department of Native Affairs who was 'admitted to the tribe' and men's business.[67] But anthropologist John Wilson argued that Stuart's role at the Port Hedland camp was, in fact, that of government spy. According to Wilson, Stuart had a mandate to 'combat white influences'.[68]

The CIS was clearly unimpressed with the Pilbara situation. In the 'Monthly Report for September' by a secret operative (perhaps even Don Stuart), Aboriginal activists were identified as ignorant pawns in a much larger game. The walk-offs were firmly attributed to the 'agitation of D. W. McLeod'. According to this report (located in one of McLeod's CIS files), the 'native boys [did] not understand the reason for the strike'.[69]

In early October the prime minister became aware of union support for Pilbara Aboriginal people. The Melbourne-based national secretary of the Sheetmetal Workers' Union wrote to Ben Chifley protesting the jailing of McLeod, describing him as 'assisting the Australian Aborigines...to secure improved working-class conditions'. The union called for 'working conditions enjoyed by white men' to be extended to Aboriginal workers too.[70] Calls in the letter were, however, dismissed.[71] But the union's solidarity with McLeod and the Aboriginal workers was to initiate a string of detailed memoranda in Canberra. Pilbara's unrest became the focus for staff within both the Prime Ministerial and Attorney-General's Offices, and their correspondence is located in one of McLeod's CIS files. In one extremely interesting internal memorandum of the Attorney-General's Department, a detailed explanation of McLeod's and Hodge's arrests on 13 August is provided. Original transcript of their court hearings is also included as a fascinating attachment. Those intriguing documents merit further examination, as follows.

On 15 November Deputy Crown Solicitor J. M. Mills furnished the Commonwealth Attorney-General's Department with a comprehensive overview of what was happening in the Pilbara. Mills' memorandum included details of McLeod's court case on 23 August (when he was sentenced to three months' hard labour after accompanying Hodge to that fateful attempted meeting near Twelve-Mile Camp). Their appeals to the Supreme Court and referral to the High Court were also highlighted. Mills described 'some evidence that McLeod is a Communist'.[72]

Most usefully, Mills also attached transcript of McLeod's Port Hedland hearing. Its contents reveal the tricky business of Wild West law enforcement in 1946. It is clear from this document that police officers prosecuting the charges (in their guise as protectors of 'natives') had constructed a strong case. Constable Tom Needle described the somewhat comical details of the day's events. Under orders from his superior officer (Leslie Fletcher), Needle had spied as Hodge arrived at the airport to be whisked away in McLeod's utility truck. Police staffing and resources were clearly problematic in Port Hedland, as illustrated by what happened next. Needle needed to hastily procure a pursuit car. Its rather surprised owner (described as a 'Dalgety's Storeman' named William Kain) drove as they chased Hodge and McLeod along rough, red-dirt Pilbara tracks. They arrived at a clearing near Twelve-Mile Camp, where Needles discovered 'abt. 100 natives congregated' with the gathering 'lined up in semi circle, bucks one side, females along side them'. Hodge was no doubt embarrassed when immediately discovered crouching behind a bush. Constable Needle testified that McLeod had not been given permission to be in a 'native encampment'. Hodge and McLeod were arrested after Needle necessarily established that 'the congregation [was not] enjoyed in any native custom when I saw them…[they] were waiting for someone to address them'.[73] In other words, this was no corroboree.

By November the walk-offs had spread to an area known as Moolyella, around 20 kilometres west of Marble Bar (the spelling of Moolyella varies in the literature, including 'Moolyalla', 'Mooleyalla' and 'Mooleyella'). Communist newspapers reported more than 100 station workers walking away from oppression and setting up the Moolyella 'co-operative camp', complete with camp committee. This organisational structure replicated that of Twelve-Mile Camp at Port Hedland. According to McLeod, this latest walk-off was a reaction to news that Dooley's horse had been stabbed in the leg while hobbled (thus crippled) by unknown parties, 'to prevent him from making an organising tour among Aboriginal station hands'.[74] Workers had responded quickly to this aggressive act by decisively implementing widened industrial action.

Communist journalist Dorothy Hewett

Dorothy Hewett arrived at Port Hedland in December 1946. She was keen to meet with Don McLeod. Her first memorable inter-action with him had been at the Perth home of her editor (Alcorn) during the winter of 1946, when news of the walk-offs was fresh. She recalled mainstream press bans on the Pilbara walk-offs, 'but in the *Workers Star* we were printing Don McLeod's dispatches from the Nor'-West as if they came from the revolutionary front'.[75] McLeod had urged Hewett and her communist comrades to send 'revolutionary cadres to the Pilbara', and her lengthy visit to Port Hedland later that year was a response to his call. She recalled the temper of the time:

> If I hadn't experienced it first hand [sic] I don't think I'd have believed the incredible hostility in this town towards the Aboriginal people. It was quite outside anything I'd ever known before.[76]

Hewett's first rendezvous with Pilbara Aboriginal people consisted of an illegal, clandestine meeting in a shed at a secret location near the Twelve-Mile Camp. It was followed by several legal visits to the camp over the next month, with permission from the Protector. Her *Workers Star* article described the setting in warm prose: 'well constructed huts…water is ample and they have dug two good wells. The camp site itself is swept clean, and the sanitary arrangements are hygienic and good'. Food and goods were shared 'on a co-operative basis' by happy and welcoming people. Hewett identified Dooley as 'their full-blood leader'.[77] Of note, she made no mention of McLeod in the article, instead attributing all progress and successes to the Aboriginal people at the camp. Indeed, the title of her reflective poem about the walk-offs reinforced that Aboriginal position. McLeod's name is listed third, although the italicised *'ands'* between each of the names infer her need to emphasise equality: 'Clancy *and* Dooley *and* Don McLeod' (her usage of italics and capitalisation have been maintained in this presentation):[78]

Clancy *and* Dooley *and* Don McLeod

[The refrain:]
Clancy and Dooley and Don McLeod
Walked by the wurlies when the wind was loud,
And their voice was new as the fresh sap running,
And we keep on fighting and we keep on coming.

Don McLeod beat at a mulga bush,
And a lot of queer things came out in a rush.
Like mongrel dogs with their flattened tail,
They sneaked him off to the Hedland jail.

In the big black jail where the moonlight fell
Clancy and Dooley sat in a cell.
In the big white court crammed full with hate,
They said: "We wouldn't scab on a mate."

In the great hot quiet they said it loud,
And smiled in the eyes of Don McLeod,
And the working-man all over the land,
Heard what they shouted and shook their hand.

The sheep's wool dragged and the squatters swore
And talked nice words till their tongue got sore,
And their bellies swelled with so much lies,
But the blackfellers shoed them off like flies.

The sheep got lost on the squatters' run,
The shearing season was nearly done.
Said the squatters eaten up with greed,
"We'll pay good wages and give good feed."

The blackfellers sheared the wool and then
Got their wages like working-men.
The squatters' words were stiff and sore:
"We won't pay wages like that no more."

The white boss said: "STAY OUT OF TOWN,"
And they ground with their boots to keep us all down.
"We'll starve them out until they crawl
Back on their bellies, we'll starve 'em all."

The sun was blood on the bare sheep-runs.
The gins all whimpered: "They'll come with guns."
But we marched to our camp, and our step was proud,
And we sat down there and we laughed out loud.

[Refrain here, then:]

The young men marched down the road like thunder,
Kicked up the dust and padded it under.
They marched into town like a whirlwind cloud:
OPEN THE JAIL AND LET OUT DON MCLEOD.

The squatters are riding round in the night
Crying: "Load up your guns and creep out quiet.
Let's teach these niggers that they can't rob
The big white bosses of thirty bob."

Our young men are hunters our old men make songs,
And the words of our people are whiplashed with wrongs.
In the tribes of our country they sing, and are proud
Of the Pilbarra[79] men and the white man, McLeod.
Our voice is lightning all over the land,
And we clench up our fists on the sweat of our hands,
For the voice of the workers is thundering loud:
FIGHT WITH CLANCY AND DOOLEY AND DON
MCLEOD.

[Finishes with refrain]

Hewett's first secretive and illegal meeting with Aboriginal people exemplifies the oppressive laws at that time.[80] Given that she was a card-carrying communist, Hewett was a prime candidate to be monitored by police. Like Hodge, she had acted illegally simply by meeting with Aboriginal people. Arrest and jailing of a white woman would likely have presented a valuable publicity opportunity for the pro-Aboriginal movement. We can only suspect that the law chose to look the other way on this occasion. Thus, Hewett did not become a martyr for the cause.

A begrudging affiliation?

McLeod's activism for Aboriginal workers continued as impacts of the walk-offs spread. Although he maintained Party membership for several years, it appears that the mutually beneficial marriage was rocky. In 1996 McLeod recounted his first encounter with a room full of communists in Perth. Whilst informing comrades about the situation up north during early 1946, he recalled that he 'fell out with them almost straightaway…they were just arrogant'. McLeod remembered the communists as fanatical zealots whose lives revolved around political pursuits at the expense of their families.[81] We can only surmise whether hindsight had hardened his opinion of comrades by 1996, or whether his position had actually been that hostile during the late 1940s.

By early September 1946 the *Tribune*'s emphasis was subtly shifting away from endorsement of McLeod as the leader or main instigator of the Pilbara dispute. It emphasised Hodge's statement that:

> …the natives are strong and determined in this battle for their rights…Their leader, Clancy McKenna, has fine qualities of leadership, and a thorough grip of the position.[82]

McKenna was also an initiated man who had lived traditionally. Consequently, he had valuable experience of life from two different perspectives – traditional cultural as well as modern white.[83] Hodge also referred to the desire of Pilbara people to establish their own enterprises, free of white control and abuse. This possible snub by Hodge and the *Tribune* writer regarding McLeod's role and influence may have been intentional. It is entirely possible that his relationship with the Party was becoming rather tenuous.

McLeod's communist membership appears to have involved a somewhat begrudging affiliation with the Party. His position within the relationship was strained, given that his utopian hopes for a communal Aboriginal cooperative clashed with Party desire for Pilbara Aborigines to work and exist within a structured industrial model of wages, conditions, unions and bosses.[84] Indeed, McLeod indicated to Max Brown after the walk-offs that communist membership 'had become more of an embarrassment than a benefit'.[85] McLeod may well have been more than pleased to be reported as distancing himself from a controlling role within the Pilbara movement.

'Things will never be the same in the Pilbara'[86]

In early 1947 McKenna was again jailed. He was found guilty of enticing 'natives' from workplaces, and sentenced to twenty months. McKenna and eight other Aboriginal activists had transported about forty people from a Marble Bar station to the Port Hedland Twelve-Mile Camp.[87] A Perth public meeting organised by CDNR called for all charges to be withdrawn. The gathering also protested the sudden government ban on work permits for Port Hedland Aboriginal wharf workers:

> As colored [sic] Australian workers have for years been working there at award rates…we consider the latest action to be a deliberate attempt to deprive them of the equality they won and to drive them back to the stations as a source of cheap labor to the pastoralists.[88]

This sudden removal of worker permits highlighted the government's keenness to remind everyone who was in charge. This penalty action also probably intimidated any other workers considering industrial action.

Union support for Aboriginal wharf workers was immediate. Port Hedland's AWU branch threatened strike action unless permits for 'half-caste' Aboriginal members were reinstated. *Workers Star* reported that if police attempted to enforce new permit rules, all wharf workers would withdraw their labour. This strategy was described as a method 'to hound the half-castes back to the stations as cheap labour for the squatters'. The AWU also softened its stance towards McLeod, by agreeing to reinstate his membership after right-wing members had 'victimised' him for supporting Aboriginal workers.[89]

A citizens' deputation including Dorothy Hewett, Bootmakers' Union delegate George Stickland and Hotel and Caterers' Union delegate Cecelia Shelley visited the Minister for Justice Emil Nulsen. *Workers Star* reported his warm reception for the group. He acknowledged that a 'miscarriage of justice might have occurred', and undertook to help McKenna and the others. Hewett informed Nulsen that eleven Aboriginal men had been jailed for attempting to remove the 'natives' from one district to another. Her description of the hygienic conditions and efficient organisation at the camp convinced Nulsen to pledge assistance to the Twelve-Mile community.[90]

Courageous and defiant Pilbara Aboriginal people inspired other groups of workers to challenge oppressive employers. In February 1947 around 200 Darwin Aboriginal workers stopped work, protesting the inequality of wages and conditions between 'black and white' in defence services, government and private employment settings. The *Tribune* reported the strike as 'spontaneous, with no leadership from whites or mixed bloods...the names of the strike committee were withheld from white inquirers to avoid victimisation'.[91] One politician suspected a more sinister influence at play in Darwin. In federal parliament Northern Territory member Adair Blain described a dominant 'huge Communist flag' at the May Day procession. He demanded immediate government action against communism because 'disruptionists [from] the south' had infiltrated the Territory's 'fertile soil for the propagation of their ideology'. Blain believed that the besieged government was 'a trapped rabbit in the coils of the communistic python'.[92]

Blain's consternation reflected the high level of activism by communists and unionists during the period. The Party widely publicised Tom Wright's 'Fight for the Aborigines' report in journals and papers.[93] The *Tribune* reported Darwin Aboriginal workers embracing the stoic efforts of Pilbara people: 'the flame lit at Pilbarra [sic] burned strongly and spread across the continent'.[94] Indeed, over thirty unions protested in support of the Darwin workers' strike, with financial assistance provided by unions and communist organisations nationwide. Motivation for the Darwin strike was almost certainly inspired by the Pilbara campaign, and this powerful example of solidarity also prompted other Aboriginal workers to strike at Carnarvon and Broome.[95]

Pilbara activists soldiered on. A High Court appeal decision successfully quashed Hodge's conviction for associating with 'congregating natives'. Hodge was represented by Fred Curran and the unanimous decision was five to zero. As a result, people who were not Aboriginal were now lawfully allowed to meet with 'natives' outside their camps unless the gathering was held 'in pursuance of native custom', in the form of ceremonies or corroborees.[96] But this small victory for basic human rights was counteracted in June 1947, when the recently elected McLarty Liberal-Country Party coalition government reminded everyone of its power. A ban on firearms for Aboriginal people at Twelve-Mile Camp meant that guns were no longer available to people whose food sources and valuable sales of kangaroo skins depended upon ownership and usage of these weapons. Licences for people already owning guns were even revoked by Port Hedland police, and weapons were confiscated.[97] The *Tribune* reported McLeod's angry response to this repressive measure. He identified the decision an arbitrary attempt 'to starve the natives into submission', whereby access to the means of hunting 'to support their co-operatives' was denied.[98]

McLeod continued to be highly irritating to pastoralists. Robert Fellowes Lukis' frustration at Munda station was typical of other lessees. Following a successful 1946 shearing season, Lukis released his Aboriginal workers to Twelve-Mile Camp, for 'pink eye, corroboree and all that'. He provided extra wages, and instructed that they be ready for collection a week later. When the overseer arrived to pick up the workers, no-one climbed aboard the truck. Lukis believed that 'McLeod had collared the lot', and it left four white station employees to work a mob of sheep requiring the labour of twenty.[99] Other Pilbara station owners had similar experiences. The Minister for Native Affairs Ross McDonald was lobbied by Port Hedland MLC Welsh and a number of pastoralists with sheep needing to be mustered and shorn. McDonald ordered that departmental officials fly to Port Hedland and negotiate directly with the obstinate Aboriginal workers. His strategy involved a deal: if workers returned to stations and completed their duties, the department would look much more favourably upon their application for governmental recognition of their 'alleged organisation' as a formalised cooperative.[100]

In August there were more arrests. Twelve Aboriginal men were locked up, following their unsuccessful attempt to rescue abused children from a station. The *Tribune* reported a station manager allowing white men to 'pester' young Aboriginal girls and terrify a young boy by shooting at him. The twelve Aboriginal men who attempted to rescue the children were arrested, charged with abduction and barred from giving evidence at their own cases. Native Affairs also 'debarred' an Aboriginal man named Ron Thompson from working. His AWU 'ticket' had been removed, meaning he could no longer work without a permit, which was duly denied. The situation was explained in the *Tribune*:

> For twenty years it has been unnecessary for colored [sic] Australians to worry about permits, exemption certificates or citizenship certificates if the union decided to give them a ticket...The "charge" against him is that he is an "agent" of Mr. Don McLeod...and that he caused a strike on Mt. Edgar station.

McLeod's vehement reaction was also reported:

> This is all ballyhoo. I never met Thompson till the other day. He had nothing to do with the departure of the Mt. Edgar people, and he is not a member of the [North West Workers' Association]. This is but another example of the petty tyranny of the Native Affairs' Department officials.[101]

The campaign continued as fifty more Aboriginal people from two stations walked to Twelve-Mile Camp. CDNR called for donations to fund a test case against the rifle permit ruling. Support from the Communist Party continued despite the McCarthy-like witch-hunt raging against them in WA. Questions were asked in federal parliament. Liberal MHR Josiah Francis pressed Labor Kalgoorlie member Herbert Johnson about the 'rampant' communist presence 'among coloured persons' in north-west Australia and threats to 'safety of the white residents'. Johnson reported that his recent trip through the region revealed no evidence to substantiate Francis' concerns.[102] Numerous anti-communist measures were implemented by governments at that time, such as the following: expulsion of communists from organisations and workplaces, prohibition of meetings, prevention of venue usage, banning of communist journalists from parliament and the Arbitration Court, attacks in mainstream press, and de-registering of unions (in one example, the Locomotive Engine Drivers' Union was de-registered in 1946 after a strike was attributed to its communist members).[103]

The WA government continued its attempts to subdue Pilbara activists. McLeod protested the arrest and fining of two Aboriginal men collecting donations for the new school established by Aboriginal people at their Port Hedland cooperative camp. Native Inspector Gribble reportedly described their fundraising as 'robbing other natives'. CDNR considered the charges and subsequent court case an exercise in government subjugation, and another warning that their return to pastoral stations was inevitable.[104] However, 1948 was a year of significant advancement for Pilbara workers. The cooperative successfully established a company named Northern Development and Mining Company Pty Ltd (NODOM). McLeod was adamant that this company was 'theirs, not mine...they were their own mob, not "McLeod's"'.[105]

Australia's security organisation watched McLeod closely, and CIS files provide useful information here. A letter to McLeod identified him as secretary of the Port Hedland union branch. Waterside Workers' Federation (WWF) official (Robertson) congratulated 'comrade' McLeod on signing up ten new members and forwarding £16 of membership subs to the Sydney head office.[106] This correspondence identifies McLeod's industrial activity on a number of fronts. A CIS dossier on McLeod also reveals his formation of an Anti-Fascist League branch at Marble Bar. This organisation was considered to be a front for McLeod to peddle communist propaganda. CIS also deemed McLeod's leading role in the CDNR to be sponsored by the Party.[107] These security documents clearly identify McLeod's active roles as unionist, communist and Aboriginal rights activist.

A significant 'Report on Survey of Native Affairs' was presented to WA parliament in mid-1948. This survey was conducted by Perth magistrate F. E. A. Bateman. He had travelled to missions and stations across the state, and his findings provide a useful snapshot of the Pilbara at that time. The report identified 600 Aboriginal people living in two groups at Twelve-Mile and Moolyella camps. Bateman explained his view about why they clustered there:

> There can be no doubt that Communistic influence brought about the position but it is equally obvious that there was a certain amount of fertile soil in which to sow the Communist seed.[108]

Bateman also cast aspersions upon the government he reported to. He argued that grievances on stations went unheard, as a lack of supervision meant that Aboriginal people had no means for recourse. Protection officers allegedly spent more time with managers 'and had little to say to them [Aboriginal workers]'. Bateman continued:

> Had the Pilbara district been adequately patrolled by an inspector acting in the interests of the natives and one who had their confidence, it is probable that their grievances would have been discussed with their employers and a satisfactory settlement reached...too little notice was taken by the Department.[109]

Bateman's conclusion about wages and conditions was also blunt:

> In my opinion a minimum wage for native workers engaged in the pastoral industry in the North-West should be fixed... stations should be compelled to supply clothing in addition to wages...Where necessary accommodation in the way of huts and amenities should be improved.[110]

And his final barb stung:

> During the 150 years of white occupation of Australia the native has continued to live in filthy squalid humpies. It would be a worthwhile achievement to end all this and it would do much towards solving the native problem.[111]

Pilbara campaign 1949

By the end of March, tensions were again high. The labour-intensive shearing season loomed, and station managers were attempting to recruit Aboriginal workers. In April 1949 thirteen more Aboriginal people from Moolyella cooperative camp were jailed at Marble Bar for 'enticing natives' to leave stations. The Aboriginal man at the heart of this matter had been 'bluffed' into returning to Corunna Downs Station, and ten men responded to a call for 'moral support' by going to get him. They (and another three) were arrested when calling out workers from other stations as a show of solidarity. McLeod attempted to represent all the men at their trials but, as usual, was refused permission to do so. He informed the *Tribune* of the workers' decision to enact a general strike as a protest action: 'Decision is that no one goes back to work unless their boss negotiates an agreement on wages and conditions with me'.[112] Demands for the release of the jailed men came from the Seamen's and Coastal, Dock, Rivers and Harbour Works unions. The Seamen's Union announced plans to ban wool handling from 'slave station owners' at Port Hedland wharves, and a harbour workers' voluntary levy of sixpence per week 'to aid the Aborigines' struggle'.[113]

It is clear that, in a variation of the old business adage, wool talked. Any disruption to its movement around the globe was keenly felt. For example, Australia's wool exports to the USSR dramatically increased in 1948. Despite keen desire to curtail communist activities in Australia, the government nevertheless maintained a very cordial trade relationship with the Soviets. Meredith Burgmann identified trade with the USSR ballooning from 0.03 per cent of total Australian exports in 1944–45 to 2.26 per cent in 1948–49. Ironically, almost all growth in sales was due to 'the heavy Russian demand for Australian wool'.[114]

Small Pilbara victories were evident. The *Tribune* reported McLeod had 'won' improved wages and conditions for eight station hands at Mount Edgar and Limestone stations. It cited 'double victory in that the station managers recognised Mr. McLeod as the Aborigines' representative in the negotiations' at long last. It was hoped that an industrial flow-on would spread these improvements across the Pilbara. But pessimism lingered about potential payback for gains made in the new agreements: 'That is why the McLarty 'Liberal' Government has unleashed a reign of terror against Pilbarra [sic] Aborigines, jailing 43 members of their co-operative'.[115] Alcorn recalled this 'new attack [as] more vicious than before, chains and revolvers used, more rank and file jailed, longer sentences'. His Perth Party branch tried to alert the public, by issuing leaflets 'giving the facts'.[116] The 'new mob' of thirty jailed Aboriginal people were convicted of enticing others to leave what the *Tribune* described as 'slave conditions', after being arrested at 'revolver point and clamped in chains to be carted off to the Marble Bar jail'. McLeod's latest attempt to represent these men at court was as usual refused, as was Perth counsel provided by the Communist Party. Magistrate Hogg did, however, allow the Native Affairs inspector to 'defend' the workers.[117]

Communist news about the Pilbara reached Canberra. An article titled 'End scandal of chained Aborigines' contained descriptions of shackled prisoners marching many miles to attend trials. The *Tribune* emphasised federal inaction regarding these human rights violations in the Pilbara and NT.[118] In parliament Doris Blackburn MHR asked Minister for the Interior Herbert Johnson a lengthy series of questions about the story. His response was predictable and short, as he reminded the House that 'control' of Aboriginal people in a state was indeed a state responsibility. Federal government held no jurisdiction, hence no role in this matter. He also suggested that stories of chained and falsely imprisoned Aboriginal people were 'exaggerated, because the natives of that area are a civilized community' not needing to be chained. Johnson, thus, placed the ball very firmly in the hands of the State.[119] A similar story had been published by the *Tribune* during March. When Senator Morrow introduced the story and accompanying photograph about chained WA Aboriginal workers into parliament, Johnson had responded accordingly, by declaring the Pilbara situation a state matter and reiterating the federal policy regarding the use of chains on prisoners as applied in the NT.[120]

McLeod's enthusiasm was not wavering. He wrote to Minister for Native Affairs McDonald, citing the 'provocative campaign' of arrests and incarceration 'intimidating us'. He deemed the February declaration of Twelve-Mile Camp as a 'Prohibited Area' a strike-breaking act, and demanded 'a halt to these persecutions'.[121] The Pilbara situation attracted attention overseas as well. The *Tribune* again reported candid publicity by Britain's Anti-Slavery Society of 'slave conditions' and 'barbarisms' involving Aboriginal people being dragged behind police horses for 'very long distances' with families following helplessly.[122]

Seamen's Union black ban

The Pilbara struggle burst onto the mainstream industrial stage in June 1949, as a most important episode unfolded. McLeod and the Seamen's Union orchestrated a ban with extreme strategic effect – they hit squarely at the vulnerable hip pockets of Pilbara's woolgrowers.

Ron Hurd was secretary of the Seamen's Union. He was also a staunch communist who joined the Party in 1929.[123] Hurd had been sent to WA to oversee 'industrial work of the party', along with Sam Aarons, who became state secretary in 1948.[124] In April 1949 McLeod, on behalf of the Aboriginal 'strike committee', began lobbying Hurd to instigate black bans on handling wool from stations where Aboriginal people were not paid and unfairly treated. The strategy was simple: hit the growers where it hurt. Shearing season loomed and the Port Hedland wharf full of unloaded wool was a potential financial disaster for pastoralists.[125] McLeod and Hurd devised a strategic campaign, prompting immediate reactions from pastoralists and government. This appeal for a trade union to support Aboriginal workers' industrial rights was most fruitful. The action propelled their fight up and into the mainstream domain of an industrial relations system created and overwhelmingly controlled by white players. In this important move the battle was waged on what was, for a brief time, a level playing field.

A series of letters between McLeod and Hurd culminated with Seamen's Union agreement to take industrial action in support of Pilbara Aboriginal workers. On 30 June Hurd wrote to Commissioner of Native Affairs S. G. Middleton informing of the black ban on handling wool from stations refusing to employ Aboriginal workers under appropriate agreements. The union stipulated that bans would remain until new employment agreements were reached. It also demanded the release of Aboriginal activists from prison. The third claim was for a new framework of Aboriginal worker organisation, sanctioned and recognised by government and police.[126] In this way, Aboriginal people could then negotiate within the white world utilising an administrative structure that those in control understood.

The effects of the bans were immediate. Wool was sitting on Port Hedland's dock, instead of inside ships sailing to overseas markets paying record prices. The power of these packs filled with greasy fleece was quite remarkable. Jailed strikers were promptly released.[127] By late July the Seamen's Union claimed victory for Pilbara Aboriginal people.[128] The Department of Native Affairs appeared to capitulate. Officials promised agreements for improved wages and conditions, matching those negotiated by McLeod three months earlier at Mount Edgar and Limestone stations. The Seamen's Union victory did not come easily and one of their impediments sprang from a surprising adversary. AWU officials had attempted to break the black bans but did not have support of their 'rank and file'. Its members chose not to toe the union leaders' line, instead rallying in solidarity to support their Seamen's Union comrades and the Aboriginal workers.[129]

Further government submission was indicated. On 24 October the *Tribune* reported that all Aboriginal men jailed for 'enticing natives' from stations had been released. Seamen's Union members were jubilant, attributing much of the success to their 'solidarity ban' on the handling of wool from unscrupulous stations. Ron Hurd said that his union would 'continue to be vigilant for the defence and advancement of native workers' conditions as we are for all workers'.[130]

But things changed rapidly once the bans were lifted. In a somewhat predictable move, Deputy Commissioner Elliott-Smith promptly reneged on his promised enforcement of new agreements for Aboriginal workers, claiming that no such undertaking existed. The keenly anticipated and supposedly negotiated deal with the government did not happen.[131] However, the success of industrial intervention by the Seamen's Union cannot be understated. Its members provided Aboriginal people full and rigorous industrial support, and dubious activity by duplicitous politicians does not undermine this significant episode displaying powerful black and white camaraderie. Indeed, some years later, a *Tribune* writer reflected that 'working class unity triumphed', as exemplified by the 'solidarity' of bans placed on black wool from unprincipled stations.[132]

Conclusion

This account of the Pilbara walk-offs concludes here. From 1949 activists splintered into several groups as Aboriginal-owned and administered company cooperatives evolved. The first pivotal years of the campaign had contributed a profound legacy that the *Tribune* reported in 1955:

> Though some of the Aborigines won their demands, the majority never returned to the stations. Under the leadership of McLeod, they banded into a co-operative to win a living for themselves.[133]

McLeod's Aboriginal rights activist methodology was unusual. He acted as mentor and facilitator – by both advising and empowering. However, although lauded as the communist hero of the movement, Graham Alcorn believed that change would have come to the Pilbara irrespective of McLeod's fierce activism. Aboriginal plans were already being formulated, and McLeod was a useful conduit into the white world. Alcorn considered that 'without him the [walk-offs and cooperatives] would not have been possible, but there would have been something'. But of particular relevance here, Alcorn identified McLeod as the first activist to '…approach the issues from the working class standpoint…[McLeod was not] a Communist who took up the native question, but a native champion who joined the Party to further that struggle'.[134]

The exodus of Aboriginal people from Pilbara stations in 1946 demonstrated dire need for drastic change. The walk-offs materialised plans of Aboriginal lawmen and organisers, and white activists such as McLeod. His profound respect for the Aboriginal activists was clearly stated:

> …many of the strikers had tasted jail life and the "ringleaders" had been in and out of jail like clockwork. Strangely enough, the Blackfellows never wilted. Nothing that either the State or the police did could shake their solidarity.[135]

The admiration was mutual. Dooley Bin Bin's comments reveal respect for the white man who fought so doggedly: 'Before the strike we were nothing…They told us to keep away from Don McLeod – he was a Communist. But he showed us how to work together…Is that a bad man?'[136] In 1957, McLeod articulated hope for his Aboriginal friends:

> If we take courage and campaign with people of good will it is not yet too late to halt the rape of a worthy people and allow

them to rebuild their shattered remnants into dignified and self-supporting citizens of the sunny land now common to all of us, and loved by black and white alike.[137]

During that same year a prominent and influential human rights activist toured Port Hedland area Aboriginal camps, as part of a wider campaign sponsored by the Anti-Slavery Society to identify human rights abuses and present them to the UN (she became Australian representative of the Society's executive in 1956).[138] Her visits were reported by the *Tribune* and the *Seamen's Journal*. Lady Jessie Street witnessed orderly sanitary camps of healthy people, sturdy housing and shared income, where committees implemented communal decisions. Street identified clear parallels between co-op lifestyles and traditional Aboriginal living, 'where each has equal status, rights and responsibilities from the young to the very old'. She praised McLeod for '[leading] them out of the wilderness and [showing] them how to stand on their own feet'. Street called for compensation, hand-back of land, and a whole new infrastructure for dealing with the dilemmas of indigenous peoples controlled by white world rules in white world settings.[139]

Postscript

In 1962 the Australian Security Intelligence Organisation (ASIO) Regional Director in WA added a confidential note to a file on McLeod:

It has been said that Don MCLEOD is a mixture of prospector, which he is, saint, which he might have been, and revolutionary, which he was...He is bare footed and wears only an old pullover and a dirty pair of shorts. His turn out is more nondescript than that of any native in his camp...[but] when he talks there is obviously much of the old fire and brimstone left and occasionally he trembles with the intensity of his feeling. He is intelligent, shrewd and very suspicious. He has a deep love and respect for the natives and this appears to be mutual. He admits…that the communists used him up and he could not stomach the discipline they tried to impose on him. He is completely single minded on rights and justice for the natives and he fights this cause with a dedication "fierce and unswerving as the zeal of saints". His weakness is this very inflexibility which makes him equate disagreement with sin… Now he is an interesting old man whose power and influence are on the wane. Nevertheless a man who is, and will continue to be long after he is dead, a legendary character of the north.[140]

Jan Richardson took this photograph of sixty-one-year-old McLeod in 1969. Referring to the photo (in email correspondence with the author on 20 April 2012), Jan commented that 'Don certainly bears the scars of the long battle'.

CENTRAL AUSTRALIA

Weapons Testing Programs

Chapter Four

I move –

[That] the proposal to establish a rocket bomb testing range in Central Australia is an act of injustice to a weaker people who have no voice in the ordering of their own lives; it is a betrayal of our responsibility to guard the human rights of those who cannot defend themselves; and a violation of the various Charters that have sought to bring about world peace.[1]

Bomb tests in Aboriginal country? Doris Blackburn was outraged. This motion by the independent MHR in March 1947 reflected deep community concern already mobilised in response to the contentious plans of the Chifley Labor government. A little over three months earlier, Minister for Defence John Dedman had provided his Canberra colleagues with a detailed proposal. A guided weapons range would be constructed in Central Australia.

Dedman assured parliament that Aboriginal people living in the testing zone would be safeguarded. But according to Mrs Blackburn, Aboriginal people would be anything but safe.[2]

∽

In what sparked a string of major controversies and even a Royal Commission, Australian and British governments collaborated to orchestrate numerous weapons testing programs on Australian soil. Over the next two decades, vast areas of hitherto remote Central Australian desert were transformed. Roads were gouged through arid country, and a township for defence personnel was swiftly constructed. Rockets were launched and nuclear weapons detonated. In Aboriginal country.

Communists and unionists pledged to wage war against the weapons research programs. They were joined in protest by a broad cross-section of Australian society. Bloody battles of World War II had so recently concluded, and so any proposal to test new weapons in Australia was bound to be met with opposition from war-weary people craving peace. That the program was to be conducted in Aboriginal country added a whole other dimension to this eclectic protest movement representing left, right and centre.

Our interest here lies with communist and unionist contributions to the movement. More precisely, focus is upon their protests about the impacts upon Aboriginal people living in or near the weapons testing areas. Ironically, the proposed projectile line stretched north-west from Woomera across South and Western Australia to cross the coastline near Port Hedland. This was straight over the heads of that other group of Aboriginal people who were busy fighting their own battles for justice in a different arena.

Three chapters concentrate on the testing programs. This chapter describes implementation and conduct of the tests, and the period of investigation ranges from 1946 until the late 1950s. During that time, Australia's federal government changed hands. Responsibility for safe implementation of the tests was, thus, in the hands of Labor and the Liberal-National coalition. The second and third chapters focus on communist and unionist protests against rocket testing and nuclear programs. Their support for Aboriginal rights and safety is identified and contextualised within the wider protest movement.

Beginnings of the weapons testing programs

The announcement in 1946 that British rockets were to be fired across Central Australia aroused surprise, suspicion and anger in many quarters. Opposition erupted from an eclectic protest movement including the Communist Party, unions, church and pacifist organisations, and women's groups. People struggled to understand how their federal government could capitulate so readily to host Britain's weapons tests on Australian soil, so soon after the brutality of World War II was finally and thankfully over.

Detailed analysis of development and implementation of the weapons testing programs is not necessary here. What follows is an overview. Peter Morton's *Fire Across the Desert* is a comprehensive account of the genesis and operation of Woomera's Rocket Range.[3] Dr Morton was commissioned by Australia's Department of Defence to write the Woomera story in 1983, and several descriptions of the rocket range here derive from his publication. Despite the pitfalls accompanying the compilation of any commissioned history, Morton's publication provides thorough description of Woomera's Weapons Research Establishment (WRE) and a solid introduction to the testing program. *Fire Across the Desert*, however, pays minimal attention to nuclear testing programs conducted during the 1950s and 1960s at Monte Bello, Emu Field and Maralinga. The reports of the Royal

Commission into Nuclear Tests are recommended as thorough and reader-friendly accounts of the tests and their ramifications.[4]

World War II had provided a grand and ugly theatre for weaponry. Britain's experience of that war was devastating, and a new military plan was urgently required. Weapons had become more sophisticated, accurate and stealthy, and Britain lagged behind. The 'guided missile age' had arrived, and that country was keen, perhaps desperate, to secure its own arsenal of high-tech weapons. Rearmament, despite Britain's precarious postwar financial position, became a top priority for that island country with raw vulnerability so keenly felt.[5]

Britain's development of a nuclear weapon began in 1947. The first of its series of tests on Australian soil did not commence until 1952. However, research into guided weapons (or rockets) proceeded quickly. By July 1945 Britain had its own Directorate of Guided Projectiles. With weapons developed and ready to fire, all they needed now was somewhere to launch them. Eyes turned to the antipodes. A rocket range 1,600 kilometres long would eventually be needed, and Central Australia fitted the British bill perfectly.[6]

Central Australia and its peoples

As Australians soon discovered, the main base for the WRE would be constructed at a remote location named as Woomera in April 1947. On today's roads, driving distance between Adelaide and Woomera is nearly 500 kilometres.

Remote desert north-west of Adelaide was speedily transformed into a defence settlement facility. A township arose in the middle of red dirt nowhere. Electricity, telephones and water supply came to the desert. Roads and airstrips progressively altered landscapes as human and physical resources moved in. And with them came the inevitability that tribal and semi-tribal

Aboriginal people would eventually experience ongoing contact with Europeans.

Rocket range trajectory sliced through the middle of two Central Australian Aboriginal Reserves saddling the borders of SA, WA and the NT. Approximately 259,000 square kilometres of land was involved. The region featured arid semi-desert with low mountain ranges, spinifex, mulga scrub and sandy plains. Movements of people, both Aboriginal and others, were governed by availability of often scarce water supplies.

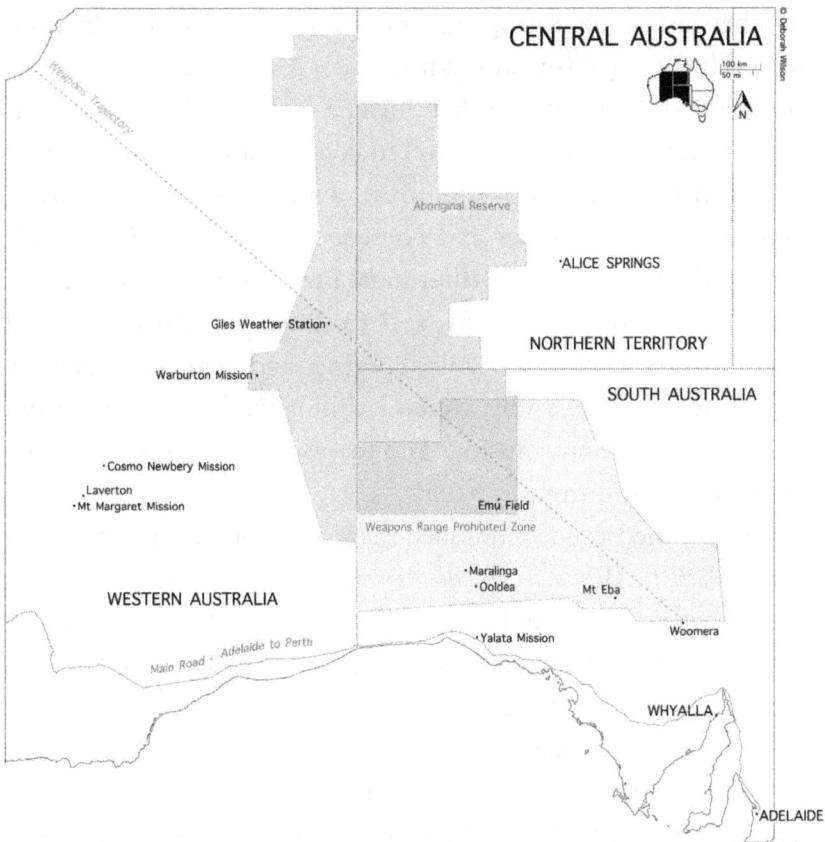

In the north-western regions of SA and the desert south of WA, many Aboriginal people were still living traditional lifestyles. They hunted, conducted ceremonies and moved camp often, largely oblivious to the white population and culture soon to overwhelm their existence. Anthropological studies of Central Australia conducted prior to, and during, establishment of the test sites, vividly described tribal life. Anthropologists such as Ronald and Catherine Berndt and Norman Tindale spent considerable time in that region, and their fieldwork is particularly relevant to the period under consideration. They contributed invaluable research into the lifestyles and cultures of many groups prior to their unsolicited immersion in European community.[7]

Aboriginal people in these areas were members of a large number of tribal and language groups. In 1942 the Berndts lived with a Pitjantjatjara-speaking nomadic group in the Ooldea area of western SA. They recorded thirteen moves within six months. Reasons for them included travel to ceremonies, deaths, firewood requirements, sanitation and stress within the group.[8] Advancing white communities and consequent contact had gradually impacted upon traditional Aboriginal life. Lands were claimed for pastoral and mining pursuits, and roads crisscrossed the rugged Australian outback. Nomadic hunting and gathering peoples, inconveniently in the way, were increasingly relocated away from traditional areas into missions and towns. Many drifted between Aboriginal and European worlds.[9]

In 1951 the Berndts published their study of cultural transition *From Black to White in South Australia*, based on fieldwork conducted between 1941 and 1944. This concentrated upon people still living traditionally and existing within complex legal, ceremonial, semi-nomadic systems. Agriculture was not practiced – hunting and gathering provided all that was required. In large part, water governed people's movements. Permanent waterholes attracted camps in the dry. People 'scattered to tribal areas' when rains came, moving often to new food sources. Ceremonies were also conducted seasonally, with people more likely to gather during times of plenty.[10]

The concept of 'country' is particularly pertinent here. The Berndts emphasised the relationship between tribes and the land. Country was not owned – it was looked after. Members of families from past, present and future held enormous responsibility. Peoples' futures were inexorably bound to the land's ability to sustain them – respect for country and its resources was vital. People lived in their own country, as their parents and grandparents had done. They expected their children and grandchildren to continue to do so forever, but this ancient process was about to cease.[11]

Anthropologists were not the only non-Aboriginal people in Central Australia. Native patrol officer Walter MacDougall was employed by the WRE in 1947, and his activities are further considered later. MacDougall recorded precise observations of tribal Aboriginal people and raised repeated concerns with government over the next fifteen years. His valuable knowledge was also shared with anthropologists. Tindale acknowledged MacDougall's guidance into remote places, far from any tracks known to white men. The patrol officer introduced him to 'new' tribes of people entirely unaware of Australia's alien white world.[12] MacDougall's knowledge of tribal life and cultural decay inspired aggressive advocacy for the people he was charged with finding, then relocating, away from the danger zones. For MacDougall though, dangers were much more likely to emanate from contact between black and white than from the detonation of a bomb.

State and federal responses to the proposed tests

South Australia's enduring Premier Thomas Playford greeted the news of a rocket range with jubilation. He believed that such a significant project (initially intended to be built at Mount Eba) would provide an economic windfall for the state. Playford thought that water could be piped from the Morgan-Whyalla pipeline along a very handy new railway line, providing invaluable spin-off water supplies to pastoralists along the route. However, the federal government was quick to identify the steep costs of locating the range at such an isolated inland spot. The range was moved to Woomera. This place was much less remote and much more convenient, being closer to Adelaide and the transcontinental railway running between Adelaide and Perth.[13] Only one SA politician actively opposed the tests. Lin Riches was a Labor MLA, and also the Mayor of Port Augusta. He announced to the local parliament that:

> Australia owes it to its Aborigines to preserve them in their own Reserves...the discharge of rocket bombs will not only be a source of danger to them, but will almost inevitably destroy the native game upon which they depend for a living.[14]

Australia's rocket range venture with Britain was formally explained in a statement to federal parliament by the Minister for Defence and Post-War Reconstruction on 22 November 1946. Twelve months of negotiations between Britain and Chifley's Labor Government culminated with Cabinet approval of the plan. John Dedman informed the House that the trajectory of guided missiles would extend from Mount Eba (moved to Woomera soon after) towards an imaginary point on the WA coast, midway between Port Hedland and Broome. The first phase would involve a 480-kilometre 'short range', with later capabilities to extend that target area. The required land was to be 'reserved'. Australia, with its vast remote spaces and favourable climatic conditions, was the only landmass in the Commonwealth capable of hosting such a program. Dedman identified SA and WA as willing hosts of the British project. He described the area involved as 'largely uninhabited', with risks to Aboriginal people as 'negligible'. He advised that the 'possibility of a missile falling on them would be extremely remote'. Further-more, he stated that any contact between workers and Aboriginal people would be 'safeguarded', to ensure their 'safety and welfare'.[15]

Minister Dedman was clearly convincing. Adelaide's *Advertiser* took him at his word with a front-page headline announcing that the 'Rocket risk to natives' was, indeed, 'negligible'.[16] The previous day, readers had learned where the bombs would fly. It published the following map featuring the 'rocket bomb range', including the small inset map identifying the proposed water pipeline from Port Augusta to Mount Eba:[17]

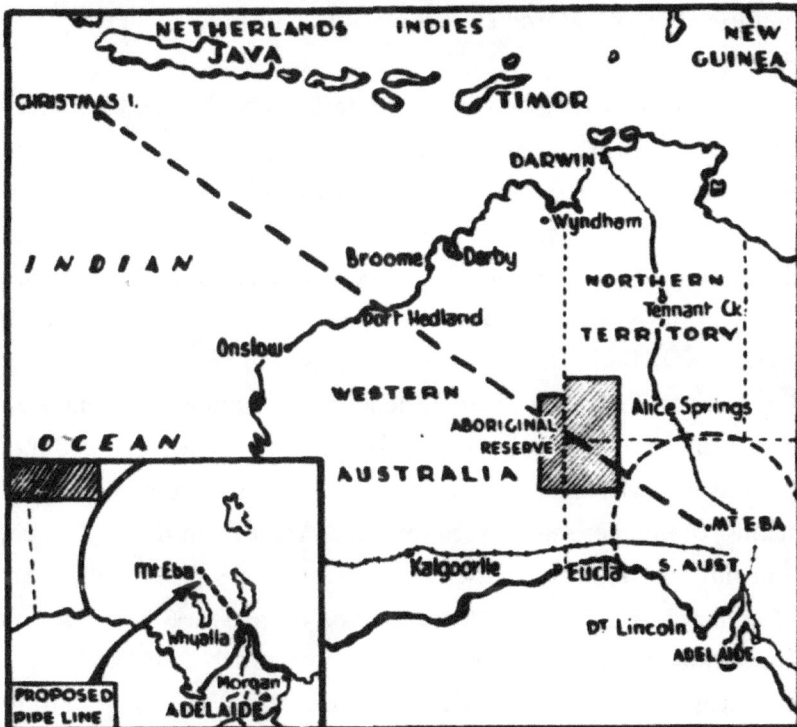

Where Rocket Bombs Will Fly

The broken line on this map traces the course of the proposed rocket bomb range. In the first instance rockets will be launched at Mt. Eba and will land in Australia. Subsequently they will be directed at Christmas Island. Inset—The proposed water pipeline.

Doris Blackburn was quick to highlight community opposition to the tests. Her allegiance to the Labor Party had ended in 1937, when members expelled her husband Maurice. Doris Blackburn's ongoing opposition to the weapons testing program was, therefore, in no danger of being hobbled by party politics. The *Tribune* reported that she had prompted Prime Minister Chifley's admission that various factions opposing the rocket range had already made representations to his Office and sent deputations to Minister Dedman. The protest movement was already visible and well underway.[18] Blackburn's loud opposition to the tests continued throughout the duration of the programs. Her politics were driven not only by advocacy for Aboriginal rights but also activism for world peace, as evidenced by her membership of Women's International League for Peace and Freedom (WILPF).[19]

Blackburn's pacifism was likely influenced by her husband's commitment to the peace movement. A CIS file-note identified Maurice Blackburn's membership of the Council Against War and Fascism in 1937. According to the file, that affiliation was the reason for his expulsion from the Labor Party. Blackburn was not readmitted to the Party until he ceased his association with the anti-war body deemed a 'communist subsidiary movement'.[20] Thus, his wife's status as an Independent Labor parliamentarian is not surprising. Doris Blackburn's independence enabled her to actively campaign against the tests. Her very public protests against the rocket range were unusual. Apart from the occasional murmur of lukewarm dissent from Canberra's party politicians, Blackburn's was the only federal voice of relentless and resolute opposition. Indeed, her contributions to the debate became regular feature articles in the *Tribune* – maverick politicians were most useful to the communist press, provided they were singing from the same hymn book.

Minister Dedman's request that Aboriginal safety and welfare be safeguarded was satisfied with the addition of five specialist members of the Cabinet-sanctioned Committee on Guided Projectiles in January 1947, including Professor A. P. Elkin, anthropologist Donald Thomson and Charles Duguid (medical practitioner, Presbyterian Church moderator and Ernabella Mission founder), and they were invited to a Committee meeting on 1 February to provide expert advice on Aboriginal protection. Their views were included in the *Report on Welfare of Aborigines Located Within the Range Area*. Duguid made clear objection to the range's site and its impact upon indigenous inhabitants. The life-long activist for Aboriginal rights was not overly concerned with the dropping of an occasional bomb; the dangers he identified lay in the broader ramifications of contact. He believed that no amount of safeguards could ameliorate the dangers presented by white men in black country. Thomson echoed Duguid's fears, but Committee members chose to ignore their learned (and invited) guests' advice. They concluded that detribalisation was inevitable, and that contact between tribal Aboriginal people and white men would merely speed that process up a bit.[21] The views of Duguid and Thomson were therefore superfluous, but lip-service had been paid.[22]

Blackburn's opposition continued. The *Tribune* published her parliamentary notice of motion in December 1946 (see the first page of this chapter for the quotation). This motion was introduced into parliament on 6 March 1947. It heralded long and passionate debate, which was suspended then eventually concluded on 1 May. Strong support for the British–Australian project by the Chifley government and Menzies opposition ensured the motion's defeat. Blackburn considered that the weapons program would commit 'an injustice to the weaker people…the "voiceless minority"'. She identified that the government was reneging on its 'trusteeship' of Aboriginal welfare:

When we are considering the establishment of a range for testing guided weapons our ideas of our own defence had better be limited by our feelings for the rights of others – the rights of the black men and women who live in Australia and from whom we took this country.

Her emotive speech continued:

...we have not shown, by our treatment of the native peoples here, that we have the right to call ourselves a civilized nation. We have degraded the dark-skinned people wherever we have come into contact with them. The aboriginal [sic] women have been subjected to much offence by the white man.[23]

Dedman moved to assure the House that the program had been thoroughly scrutinised. The first 480 kilometres of the range were not even, he claimed, within Aboriginal reserves. He described the number of Aboriginal people within the area as 'comparatively small', with the estimated 1800 Aboriginal people equating to only 'about one every 50 square miles'. The Minister did, however, concede that 'at times the natives may congregate in one spot'.[24]

The Committee on Guided Projectiles report was discussed in parliament. Dedman announced that it supported government arrangements safeguarding people living within the range area, and that criticisms of the plans by Duguid and Thomson were unfounded. Ramifications of contact with 'native' Aboriginal people were to be just another step in the 'inevitable' process of detribalisation. The report found that 'their [weapons tests'] only effect would be the putting forward of the clock regarding detribalization [sic] by possibly a generation'. Dedman assured the House that the appointment of patrol officers in the area would sufficiently control any damage that contact might create.[25] But for Blackburn, contact implied the gravest danger:

> ...the real danger to the natives will not be the falling projectiles but their probable contamination by the white people who go into that area.[26]

Extensive contact would require supervision. But the appointment of just one patrol officer 'to supervise an area which would easily contain England and Wales' highlighted the naivety and ignorance of governmental administration.[27]

Anthropologist Thomson could not let Dedman's public opinions pass without comment. In May 1947 he wrote a booklet for the Melbourne-based Rocket Range Protest Committee (this organisation is important and will be examined in the next chapter). In *The Aborigines and the Rocket Range*, Thomson identified government smears of the anti-testing protest campaign:

> Charges of communism, of irresponsibility towards the defence of Australia, have been dragged like a red herring across the trail, to confuse what is a separate and clear-cut issue. I am not a Communist, and as an Australian who knows the aborigines [sic] and who has served his country, I claim the right to be heard.[28]

Thomson argued that consequences would be 'fatal' for the Aboriginal people – a 'disaster' rivalling Tasmanian and Victorian black pages in Australia's history. He described his token participation in the projectiles Committee meeting, claiming to have been summoned with only a few hours' notice and no briefing about the discussion topic. Thomson recalled that when he and

Duguid entered the room, 'it was clear that [our] presence was a mere formality in deference to the instructions of the Minister'. Warnings about contact in the Western Desert spelling disaster for Aboriginal inhabitants were 'not palatable' to Committee members, but Thomson was sure that 'posterity [would] prove the truth'.[29]

Weapons testing and national security

Potential sabotage at the rocket range provided ideal opportunity for soapbox theatrics. Fears of communists were loudly articulated by anti-communist politicians. A Canadian Royal Commission had recently investigated Soviet espionage activities, and many Australian politicians were keen for a similar process in their country too. Joseph Abbott MHR introduced a matter of 'urgent public importance' in March 1947; namely, safeguarding secret details of the 'rocket projectile experiments' from 'leakage' to 'foreign powers'. Abbott was keen to initiate a communist witch-hunt. Protection of state defence secrets provided perfect justification to launch a very proper and legitimate security exercise, with the happy coincidental spin-off that the odd communist spy or two might be flushed out.

Abbott argued Australia's need to heed Canada's experience. Spies exposed by its Royal Commission were all members or sympathisers of the Canadian Communist Party. Abbott told parliament that this should be 'a warning to us that, in regard to our research work [the weapons tests] in Australia...no Communist or person with Communist sympathies is given access to the findings'. He went on to name names of dubious Australian persons and organisations, paying particular attention to the Australian Association of Scientific Workers and identifying a number of members as communists.[30] Victorian MHR Thomas White echoed Abbott's push for a Royal Commission:

Any frustrated person, any failure, finds a welcome and a haven in the Communist party. Many so-called Australian Communists do not know what communism is all about, but they are the willing dupes of the real Communists. We must have a royal commission to find who those real Communists are and what they are doing.[31]

Fear of communism was palpable. White flagged the possibility that communists were ensconced in high-ranking public service positions. He even targeted prominent Melbourne schools 'where veiled communism is taught'. White warned that communists were not just the 'wild and woolly men in trade unions who want to disrupt the country'.[32] Others also supported a Royal Commission. Percy Spender MHR warned darkly:

The Communist party here is one integer of a vast organization [sic] which, in a sinister and ruthless manner, is ready to use any means open to it, even in countries that fought with it, to advance its international needs.

As did Rupert Ryan MHR:

The Communist movement here is strong and virile...they are pledged irrevocably to Russia itself. We should take extensive security measures at once.

And Henry Gullett MHR:

[Australia's Communist Party] today is nothing more or less than the intelligence wing of Soviet Russia...engaged in ferreting out defence secrets and in "fifth column" activities....There are two types of Communists in this country...the more intelligent sort [of] the half-baked university professor type...[and the] "dopes" or "boobs".[33]

Protest organisations

Initial rumours about long-range weapons testing in Central Australia prompted the hurried formation of a protest body in South Australia. Members representing a diverse spectrum of organisations established the campaign committee. These included the Society of Friends (Quakers), Women's Christian Temperance Union, Howard Reform League, Aborigines' Friends' Society, Council of Churches, Socialist League, Federation of Scientific Workers, and Adelaide's Common Cause (a group established in 1943 which advocated greater unity in the war effort and postwar reconstruction, and headed by Duguid). Common Cause members circulated petitions throughout SA in August 1946. They also wrote letters to Australian and British politicians, League of Coloured Peoples, Anti-Slavery League and Aborigines' Protection Society, and British and Australian newspapers. Common Cause protested the dangers for Aboriginal people and threats that preparation for another war posed to mankind.[34]

Duguid quickly became a very annoying critic of government plans. He began prying about the proposed rocket route early in 1946, and questions were soon asked about whether Duguid was driven by humanitarian concerns or communistic zeal. Duguid was definitely a champion of Aboriginal rights, but it seems unlikely that political affiliations figured in his activism. Indeed, he provided his own last word on the subject. When interviewed in 1980, 96-year-old Duguid was adamant that he had never been a Communist Party member.[35]

Duguid's non-partisan Common Cause social reform agenda merely moulded to embrace needs of Aboriginal people in the firing line, but Army Intelligence believed otherwise. One report identified communist infiltration into a range of organisations, including Common Cause. It also highlighted Don McLeod's activities in that other Aboriginal rights activism hotspot in the Pilbara. These examples were cited as clear evidence of insidious activities by desperate communists. But the report's description of Duguid's organisation as a hotbed filled with reds was unfounded. Only three members of Common Cause, with minimal influence, were actually suspected as communists.[36]

A Melbourne Rocket Range Protest Committee meeting on 31 March 1947 was attended by 1,300 people. They hailed from forty-six very different organisations, including trade unions, church groups (including Quakers), pacifist groups and the women's temperance movement. A Military Intelligence spy reported the Communist Party as one organisation 'associated with the gathering'. But communist participation did not mean communist control. The spy reported that 'although supported by the [Communist Party], the meeting does not appear to have been influenced by the Communists'. An almost unanimous vote called 'to abandon the rocket project in the interests of the aborigines [sic] and world peace'.[37] Victoria's Christian Pacifist Movement endorsed this sentiment, and Reverend Robert Green wrote to the prime minister that he was:

> ...asked to point out that this protest came from united action by 46 organisations of which the Communists were but one. The Communists did not initiate the move nor did they in any way dominate the action taken.

Green acknowledged that the Rocket Range Protest Committee and its affiliated organisations collaborated in the 'interests of world peace and international good will [and for] the sake of the Aborigines'. He insisted that calls for the abandonment of tests not be linked with any communist direction.[38]

Duguid was one of the speakers at that Melbourne protest meeting. His lengthy address was published by the Rocket Range Protest Committee. Duguid reinforced Thomson's comments about their sham appearances before the Committee on Guided Projectiles. He said they 'realised that reason and argument have no effect against closed minds. The military mind was made up long ago. In my opinion the people have been fooled'. Duguid's closing sentiment was foreboding:

> ...my hope is that you will all see in the proposals a final token of Australia's disregard of her minority race. Shot and poisoned as they were in the early days, neglected and despised more lately, must our Aborigines now be finally sacrificed and hurried to extinction by sudden contact with the mad demands of twentieth century militarism?

Attendees heeded Duguid's call. In one of two resolutions, those present:

> ...earnestly and respectfully [urged] the Australian Government to abandon all projects of this nature, which violate the policy of the United Nations in regard to primitive races and Australia's claim to international status, with responsibility for native races in the South West Pacific.[39]

The March 1947 meeting was a pivotal turning point for the protest movement. A Gallup Poll conducted during that month identified opposition to the tests primarily involving fears about harm to Aboriginal people. The focus of protest was about to shift, with an 'easing' of the Aboriginal issue into the background from that time onwards, as pacifist arguments about worldwide armament build-ups drove most protest actions.[40] But as identified in following chapters, while peak protest bodies may have been changing tack towards pacifist concerns, communists and unionists maintained focus upon Aboriginal rights, as rockets then nuclear weapons were tested in Central Australia.

Pastoralists were singled out for special treatment in federal parliament. Almost identical Dorothy Dixer questions were asked in the upper and lower houses on 25 November 1947. And nearly identical responses were dutifully issued by Minister for Munitions (Senator John Armstrong) and his Lower House representative: 'pastoral pursuits' of graziers unlucky enough to be farming in or near the rocket range would be guaranteed, and pastoralists were assured that their safety was tantamount and grazing capabilities would be protected. 'Interference' would be 'reduced to a min-imum'. Armstrong assured concerned members he was 'taking a keen personal interest in these matters, and that the interests of all concerned will be safeguarded'.[41] The pastoralists had friends in high places. They, their land and their stock would be fine.

∞

The township of Woomera was built upon desolate red earth at breakneck pace. A sealed road now connected this newest Australian centre with Adelaide. Electricity, telegraph lines, drainage, water, houses, offices and warehouses were all speedily established between the new airfield and railway, with the rocket 'rangehead' a safe 32 kilometres away. In April 1947 the Long Range Weapons Board decreed that nomenclature for this new centre should incorporate an Aboriginal word. *Woomera* (a type of spear thrower) was chosen. But, as was later identified, the desert people of the central desert area actually used an entirely different word to describe their spear thrower – *miru*. Woomera was a word used in eastern Australia.

By mid–1950 Woomera's population was 3,500. A compre-hensive range of services and shops greeted workers and families moving into the area. Thousands of bombs were exploded on the range from late 1947 onwards. Guided missile tests began in late 1949, and continued over several decades. However, the weapons testing story took an abrupt turn in 1953 when nuclear weaponry was first detonated on the Australian mainland.

Nuclear weapons testing program

The first central desert nuclear test was conducted in October 1953. But this was not the first to occur in Australia over what became a twelve-year nuclear program. The initial detonation site was at Monte Bello Islands, 120 kilometres off the north-west Australian coast. There, *Operation Hurricane* exploded a nuclear weapon in the hull of an ageing British frigate on 3 October 1952. Significance of that blast was identified in the 1985 Royal Commission report about the testing program, whereby 'UK joined the United States and the USSR to become the world's third nuclear power'. The Commission identified several other more disturbing characteristics of that first atomic blast. It highlighted 'scant attention... paid to the location of Aborigines during the Hurricane test'. The report cited a dubious local demographic document that 'British authorities [had] appeared to rely upon'. It apparently listed '715 [white] people...and detailed enumeration of hens, ducks, cattle, horses and sheep' in the north-west danger zone, while totally ignoring the real (and known) presence of Aboriginal people.[42]

Nuclear test rumours abounded. Prime Minister Menzies was increasingly pressured to make clear exactly what would be happening. He assured parliament that all Australian newspapers would have equal access to information about imminent atomic explosions. The public would know all they needed to know. Menzies guaranteed that any restrictions regarding the program's security would apply equally to all media organisations.[43] Scaremongering in the press heightened government pressures. Newspapers reported that clouds of nuclear particles could drift across the continent to the densely populated east coast for up to five years. Minister for Supply Beale was forced to refute rumours that live animals would be used in experimental nuclear blasts. Menzies resolutely swept away any threats to human safety: 'I have stated repeatedly that the important tests...will not be associated with any danger to Australian lives'.[44]

Menzies told parliament he did 'not believe that there are any fears in the mind of the Australian public [regarding the tests]'.[45] In response to a Dorothy Dixer question by MHR Gordon Freeth regarding a mid-October delay to testing, Beale squashed rumours of government capitulation to public outcry about nuclear fallout dangers. He attributed the real reason for the postponement to scientific personnel controlling the blast's timing. In a faithful toe of the Party line, he echoed his prime minister:

> I do not believe for one moment that the Australian people are anxious. The tests are quite safe. If they were not safe they would not be taking place. Furthermore they are part of the defence of the free world, and I believe…that all Australians are glad to play their part in such defence.[46]

The patriotism card was now in play, and public opinion was about to be tested. The first nuclear weapon was detonated in Central Australia, just one day after Beale's stoic statement.

∞

On 15 October 1953 the first of two *Operation Totem* nuclear weapons exploded at Emu Field in the Great Victoria Desert. This was nearly 500 kilometres north-west of Woomera. The governments of Britain and Australia wanted to compare two types of atomic weapons, so the second test was duly conducted on 27 October at the same location. Six days after the first Emu Field test, Menzies again moved to nullify any concerns about safety. He also added just a hint of fear to his campaign:

> The tests are conducted in the vast spaces in the centre of Australia…[if Australia does not conduct the experiments] believe me, the enemy will conduct them…The greatest risk is

that we may become inferior in potential military strength to
the potential of the enemy.[47]

The testing program rolled on, and the Menzies government
justified increasing expenditure. In 1955 Minister for Supply
Beale announced the next year's program estimate as £8,551,000.
This was £500,000 higher than the previous year, and a doubling
of annual monetary commitment since the tests were costed in
1948. Total program expenditure to 1955 was £54,000,000. Beale
regarded this spending as Australia's vital contribution to 'the
welfare of the free world' and 'prevention of a third world war'.
Indeed, he declared Australia's 'merciful service to humanity'.[48]
Beale informed parliament that Britain was deeply impressed and
thankful for Australia's contribution to its defence. The spin-off
for Australia was that 'if Britain went under, we should be in
deadly danger...a lot of money will be spent in the interests of
Australia and the free world'. Beale also comprehensively identified
Australia's allegiance to Britain when quoting part of a speech
by Governor-General Sir William Slim where Slim said: 'My
Government is co-operating with the Government of the United
Kingdom in the testing of nuclear weapons. They will, consistently
with the safety of the civil population, continue to do so'.[49] But not
all parliamentarians were convinced. In 1956 Henry Bruce MHR
identified Australians as 'guinea pigs for the United Nations'. Menzies, however, responded in customary manner that atomic tests on
Australian soil were 'directly relevant to the safety of free men'.[50]

Beale faced mounting concern in the scientific community. He
again assured parliament that testing would be conducted 'with
the most careful regard to safety'. Beale also pledged full confidence in the abilities of two native patrol officers – MacDougall
and Robert Macaulay (who was appointed in August 1956). Their
seemingly impossible mandate was to roam the huge and remote
77,700 square kilometres of desert across SA and WA, looking

for Aboriginal people at risk within the target or fallout zones. That they managed to coax people away from their land without duress or force is surprising. Beale boasted that 'No aborigine [sic] has been forced to evacuate his tribal territory'.[51] The government line was that Aboriginal people had willingly walked away from their country, traditions, ceremonial and burial grounds.

An observation made in the Royal Commission report about MacDougall is noteworthy. He was one of very few non-Aboriginal people who knew the country and many of the people who roamed it. The report identified the contempt with which MacDougall's invaluable knowledge and relationships with Aboriginal people were treated:

> Officials of the [Weapons Research Establishment] withheld information from MacDougall, they tried to silence him, and they discredited him. Such was the relationship between the one person who knew about Aborigines and was concerned with their welfare…It was in this environment of uncertainty and conflict that MacDougall had to conduct his patrols during the [Maralinga] tests.[52]

Exacerbating this was the 'chaotic' nature of ground patrols involving new recruit officer Macaulay. This 23-year-old anthropology graduate had rarely been out of Sydney. His mandate was to patrol thousands of square miles of desert. Macaulay (who commenced employment ten days before the first nuclear test) was not even supplied with a vehicle or radio. He knew nothing of the region's Aboriginal peoples or the country he was now patrolling, and had no briefing on the tests or dangers.[53]

Macaulay and MacDougall faced an impossible task. Two men didn't have a hope of clearing all Aboriginal people from the huge danger zone. And consequently, as the Royal Commission found, we will never really know how many people were affected by radiation sickness or the actual detonations.

Maralinga

Late in the afternoon of 27 September 1956, the first in a series of atomic weapons was exploded on the Maralinga Range. *Buffalo Two*, *Three* and *Four* were subsequently detonated on 4, 11 and 22 October. Maralinga was the new testing site. The program had moved from Emu Field to this much more accessible area with better water supplies.

The 1985 Royal Commission established that ground and aerial searches for Aboriginal people were conducted in a 275 kilometre radius of the firing sites. It found these searches to be grossly incompetent hit-and-miss affairs. Poorly resourced and incorrectly targeted searches were conducted intermittently, based upon completely inadequate knowledge of Aboriginal movements and behaviours. The Commission identified that numerous reports existed about Aboriginal people walking in groups across the area, but these were ignored. The author of those reports – MacDougall – was considered a most reliable source. He had continued to warn the testing controller of significant numbers of nomadic people moving, as per usual, throughout their traditional hunting and ceremonial lands. His observations continued as the tests were planned, and then conducted.[54]

Six conclusions about the effects of Maralinga *Operation Buffalo* nuclear tests on Aboriginal people were presented in the Royal Commission report. They highlighted abject failures by British and Australian governments to protect and respect Aboriginal people, land and culture. This is a summary of key findings:

(a)   Overall, the attempts to ensure Aboriginal safety...demonstrate ignorance, incompetence and cynicism...if Aborigines were not injured or killed as a result of the explosions, this was a matter of luck...

(b) [the] site was chosen on the false assumption that the area was not used by its traditional Aboriginal owners...sightings of Aboriginal people [were] discouraged and ignored.

(c) ...construction of the Giles meteorological station and roads brought intruders and detrimental effects to the [Aboriginal] people north-west of Maralinga.

(d) Native Patrol Officer MacDougall was placed in an impossible situation...The affairs of a 'handful of natives' counted little compared to the interests of the British Commonwealth of Nations.

(e) The Pom Pom [Milpuddie family] incident demonstrated that flaws existed in the security system at Maralinga.

(f) For the Milpuddies the experience caused great concern and it distresses Edie Milpuddie today...[the possibility exists that] the contaminated area resulted in injury to them.[55]

The tribal Milpuddie family referred to in the Report had wandered into a radioactive site several years after tests had been conducted. Their story is further described later.

∞

In late 1957 *Operation Antler* was conducted at Maralinga. This last major nuclear test program on Australian soil involved exploding three bombs, on 14 and 25 September and 9 October. These tests were code-named *Tadje*, *Biak* and *Taranaki*, representing the locations of each test.

The Australian government continued to pay lip-service to Aboriginal protection. On 2 October Beale again assured parliament that tests occurred with 'complete safety'.[56] Comments in the 1985 Royal Commission report regarding this politician's inept activities were scathing – for example, 'But still Beale bumbled on'. Beale's continued denials about Aboriginal people in the

Prohibited Zone were described in the report as his 'falsehoods'. One of these falsehoods regarded the location of Giles Weather Station. Beale suggested it was nowhere near an Aboriginal watering place, but that is exactly what that place was. He also claimed that contacts between Aboriginal people and white workers were 'carefully controlled'. Evidence presented to the 1985 Commission contradicted this claim. Numerous examples of gross negligence were presented, including an incident where workmen photographed a 'native birth'.[57] Commission findings were damning:

> [Aboriginal] people continued to inhabit the Prohibited Zone as close to the test sites as 130km...[they also] continued to inhabit the Prohibited Zone for six years after the tests. When they were told to leave the Prohibited Zone, some of them perished.

∞

Worldwide concern and protest against nuclear testing culminated with the declaration of an international moratorium in Geneva (signed by the UK, USA and USSR) in 1958. The testing of nuclear weapons was banned until 1961.

∞

Communist and unionist activism against the weapons testing programs was an integral aspect of these campaigns, and this is examined in the next two chapters. The discussion begins as colourful communist protest methodologies reveal not only orthodox, but also more unusual and creative, outlets of articulation for Aboriginal rights.

Chapter Five

Rocket Tests Danger To Our Aborigines

The *Tribune*'s headline was dramatic and ominous. Rockets armed with bombs would be tested in country where Aboriginal people still maintained nomadic hunter-gatherer lifestyles. The Communist Party, unions, churches and an eclectic assortment of community groups were collaborating in protest against the proposed rocket range. The article warned that bombs could conceivably 'land in the Aborigine reserves'. Bigger-picture fears were also presented, with the *Tribune*'s writer bleakly suggesting that surely weapons tests were sound indicators of preparations for another war?[1]

∞

Opposition manifested in many typical forms. Public meetings, marches, letters and newspaper articles variously condemned Woomera's programs, and these are discussed later. However, before moving to that section, several more unusual characters and their methods of protest will be examined. The cultural vitality of the time is highlighted as three communists – poet, playwright and artist – reacted to the news that guided missiles would soon fly over Aboriginal reserves.

'Where is the Dead Heart of Australia?'

Nearly three months after the *Tribune* article appeared, a new story about the dangers for Aboriginal people was published by an intriguing, but minor, poet. An impassioned plea by 'Rickety Kate' was published by the *Tribune* in November 1946. Communist poet Minnie Agnes Filson adopted her widely-known pseudonym to advocate abandonment of tests for the sake of tribal Aboriginal people. Filson's compassion was not surprising. Her personal battle with profound disability likely influenced this emotional call for Aboriginal safety, as rheumatoid arthritis during her early twenties had manifested into devastating adulthood paralysis. Filson spent most of her time bed-ridden or reclined on a couch, while friends and family members transcribed her poetry and other writings for publication in newspapers, literature collections and schoolbooks.[2]

Filson's *Tribune* contribution 'Where is the Dead Heart of Australia?' juxtaposed beauty and destructive peril. She began by describing the glorious Australian landscape and rich culture of its 'small nation' peoples. Filson believed that Aboriginal lands and lives were violently threatened by the weapons program. She foresaw 'bomb craters in the country of a people **whose culture included no organised warfare** [Filson's bolding]'. For this passionate writer, the coming of 'civilisation' was obscene:

Some of us heard the laughter and the singing change to the awful silence which follows after the cataclysm. We saw the Sacred Stones defiled; we saw the camps of the white men at the water soaks; we saw the caravans crossing the ancient tracks laden with food and scientific instruments and booze; and we saw serenity in a people replaced by fear and cunning and bewilderment; and we saw the rape of their women.[3]

Filson's lengthy article radiated passion and determination. She believed that Australia's government had two choices: either kowtow to the mother country by hosting Britain's defence program, or summon the courage to stand up for the human rights of its indigenous population:

There are some of us who will not rest until this nation stands by its solemn commitment to humanity in general and to the small nations...**in particular** [Filson's bolding] to this small nation, whose life is threatened with extinction [we] will not cease to demand that Government in the name of its people should make some avowal of faith in the future by refusing to allow these tests to take place anywhere in Australia. Should the Government have the courage to make a gesture so divorced from fear and so identical with its pledge to humanity, this could be our finest hour. Or is the heart really dead?[4]

An epic poem (about an Aboriginal dreamtime story) entitled *Bralgah: A Legend* had vividly portrayed Filson's fascination with Aboriginal culture and language two years earlier. This was published (in her third book) by the Jindyworobak group in 1944 (Jindyworobak writers and artists incorporated Australia's landscapes and peoples into the country's literature and artwork, and included Aboriginal culture).[5] Filson considered this a very important piece of work that promoted and celebrated the beauty and power of Aboriginal stories.[6]

Filson's keen interest in Aboriginal people began many years earlier. She collected newspaper clippings and written notes about Aboriginal languages and words as a teenager in 1912, including her great-uncle's compassionate and insightful articles about Aboriginal people published in the *Goulburn Evening Penny Post* in 1913. Her lifelong commitment to social justice was evidenced in writing for Sydney's Radio 2KY, which was owned and operated by the NSW Labor Council and known as the 'trade union station'. Filson contributed letters to a program called 'Mrs Grey's Women's Session' from the 1930s until the progressive and controversial program ended when Mrs Grey died in 1946. Filson's communist membership officially commenced at around this time, although she had already been a supporter for many years. This affiliation with the Party was, however, short-lived. Her great-nephew related that membership had 'put at risk' his grandparents who were living in the USA:

[Minnie's brother-in-law William Stuart Long] was really spooked that Hoover's FBI would realise that he and Ruby [Minnie's sister] were related to a Communist in Australia...they became paranoid about...losing their American citizenship.[7]

Filson's membership came to an end: 'She was very brave but in the face of McCarthyism and Menzies would have been cautious'. However, her progressive free-thinking and openness to many philosophies and theories continued throughout her life.[8]

An ASIO report written about Filson's son in 1950 indicated that she was not considered a threat to Australia's security. It identified Filson 'a literary student of some note' who had been 'confined to her bed for the past 25 years'. The officer added, 'it is reported that she is unaware of her son's associations with the

Communist Party'.[9] Seemingly, the subversive capability of a woman with profound disability (unlike that of her able-bodied son) was not a possibility as far as ASIO was concerned. But given that this report also identified Minnie's keen intellect and published body of poetry, perhaps the officer should have taken a closer look.

High drama at New Theatre

Filson's powerful *Tribune* propaganda supporting Aboriginal rights was followed by another writer's dramatic interpretation of testing program's dangers. Communist playwright Jim Crawford articulated his commentary in a speedily-created new play titled *Rocket Range*. It was staged at Sydney's left-wing New Theatre in March 1947.

Before moving to a discussion about Crawford's play, a short introduction to New Theatre is timely. It formed in 1932, and is now the oldest continuously performing theatre in Australia. New Theatre was established by worker organisations and initially presented short sketches known as 'agit prop', or agitational propaganda. Other New Theatres were later established in Melbourne, Brisbane, Adelaide and Perth. While dramatic productions involving political themes were regularly presented, New Theatre also featured many mainstream plays by internationally acclaimed writers as diverse as Shakespeare, Tennessee Williams, Jean-Paul Sartre and George Bernard Shaw. It also maintained a strict policy of presenting Australian socially relevant content by writers including Frank Hardy, C. J. Dennis, Mona Brand and Dymphna Cusack.[10]

Left-wing theatre attracted a diverse audience. ASIO officers also keenly observed what they considered to be communist propaganda camouflaged within theatrical amusement. There are over 900 pages in ASIO files on New Theatres in Sydney,

Melbourne, Adelaide and Perth. Security officials clearly recognised the power that creators of theatrical propaganda could exert. ASIO considered New Theatre to be an Australian version of its Russian counterpart that offered free amusement for workers while insidiously promulgating propaganda messages. Class struggle was the key to New Theatre's popularity. Audience members became drawn into the struggles of the masses via dramatic appeals to their hearts and consciences. And as far as ASIO was concerned, those audiences were chock full of communists and their travelling companions.[11] When Jim Crawford's latest production opened to a packed house on 14 March 1947, there is little doubt that at least one audience member was there to observe more than just the play.

The *Tribune* introduced *Rocket Range* to readers. Crawford's theatrical representation of white man's impact on Aboriginal land was described as 'a hard-hitting indictment of the Evatt-Chifley policy [throwing] into sharp relief the lack of understanding by the authorities of our Aborigines'. The article summarised the plot:

> Sent as labor spy for the builders of the rocket range, the white man kills game needlessly, takes lubras as he wishes and, crowning blow of all, whips the lubra "because she smells". The play moves to a climax with a killing, the visit of a policeman, further killing, and the chained Aborigines being led off the stage as the young lubra wails beside her dead mate.[12]

Rocket Range features three scenes set in 'an Aboriginal encampment' at night or dusk. Crawford's script-notes emphasise the 'considerable importance' of lighting and music during breaks between scenes – the full impact of the storyline, thus, reinforced by dark atmospherics. There are seven characters. Six are Aboriginal (an elder, two 'warriors', two girls and a 'black tracker') and one is a white policeman. The Aboriginal roles were all played by white actors with darkened skin (Aboriginal people did not play Aboriginal roles until relatively recently).[13]

Crawford's crafting of the dialogue in *Rocket Range* is particularly interesting. He dictated his strategy at the opening of Scene One: 'The [tribal] Aborigines' talk is given straight. Pidgin is used only when they are retailing [retelling] remarks of white men'. This strategy ascribes value and agency to noble tribal Aboriginal characters, as they tell their stories in articulate and sophisticated English. Crawford relegated the less civilised conversation (pidgin) to any Aboriginal comments about the story's villains – the clumsy and ignorant white men. This tactic is clever. It immediately informs the audience that the Aboriginal discourse is much more logical and intelligent, or cultured perhaps.

The play begins with discussion among Aboriginal characters about recent observations of a white interloper in the desert. In the play's singular comical moment, Gimbin the elder asks 'How on earth are we ever going to absorb him?'. Crawford made sure that the audience appreciated his version of Aboriginal culture. He did this by inserting snatches of dialogue explaining aspects of Aboriginal life – for example, the roles of (and respect for) elders, law, hunting and gathering practices, and the significance of totems and the Dreamtime. Whilst this strategy does contentiously position Crawford as a white man telling Aboriginal stories, we can guess at his motives. It is highly likely that he was attempting to explain this culture to a less-informed Sydney theatre audience.

We learn that the white interloper has stolen away a young girl from the tribe. He broke traditional law by camping with the girl beside a waterhole where women's business bans the presence of men. The young girl returns to the tribe that evening. She has been beaten by the white man. Kajabbi (a young man in the tribe who learnt English while stolen away to slave for tin miners) goes to find and speak with the white man, who explains what is about to happen in the desert. Kajabbi relays the white man's pidgin version of this information to the others in the tribe: 'This place belong big gubment feller now...belong Prime Minister'. Crawford's script continues:

> This feller place Rocket Range now...He said – "Big budgeree"[14] feller Rocket live longa here soon. He go "Wheeeeeeeh" [WAVING HIS ARMS] Then he go – Boooooooooom! When he go Boooooooooooom! no more man, no more woman, no more piccaninny, no more kangaroo – no more nothing all about. Him all dead longa Rocket.

Gimbin's response to this terrible news sees the Aboriginal elder's script-lines return neatly to proper English: 'Incredible! Good God, the man must be a raving lunatic'. The tribe consider their options in light of this terrible new predicament. They decide that this 'murderous-minded lunatic' should be killed.

Crawford's instructions for the final scene are clear: 'This scene should be played quickly and violently'. It is set on the day after the white man has been killed. A policeman and 'black tracker' enter. One of the Aboriginal men is wounded then shot dead while reaching for his spear. The policeman throws a chain to 'black tracker' Jacky and his pidgin instructions are: 'You gettim spear, you gettim nulla-nulla belong those feller. Then chain them up, d'you hear?'. The script describes what happens next:

> Jacky collects spears and boomerangs and lays them at policeman's feet. He then commences to loop chain around Aborigines' necks as the policeman rolls Namalka's body over with his foot and looks at him.

The policeman ensures that Jacky is a reliable witness. He feeds him an intimidating version of the truth: 'You bin seeim this feller throwim spear longa me? You bin seeim that, Jacky?'. Jacky complies with 'Yes, Boss'. *Rocket Range* concludes as chained Aboriginal characters are led off stage. The policeman reloads his gun and buckles his spurs as *Advance Australia Fair* is played in the background.

∞

Rocket Range is powerful political propaganda. Aboriginal people are respectfully portrayed within ancient culture of deep knowledge and spiritual wonder. White men are presented as ignorant, violent and uncivilised thugs who rape women, kill men and chain necks. Woomera's rocket range is depicted as the ultimate white weapon threatening tribal Aboriginal people. Playwright Crawford artfully draws his audience into the dark and ominous plight of desert Aboriginal people. Blame is pinned on all white players – the government, police, miners and range workers. There is no happy ending. If Aboriginal people are forced from the desert, Crawford's script warns of lives ruined by starvation and permanent loss of culture.

New Theatre's production of *Rocket Range* was hailed in mainstream press. The *Sydney Morning Herald* reported the play 'impressively produced', with a script creating:

> ...an eerie atmosphere [enabling] the observer to live in the world of the first inhabitants of the Continent, and to see the white man's power and ruthlessness through their sad and bewildered eyes.

Rocket Range and two other New Theatre plays received high praise as 'alive, relevant and challenging'.[15] Admiration for the left-wing company's productions was however short-lived. Between 1948 and 1961, the *Sydney Morning Herald* refused to accept advertisements for New Theatre plays, and this dearth of publicity adversely affected audience numbers when Cold War fears had already created a tough business environment for this radical theatre.[16]

Crawford did more than write plays. In Melbourne's communist *Guardian* two months later, Crawford claimed to have identified an ulterior motive behind development of the rocket range. He alleged that 'big meat combines have eyed this country hungrily', and that provision of territory for the weapons project provided ideal opportunity for seizure of Aboriginal land by 'forbidden white men'. According to Crawford, the northern range zone boasted 'some of the finest pastoral country in Australia', and government intended to 'facilitate this grab'. By removing Aboriginal people from this vast area, the government was saving pastoralists the usual problem of 'clearing off the aboriginal [sic] tribes in the manner usual to Australian capitalism'. Crawford wrote passionately:

> The central core of tribal unity, tribal culture and the tribal will to live is based on the rocks, trees, lagoons and sacred places of the tribal domain. To divorce the aborigines [sic] from these is to divorce them from their sources of life.[17]

Crawford was also a communist educator. His CIS file detailed a number of Sydney Marx School sessions where he lectured about the 'primitive communism' of Aboriginal people.[18] In an article published by the *Guardian*, Crawford explained why he wrote *Rocket Range*. He hoped that it provided insight into 'clan communism' of tribal Aboriginal people, whose lifestyles were disrupted by ignorant authorities. Crawford argued that *Rocket Range* was a stark reminder of the dire need for Aboriginal people to continue cultural practices on their own lands. He believed that white intruders needed to tread lightly and think carefully before every potentially damaging move they made.[19] *Rocket Range* reached international audiences too. A CIS officer reported that the play was later produced in Budapest by the Australian delegation to the World Youth Congress.[20]

Another contemporary theatre commentator echoed Crawford's pleas. In *New Theatre Review*, Maxine Bucklow described Aboriginal land and culture placed in jeopardy by the tests, and called for vigorous protest 'against this criminal intention'. Indeed, the *Review* editor deemed the weapons program to be 'one of the most important issues in our country today – especially as it affects the future of the aborigine [sic]'.[21]

Commentary in caricature

Another communist expressed his protest to the weapons tests in artistic form. In this example, caricature articulated the message. Noel Counihan was one of the best-known social realist artists in Australia. His dark art during the 1930s reflected observations of working people suffering enduring legacies of the Depression. Counihan's caricatures featured regularly in the *Bulletin* and the communist *Guardian*. His artistic commentary turned to the impact of the rocket range in 1946. On 5 November the *Tribune* published his cartoon:[22]

THE AUSTRALIAN: You will drive us from our source of life.
THE IMPERIALISTS: Life! Who said we are interested in life?

The Aboriginal man is portrayed as strong and proud. He carries a boomerang and spear with *miru* (spear thrower), indicating that he is a hunter for his tribe. Behind him stand a number of people, including women and children. He appears to be the group's representative confronting rocket range workers. By contrast, the white men are depicted as overweight and short. One holds a gun and looks intimidating. The other appears somewhat goofy, with bulging eyes indicating surprise or perhaps fear. In comparison, the Aboriginal man stands tall and looks physically powerful and handsome. He stares down at the man with the gun and bag full of rocket plans. His physique dominates the caricature, radiating power and the stoic presence of an Aboriginal warrior.

Counihan embraced communism early and joined the Young Communist League in 1931, when a teenager. Later membership with the Party often inspired his work. Counihan's drawings, paintings and sculptures regularly depicted the injustice and struggle of marginal or oppressed groups. Art historian Bernard Smith considered that 'the party gave him eyes'.[23] The Party also actively supported Counihan and his art. In 1945 it featured his work at an exhibition marking the twenty-fifth anniversary of the Party, and also purchased a painting to support this 'progressive Artist'.[24]

Being a communist was a badge of honour for Counihan. His relationship with the Party was never concealed and his artistic commentaries on life were presented to the public on that basis. While radical politics frosted his reception within Australia's circle of artistic critics at times, Noel Counihan was, nevertheless, extremely successful. Indeed, by the end of 1946, Counihan was one of the most recognised, respected and admired artists in Australia.[25] Although best known for paintings and linocut prints, Counihan's caustic cartoon commentaries made him an invaluable conduit of communist propaganda. Between 1944 and 1946, his satirical political caricatures featured weekly in Party newspapers.

A conservative *Tribune* commentator

Two weeks after Minnie Filson's impassioned call for weapons tests to be abandoned, a more unusual article appeared in the *Tribune*. A communist journalist had interviewed (then published) the remarks of a much more conservative opponent of the tests.

This interesting article was published in the *Tribune* four days after Minister for Defence and Post-War Reconstruction John Dedman furnished parliament with details of the weapons programs. The newspaper had secured an interview with A. P. Elkin (Professor of Anthropology at Sydney University). Elkin had provided contributions to the communist newspaper on a number of previous occasions. His endorsement (in a 1945 *Tribune* edition) of a Party initiative that government provide a mobile medical unit for Aboriginal people in remote areas was particularly supportive.[26] Elkin, a prominent advocate of assimilation, weighed into the weapons testing debate by suggesting to the *Tribune* that the allocated £6,000,000 could be much better spent acquiring education and land for Aboriginal people in Central Australia. Elkin believed the 'bomb testing course' to be Britain's way of keeping up with the Joneses – whatever America had, Britain had to have too. He said:

> America has a bomb range, so now apparently Britain has to have one and the authorities are going to spend six million pounds providing it.[27]

Elkin warned that 'natural water and food supplies would be endangered and would possibly disappear' if real war-heads and 'gamma rays were exploded on the Warburton and other ranges'. He called on the Department of Native Affairs to address the welfare of the estimated 2,000 Aboriginal people living along the projectile line. Despite this rather radical sentiment, Elkin also articulated support for the government's conservative assimilation policy. He presented an alternative proposal if the tests proceeded. If tribal Aboriginal people were to be relocated away from the danger zone, Elkin suggested that they could seize golden business opportunities by growing vegetables and meat for 'scientific outposts' monitoring the tests in the bush.[28] Thus, despite his clear opposition to the weapons program at this time, Elkin's worst-case scenario for tribal Aboriginal people was still a win-win for assimilationists. Even if the tests proceeded, Aboriginal people could be removed from the desert, to be then successfully immersed within the white world of agriculture and commerce.

Elkin's most cordial relationship with the *Tribune* contrasts with comments he made about two of his colleagues at that time. In correspondence between Elkin and the Committee on Guided Projectiles Chairman (L. E. Beavis), Elkin linked Donald Thomson and Charles Duguid to the Communist Party. It is likely that Elkin smeared the reputations of the Committee's two advisers in order to undermine them, as well as the wider protest movement. Elkin told Beavis that Thomson 'seems to be well thought of by them [communists]'. He considered Duguid would be 'used by them', and described his writings about the weapons program as 'Dr Duguid dressed in red'.[29] Given that Elkin had provided commentary to the *Tribune* previously, where his recommendations and contributions to public meetings were reported most positively, it is clear that Elkin too was 'well thought of by them'. While mischievously linking Thomson and Duguid with communism, Elkin was probably lucky that his fellow Committee members were not *Tribune* readers.

It is interesting to note that although Elkin was never known to be a member of the Party, his political activism had already meandered to the left. He was identified as a well-known supporter of Russia against the Nazis, who had chaired a meeting of the Friendship with Russia League in 1945. His left-wing associations were evidenced 'most damningly' by his membership of the Australian Association of Scientific Workers. This organ-isation was regularly placed under the spotlight by Australia's security organisations, and many of its members were considered politically suspect.[30]

Australia's broader scientific community faced a number of challenges during the decade following World War II. In an article examining the compromising impact of overt communism on the careers of two scientists, historian Phillip Deery argued that during the Cold War years, most Australian scientists were either members of the Communist Party, or enthusiastic travelling companions. This period proved challenging for many seeking academic posts, and security files were compiled on those deemed politically risky. These, of course, included scientists conducting research for nuclear or weaponry programs. A typical case was that of 'Dick' Makinson. By publicly declaring Party membership in 1946, Makinson stymied his own professional career for the next decade. His many applications for academic positions in specialty fields of radio and nuclear physics were repeatedly rejected for seemingly spurious reasons. Another nuclear physicist (Thomas R. Kaiser) is also discussed in this article. His overt communist status created very similar problems to those of Makinson. It appears that Australia's security organisations collaborated most effectively with government instrumentalities, ensuring that questionable identities did not infiltrate into top-secret programs.[31]

Elkin's opposition to the rocket range was short-lived. Indeed, that disapproval transformed into full-fledged support. Six months after his anti-tests comments appeared in the *Tribune*, Elkin back-flipped to deliver a government-endorsed statement supporting the range. This about-face buttressed a collaborative attempt by Elkin and the government to bring 'futile protests' to an end, given Elkin's revised belief that no harm would come to Aboriginal people. In his article for the *Sydney Morning Herald*, Elkin argued that central desert missions were already successfully assimilating tribal people as part of a necessary 'civilising' process, and he expressed complete confidence in the patrol officers' abilities to protect remaining nomadic desert peoples.[32] Indeed, a month later the *Canberra Times* reported Elkin saying that 'emphasis on the danger to the blacks was overdone'.[33]

Anthropologist Geoffrey Gray argued that Elkin was indeed a man who did not tend to rock the boat, but that he was also a pretty wily tactician, considering himself the eminent 'guardian' of Aboriginal people. He credited Elkin's political manoeuvrings with securing the employment of the two 'native patrol officers' deployed in the Woomera area, but tempered this with the view that Elkin 'often inflated' his importance, and was probably his own biggest fan.[34]

Communists and the Australian peace movement

Activists opposing establishment of the rocket range were also participants in a broader mushrooming anti-war movement. During the late 1940s, Australian pacifists formed a number of new associations at state and national levels. Delegates travelled to domestic and international peace conferences. The face of Australian peace activism changed significantly during this time, and it is important that these anti-war bodies be included in this discussion. Most of Australia's peace groups were widely considered to be communist fronts. A brief introduction to these peace organisations contextualises examination of the wider anti-nuclear movement in the following chapter.

Australians joining the peace movement hailed from all walks of life. Their objections to the weapons programs, while encompassing the need to protect Aboriginal people, also incorporated global arguments about world peace and disarmament. It is important to identify who these people were and what they were fighting for. Communists formed a significant sector of the anti-war movement, and their roles will be discussed here within broader themes of that activism.

By the late 1940s peace councils were being established in Australian states. During 1949 (when the peak Australian Peace Council formed) two interesting things happened. Firstly, in the midst of Cold War hysteria about all things red, the Chifley government's much lauded new security organisation – ASIO – sprang to life. This new spy-catching body didn't remain under Labor Party control for long, as the second interesting thing occurred. In December government changed hands, and Robert Menzies became Australia's new prime minister.

Communist general secretary Lance Sharkey enthusiastically endorsed the growing peace movement, while distancing his Party from control of the process:

> We Communists do not want to "boss" such a movement or order it about, nor define its policy or dictate its tactics; we want to see a broad mobilisation of peace-lovers fighting on a broad programme, directed against aggression in the interest of the overwhelming majority of mankind. The Communist Party will take its full share of the work of such a movement and give its fullest support to it.[35]

Alec Robertson was a Party member (and Party National Executive member) and journalist (including editor of the *Tribune*) from the 1940s onwards. In a reflective article, he noted his belief that communists and trade union officials embraced the peace movement because they needed to consolidate the ground achieved over the previous few decades. Robertson argued three main reasons why such significant energy and resources were directed by communists into the peace movement. Firstly, fears of a war being waged against the USSR by the USA and their allies produced a defensive need to prevent their soviet comrades becoming the new target. Secondly, new knowledge of China's successful revolution filled communists in Australia and overseas with hope and confidence for successful global communist movements. World peace held the key to the ongoing spread of communism. Thirdly, with the election of the Menzies Government came a new danger of right-wing attacks on basic rights of association and political affiliation.[36]

The Australian Peace Council (APC) was formed in Melbourne by a group of communists, religious leaders and future Labor politician Jim Cairns (then a senior lecturer in economic history at the University of Melbourne) in July 1949. The first three organising secretaries were all Communist Party members.[37] Cairns recalled that the APC was significantly controlled by the Party – he parted company with the peace body a year or so later, but although identifying 'very authoritarian' communist influence, denied this as the reason for his departure.[38] By September the APC had formulated a policy, manifesto of objectives and program of action. Its report for that month described the new organisation as 'non-party and undenominational', with 'about 70 representative citizens drawn from all States [sic]', including unionists, representatives of religions, writers, scientists, housewives and politicians. Understandably, communists were not included in their itemised list. The APC's manifesto identified fears of another world war, and endorsed the Charter of the UN signed four years earlier. By promoting peace and disarmament, the APC view was that people power would overcome government efforts to gear up for new wars.[39]

By 1950 many Australians were fully engaged in the movement to ban the nuclear bomb. The NSW branch of the APC had formed to join the fight, and communist WWF heavyweight Jim Healy was a prominent member.[40] Over 200,000 signatures were added to petitions (circulated predominantly by communists) as part of the World Peace Council's 'Stockholm Appeal', which attracted up to 500 million signatories world-wide calling to ban the bomb. A Peace Congress that year in Australia involved rallies of up to 12,000 people in Melbourne. Robertson considered the Congress as 'underwritten by the CPA', with significant communist organisation and funding of the events. Indeed, he believed that the peace movement, more generally, 'was in effect, the conscious Left [consisting] almost entirely of communists and their supporters'.[41]

Following attempts by the Menzies government to ban the Communist Party in 1950, via its Communist Party Dissolution Bill and unsuccessful 1951 referendum, communists decided to re-brand their peace activism. Propaganda became softer. Hard-line revolutionary slogans and provocative statements were replaced by community and peace-friendly meetings, films and printed material designed to promote peace – minus the need for revolution, strikes or other militant activities. Robertson recalled that peace was the important issue for communists during the 1950s, and vitriolic Party rhetoric took a back seat.[42] But in 1947, communist propaganda was still littered with emotive hard-line diatribe. As this next example illustrates, anti-weapons testing literature in the late 1940s was rugged and inflammatory – indeed, anything but soft.

A little red book

In early 1947 the SA State Committee, Australian Communist Party published *Rocket Range Threatens Australia*. This vividly red booklet was written by state secretary Alf Watt. It warned that 'juggernauts of mass destruction' would 'violate' the Central Australian Aboriginal Reserve, as white men infiltrated sacred tribal lands. Watt argued that traditional owners of the land would be 'sacrificed, and the crime [was] to be committed in the name of peace and freedom'. Watt labelled SA Premier Tom

Playford's support for the weapons program as yet another attack by the 'leader of the dreary old men who guard monied interest and privilege against the people'.[43]

Alf Watt's sixteen-page booklet attacked the rocket range on several fronts. The first section highlighted dangers to Aboriginal people. Noel Counihan's caricature (presented and discussed previously) powerfully illustrated Watt's argument. He cited Donald Thomson's recommendations that tribal people be 'segregated' to protect them and their culture, supporting the anthropologist's call for reserves to be legally owned by traditional owners.[44] Watt's arguments against the rocket range then moved to the program's exorbitant costs and Australia's foreign policy incompatibility with global moves for peace. He advocated Australian severance of relationships with British and US 'millionaires'. Watt argued it should instead embrace friendship with 'peace-loving peoples' such as the Soviets, and become loyal to the UN. With disarmament completed and armed forces redundant, funds could instead be channelled into smaller peace-keeping organisations. Watt's utopia would, of course, improve living standards for all, as taxes diverted away from defence into social programs. He urged communists and like-minded friends to spread the word through their unions, workplaces and organisations. Watt pleaded 'we cannot fight for peace by preparing for war'.[45]

Distribution of Watt's little red book reached Canberra, where Victorian Liberal MHR Thomas White was quick to alert the House. He warned that people protesting the tests and protecting Aboriginal people were mostly 'supported by Communists with other intentions'. White said that *Rocket Range Threatens Australia* directed unions to create industrial mayhem. He warned that the pretence of communist concern for Aboriginal welfare disguised 'sinister support behind the protests against the establishment of the range'.[46]

Suspicions that testing program opponents were likely communists occasionally caused investigations to veer off course. A number of important figures were closely viewed through suspicious government eyes. As illustrated in the next example, the activities of well-known anthropologist Fred Rose were loosely investigated, with shreds of evidence hastily pasted into a montage that didn't match.

Fred Rose and Chinese whispers

In 1947 Australia's security was managed by CIS. Any hint of communist interest in the weapons testing program was immediately investigated, but in the heat of pursuit, things did not always go smoothly. One such instance provides a good example of what can go awry when Chinese whisperers get the words wrong.

Frederick Rose was a person of interest for several reasons. He was a suspected communist Englishman married to an East German woman. He had also recently collaborated with communist doctor Alex Jolly to write an anthropological paper about the plight of Aboriginal people in the remote north-west. Their revealing work had been warmly embraced by comrade Katharine Susannah Prichard, who forwarded a copy to Moscow for publication in the Russian *International Literature* journal.[47] Rumours reached the CIS that Rose had been appointed the Communist Party's official anthropologist. High-level correspondence ensued, as CIS Deputy Director Alexander alerted his superior to what he thought was Rose's appointment to the 'Rocket Bomb Committee'.[48] Here, he believed that Rose was a member of the government's Committee on Guided Projectiles. However, a quick look at the Committee's recently released *Report on the Welfare of Aborigines Located Within the Range Area* would have immediately informed Alexander that Rose was most certainly not a member. Indeed, a copy of this report was handily located (but obviously not read) in one of his own security organisation's files.[49]

Two months later Alexander told the CIS Director that his previous correspondence about Rose had been incorrect. He also attributed responsibility for this inaccuracy to his incompetent 'informant'. At that time, Fred Rose was actually a public servant holding sole responsibility for the NT section of the Department of Post-War Reconstruction. In a bid to wipe the egg off his rather embarrassed face, Alexander suggested that the all-too-eager informant had confused Rose's non-existent membership on the government committee with another role on a non-existent Communist Party 'Rocket Bomb Committee'. Most unfortunately, however, he told his Director 'it is not possible to contact my informant' to pursue the matter further.[50] We can only wonder whether this mystery informant actually existed, or whether Alexander had created a smokescreen to hide his own inadequacies.

This was not the first time Australia's security watchdogs had Rose's story wrong. He was working as a meteorologist in Broome in 1940 when Military Intelligence forebodingly reported Rose to be a 'suspicious character [allegedly] mapping the coastline'. Eleven years later ASIO provided this rather embarrassing correction:

> ROSE was in charge of the Signal Squad of the BROOME Home Guard, and on the occasions he was thought to be mapping the coast-line, he was in fact carrying out Signal exercises with other members of the Home Guard.[51]

Prichard's letter accompanying Rose and Jolly's manuscript to Boris Suchkov (editor-in-chief at Moscow's *International Literature*) is noteworthy. It is located in one of her CIS files. She informed Suchkov that she was also forwarding 'some poems by a young Queensland poetess, Kathleen Watson'.[52] It is assumed that she referred to Kath Walker (now known as Oodgeroo Noonuccal), who heartily embraced communism and applauded the Party's vehemently anti-racist policies during the 1950s.[53] Aboriginal poetry had, thus, obtained international exposure.

Fred Rose had been viewed with suspicion. Governmental responses to his potential infiltration of national security are illuminating, and provide a very useful segue to the next discussion. As fears of communist incursions at the rocket range increased, government reactions intensified. They culminated with the introduction of a remarkable piece of legislation, aiming to stop communists and unionists in their tracks.

Red rumours of black bans

Industrial action by communist-run unions at Woomera was the last thing the federal government wanted. Thomas White had already warned his parliamentary colleagues about communist incitement of unions at Woomera, and in mid-May 1947 he added fuel to his fire. White revealed reports of threats by fourteen 'communist-run' unions to declare the weapons testing range 'black', thus depriving the worksite of workers. Rumours were also circulating about plans for communist sabotage of the range. White told parliament this would occur 'if they thought it was in Russia's interests to do so'. Harold Holt MHR echoed these concerns and joined others calling for a Royal Commission into communist activities. In reply, Labor Prime Minister Chifley unequivocally endorsed CIS capability to satisfy Australia's needs for security, with its robust investigations entirely adequate to keep tabs on communists. Chifley believed a Royal Commission was unnecessary.[54]

Union opposition to the tests had been voiced early. Over two months before parliamentary announcement of plans, the T&LC in South Australia passed a resolution calling for abandonment of the program. Communist newspaper the *Guardian* recorded protests by the WWF, BWIU, Hotel Club and Restaurant Employees, Sheet Metal Workers', Boiler Makers and NSW Nurses. It also published a WWF letter to Prime Minister Chifley calling for governmental protection of Aboriginal people, as the rocket range 'represented a physical as well as spiritual threat to tribal existence'.[55]

Rumours of black bans at the rocket range were published in the *Sydney Morning Herald*. It reported right-wing union leaders condemning communist efforts to impose bans on work there. The article identified left-wing unions using Aboriginal safety as a ruse, disguising their real agenda in 'a mere smokescreen for their sinister activities'. This grand plan was for the communist 'agents of Russia' to delay rocket research, so the Soviets would not be left behind in the arms race. The newspaper also reported ACTU President Percy Clarey (also a Victorian Legislative Councillor) advising all unions to disregard the proposed bans, with any policy or action on the weapons tests to come from his peak union body only. Clarey's position was backed by NSW T&LC Secretary Robert King (coincidentally a member of that state's Legislative Council). King argued that communists were attempting to deprive thousands of building workers of 'useful employment'. Furthermore, he believed that 'while pretending to be concerned about the future of the aborigines [sic], these people are prepared to betray the future of the people of Australia'. AWU Secretary Tom Dougherty's blunt reaction to these comments was reported:

> The local breed of Communists would not have the guts, as they do not have the desire, to interfere in the activities of Russia. They should be permitted no say whatever against the actions of our elected, democratic Government on our future defence.[56]

Labor's Federal Executive met that same day. In light of White's ominous warnings about a union black ban upon the test site, members moved quickly in a show of political solidarity. The following resolution was carried unanimously:

> The Federal Executive of the ALP congratulates the Prime Minister and Dr. Evatt on the firm stand taken by the Government against the proposed black ban on the rocket range project. It is apparent that the propaganda recently issued by the Communist Party in connection with this undertaking is for the sole purpose of defeating Australia's Defence Policy in the interest of a foreign power.[57]

Evidently, the little red book had done its job very well. Not only cited in parliament by White, *Rocket Range Threatens Australia* was now ascribed significant agency by the Labor Party as a powerful piece of political propaganda threatening to bring down Australia's defences. Alf Watt was probably quite chuffed with his efforts. His little red book was now famous or, more fittingly perhaps, infamous.

Harold Holt chose to ignore prime ministerial faith in Australia's security system. In parliament two days later, he changed tack a few degrees, moving that 'a public inquiry' be conducted into communist objectives and activities. Holt believed that the Party's 16,000 members controlled a vast web of political activity and communist newspapers. Communists had also infiltrated to control and exploit the most powerful unions in Australia. Holt said the Party was working to 'smash our democratic institutions with its proletarian revolution'. He argued that relatively small numbers of members belied the power of the communist machine:

> ...from what we know of the energy and ability of their leaders who possess the fanaticism of zealots it can be described as one of the most powerful political organizations [sic] in Australia at the present time.[58]

Labor Attorney-General Evatt had a similar view about communist motives. He believed that communist opposition to the rocket range was not driven by need to protect Aboriginal people. Evatt considered the 'primary object' of the Party was 'to terminate the project'. He further believed that communists wanted to stop the 'defence' program, because it was preparing Australia for war with Russia. Aboriginal needs were being conveniently hijacked by radicals as an excuse to oppose the project. Opposition Leader Menzies added gusto to the debate, by grimly describing communists as 'the apostles of class war'.[59]

Communists, unionists and bad press

Community angst about the proposed weapons tests was mounting. Media coverage incorporated considerable commentary about the growing protest movement. Press coverage of the protests was initially strong, but soon decreased significantly. After covering the first rush of protests, mainstream newspapers fell in with the federal line, henceforth distancing themselves from any activism deemed remotely red.[60]

Despite the fact that such an eclectic collection of groups and organisations were collaborating to jointly oppose the tests, the Communist Party was regularly singled out in the press as the menacing puppeteer of protest action. Communist and unionist opposition became ideal anti-left fodder for mainstream newspapers. The *Tribune* lambasted the *Daily Telegraph*'s reportage of the Party's position on the tests, for having 'severely mutilated' a Party statement. The *Sydney Morning Herald* was roasted for running a 'scurrilous cartoon against the Communists'. BWIU President Ted Bulmer was also angry. He accused the *Sun* of distorting his comments about the weapons program. When asked by that newspaper about BWIU's possible intentions to black ban rocket range work, Bulmer had ardently refuted those rumours.

According to Bulmer, the *Sun* ignored his statement and reported that 40,000 BWIU members would participate in protest actions and bans. Bulmer was adamant he told the *Sun* that no decisions had been taken about work at the rocket range site. He pointed out that the union's Federal Council had not even met to consider the issue, let alone vote on any action.[61]

Mainstream media was not the only antagonist of the Party. Sheetmetal Workers' Union federal leader Tom Wright told the *Tribune* that while members vehemently opposed the weapons tests, solidarity of other 'comrades' was questionable. Wright named the Federated Furnishing Trades Society and NSW Labor Council as collaborators in Menzies' creation of 'anti-Communist and anti-Russian propaganda over objections to the proposed rocket range'. Wright urged union solidarity against the tests and advocacy for improved Aboriginal rights, nutrition and health.[62]

One Victorian union was a clear supporter of a range site black ban. Victorian Building Trades Federation secretary Don Thomson called for bans in mid-May 1947. His arguments incorporated advocacy for Aboriginal rights and pacifist sentiment. His union counterpart in South Australia echoed these calls, lobbying the T&LC to coordinate blanket industrial action.[63] Meanwhile, the *Argus* was clearly no supporter of union bans. It ran a front-page headline declaring 'Country-Wide Probe Into Disloyalty: Unionists as Tools', and an article describing a 'deliberate plot...to sabotage Empire defences...being directed from outside Australia'.[64]

Communist motivations

Australia's government had been quick to cloak communist opposition to weapons testing with more sinister motives. Communist protests were linked to Russian collusion and espionage, even to possibilities of sabotage. Federal politicians viewed their intentions as insidious and dangerous. Communist calls for Aboriginal people to be protected and supported were ridiculed, as nothing more than a paper-thin ruse for sinister agendas.

In response to media accusations of protest camouflaged as communist plot, Duguid told the *Tribune* what was really going on. He explained that the need to protect sacred Aboriginal grounds from the weapons testing program had bonded an eclectic group of organisations together for common purpose. Duguid argued that protestors were most certainly not part of a 'red plot' by the Communist Party.[65] Melbourne's *Argus* editor begged to differ:

> Opponents of the plan form a motley army, but behind the pacifists, the day-dreamers, and the humanitarians, it is not difficult to perceive the directing hand of the Communists who are determined not to see any offensive weapon in the hands of the non-Communist nation if they can help it.[66]

Communist motives were frequently discussed in federal parliament. Adair Blain's comment typified the rhetoric. The NT Independent MHR feared a rising tide of communism spreading through the world, 'like an amorphous mass'. Blain believed every Commonwealth department was 'riddled with Communist cells'. He accused 'communist clowns' of deviously procuring the support of religious organisations, by climbing into bed with missions in South Australia (probably referring here to Duguid's fierce opposition to the tests):

> They used the cause of the black man – though they have no more genuine sympathy for the aborigine [sic] than they would have for a bandicoot – as a means of stirring up opinion among civilized sections of the community against the guided weapons range project.[67]

Blain insisted that communists were insidious: 'Atheistic to the core, but they play on the feelings of religious people...to further their nefarious ends'.

So what conclusions can be made about communist motivations? Two commentaries published during the 1960s by a communist turncoat and a priest presented very similar arguments about what drove Party activists, with complete disregard for any humanitarian motives. In the first of these examples, an ex-communist's comments about the Party's role during early days of the testing program clearly display what can happen when passionate allegiances die.

In a fierce duplicitous attack on his former Party, Geoff McDonald's scathing 1969 publication described what he believed were the real communist agendas, hidden beneath superficial support for Aboriginal rights. The bitter ex-comrade was convinced that the weapons testing protest was riddled with ulterior motives. McDonald had been a Party member between 1948 and 1960, and felt well-placed to comment upon its opposition to the program. In a contemptuous diatribe, McDonald argued the communist role in Aboriginal rights as a divisive program, 'designed to fragment' the country. He believed the Party's long-term plan was to establish a separate Aboriginal 'nation'. According to McDonald, vigorous Communist Party protest campaigning in 1946 and 1947 '[made] use of the name of aboriginals [sic] to sabotage Australian defence'. He argued that the real motive was to prevent Australia from becoming a 'strategic base of US imperialism', with the Woomera campaign drawing unions into the communist 'united front', by disguising their agenda and using Aboriginal rights as their 'cover' issue. McDonald argued that this method successfully enabled communists to weasel into leadership of unsuspecting groups, transforming them into communist 'front' organisations. Disillusionment with the Party he once embraced left no room for niceties, as evidenced by McDonald's barbed conclusion: 'It will be found that Communists are the greatest "racists" of all'.[68]

Suspicion about communist motives was also stated in an article published by the Catholic Church's Institute of Social Order in 1963. Jesuit priest W. G. Smith believed that the weapons testing program provided communists with perfect propaganda and recruitment opportunities:

> The Party...took avid advantage of the opportunity to suck into their orbit organizations [sic] and individuals interested in the welfare of the Aborigines. The communist leaders were clearly intent on the development of a "broad front" program to influence suitable organizations [sic] and individuals, a policy they have pursued relentlessly ever since.[69]

Party membership figures, however, do not support Smith's interpretation. After reaching its membership high of 23,000 in 1944, numbers decreased significantly. For example, by 1947 membership had fallen to 12,108. In 1952 this slipped to about 6,000. By 1957 Communist Party membership numbered only 5,850. Davidson attributed this drastic fall in numbers to 'sectarianism' within the Party and 'Cold War persecution'.[70]

The ultimate gag tool

In an extremely contentious legislative move, the federal Labor Government devised a new law denying freedom of speech for Australian citizens wanting to articulate opposition to the testing program. Indeed, this legislation held potentially dire ramifications for anybody uttering or writing anything vaguely related to Australia's defence. The power of this Act was immense. And, its efficacy was spot-on.

Protests and boycott threats to the rocket range prompted this decisive government action. In what the *Tribune* described 'the death knell of free speech in Australia', parliament rushed through the Approved Defence Projects Protection Bill in June 1947. This legislative gag-tool prevented people or organisations critically commenting about the nation's defence policy. Penalties for transgression were significant, with up to a £5,000 fine or twelve months imprisonment. The *Tribune* reported Attorney-General Evatt's belief that provisions of the Crimes Act were insufficient safeguards of the testing project, hence the need for this aggressive and extremely specific new law.[71] Not surprisingly, Doris Blackburn disagreed. She considered the new legislation entirely unnecessary, with the Crimes Act more than sufficient to protect the rocket range. For Blackburn, this new law was an undemocratic attack on civil rights. Country Party MHR Bernard Corser questioned Blackburn's motives, by later alleging in parliament that Blackburn supported the Communist Party. Blackburn responded by hotly refuting his claim.[72]

Evatt's Bill intended to protect the rocket range, but communists believed the potential power of this new legislation to be far more insidious. The *Tribune* warned that government would now be able to declare 'any work' an approved defence project. This meant that the new Approved Defence Projects Protection Act outlawing public comment could extend, for example, to unionists striking for better wages and conditions at a worksite not remotely connected with Australia's defence. According to the *Tribune*, any worksite could be deemed an 'approved defence site'. Thus, unions could potentially be stymied at all levels of industrial action whenever government chose to close down their coverage, via enforcement of the Act. The *Tribune* reported that evidence of 'Dr. Evatt's super-snoopers' would be sufficient to jail people for twelve months, if they even commented about defence funding levels. The *Tribune* predicted that this 'fascist' legislation would invoke 'a tremendous storm of protest'.[73]

Objection to the Act was also voiced by the Rocket Range Protest Committee. Resolutions carried at a large Melbourne meeting were conveyed in a letter to the prime minister. As well as calling for cessation of governmental violation of Aboriginal rights in the area affected by the tests, the group articulated support for views of the Australian Council for Civil Liberties. On this basis, the meeting voted unanimously to denounce the Act as 'imposing radical limitations on freedom of speech and writing and as rendering citizens liable to heavy penalties without any right to trial'.[74] But despite continued protests, the Bill's legislative teeth cut through, with the Act becoming law on 12 June 1947. Its powers soon hit the mark, producing a significant decrease in protest against the tests.[75]

However, in a bold reactionary move the Rocket Range Protest Committee organised another Melbourne public meeting on 24 August (advertised as 'Rocket Range, Aborigines and You'). Speakers included Duguid, Blackburn, Doug Nicholls and Council for Civil Liberties founder, Brian Fitzpatrick. The meeting passed two resolutions calling for the government to protect Aboriginal people and stop violating their rights, and protesting the Act as an outlandish legislative over-reaction to security needs at Woomera.[76] Fitzpatrick was to become a member of the Protest Committee, and his movements were followed with great interest by the CIS and ASIO, which compiled a total of seven files about him. It is likely that he was never a Communist Party member, but Fitzpatrick's sympathies definitely aligned with left-wing political groups he engaged with (such as the Melbourne University Labor Club, Left Book Club, and Australian Soviet Friendship League). An ASIO dossier described him as 'associated with [the Communist Party] for about five years', highlighting 'reliable information from an ex-member' that Fitzpatrick was:

> ...considered too unreliable for Party membership and could be used more advantageously in frontal activities as a non-Party member. Holds same views as Party members.[77]

Fitzpatrick was a man to be watched. His active role on the Rocket Range Protest Committee gave security agents even more reason to observe any of his (now illegal) protest activities closely.

In early September the ACTU added its voice to calls for repeal of the Approved Defence Projects Protection Act. At its annual Congress in Melbourne, members demanded the 'so called' protection legislation be removed:

> [The Act]...completely abrogates the peoples' democratic rights to freedom of speech...oppressive in its application against working class organisations which may criticise "approved defence projects" or trade unions striking for higher wages or improved conditions on such declared "approved defence projects". We demand the repeal...in the interests of freedom of speech and democracy as defined in the Atlantic Charter.[78]

A year later, unions were further outraged when federal bans on union official visits to Woomera's rocket range site were imposed. The *Tribune* described this move a 'Smear on Labor'.[79] Security authorities were warned to keep eyes peeled for miscreants attempting to infiltrate the area. Communist and unionist Donald Thomson (a person of interest to Australia's security organisations since 1935) was a prime suspect.[80] He was also one of the union officials refused entry. According to a CIS dossier, Thomson planned to 'obtain access to Woomera, probably through gaining employment...all officers were requested to keep a lookout for him'. His 'special mission' allegedly involved a name change to procure access to the range. Photographs of Thomson were immediately forwarded to Woomera, along with a polite suggestion from the CIS Director that checks of personnel entering the area might be a good idea.[81]

∞

In the late 1940s, Australia's security systems underwent major overhaul. The Woomera project provided urgent impetus for Chifley's government to establish a new independent and powerful security organisation. Defence bodies in Australia had been urging the creation of a dedicated 'defence security organisation' since World War II concluded. This new body would be capable of investigating subversive groups, tracking suspect aliens, and interning them if necessary during wartime. In order to stop spies conveying their secrets to Moscow via the Soviet Embassy in Canberra, the government moved quickly to set up this new body. The Australian Security Intelligence Organisation was established in 1949.

Australia's reputation in the USA was significantly damaged in May 1948, when doubts about security led to a ban on classified transmissions from the USA to Australia. According to David McKnight, Australian embarrassment was intolerable:

> The ban hit hard at the UK–Australia project to test missiles…the Woomera project depended for its success on a flow of classified technical information from the United States to Britain which it shared with Australia. The Americans made it clear to the British that unless the security situation in Australia was improved the ban would stay.[82]

Dangers to the Woomera site posed by communists and unionists made a surprise re-appearance in parliament some years later. An official with the Plasterers' Society of SA had been refused admission to the rocket range in 1948. This made Jim (James) Cavanagh a person of great interest to the Liberal Party when he nominated as ALP Senate Candidate in 1961. Harold Holt (then Federal Treasurer) informed the House that 'twelve or thirteen officials' applied to visit the range in 1948, with only 'six or seven' allowed onto the site. Cavanagh (as one of those banned from the range) had threatened to call a mass walk-off at Woomera unless all officials were allowed on-site. Holt provided evidence suggesting that Cavanagh (and the other five union officials) were rejected because they allegedly associated with 'elements believed to be subversive to the community'.[83]

Holt's inference that Cavanagh was a communist sent the ALP into immediate damage control, with their Senate candidate's future hanging in the balance. Opposition Leader Arthur Calwell backed Cavanagh's claim that he had never been a member (or even like-minded friend) of the Communist Party. To reinforce his argument, Calwell informed the House that Cavanagh had, indeed, been allowed access to the Woomera range when he and twelve other union officials visited in 1959. That, said Calwell, was at a time when the most extreme version of weapons – nuclear – was being tested. Cavanagh's security credentials, he suggested, were surely sound.[84] Not to be deterred, Jim Cavanagh did go on to win his Senate seat in 1961, and remained in parliament until 1981. Between 1973 and 1975, he served as Minister for Aboriginal Affairs in the Whitlam Government.

∞

In the next chapter, focus is upon the nuclear testing program. Protests for peace and Aboriginal rights intensify as Britain and Australia prepare to detonate the first atomic bomb in the central desert during 1953.

Chapter Six

The Government has said the tests won't hurt a living thing...

In April 1952 the Women's International League for Peace and Freedom organised a protest meeting in Melbourne. Aboriginal woman Margaret Tucker moved that scheduled British atom-bomb tests at Maralinga be abandoned. The *Tribune* reported her trepidation: 'The Government [sic] has said the tests won't hurt a living thing, but my people are the last who would believe Government [sic] promises'. Tucker argued that money being poured into these 'war preparations' be used to address Aboriginal needs. Meeting participants condemned the tests as 'one more betrayal of our responsibility to guard Aboriginal and other human rights'.[1]

∞

In this chapter, radical activism features within the broader movement protesting atomic tests in Aboriginal country. The discussion begins as Australians contemplate impending blasts in the South Australian desert.

Radical activities and ASIO observations

Protest meetings were conducted throughout the country. At Sydney's Domain communist journalist Rupert Lockwood spoke to a large crowd. ASIO operative 'R. W. W.' was also present, and his/her report about the gathering included a copy of the communist's speech. The operative noted Lockwood's recent return from several weeks 'with the workers' on the rocket range. Lockwood delivered a sarcastic attack upon flimsy employee security-screening systems at the test site, whimsically telling the crowd:

> The reds are everywhere. The reds are in the wardrobe, the reds are on the rocket range and W. C. Wentworth [MHR, and outspoken opponent of communism] is singing that old song, 'When the Red, Red Rocket goes Buzz, Buzz, Buzzing along'. I can see only one solution to this grave national problem and it is one with which everyone here is in agreement. Workers wherever they are are unreliable...Let Menzies go there, let Beale go there...pick and shovel work should be done by the most reliable anti-communist workers of Australia.[2]

Rocket range construction and maintenance workers who Lockwood had met were covered by one of Australia's largest unions. The AWU voiced strong opposition to nuclear testing on Australian soil, and general secretary Tom Dougherty considered Australia to be an ignorant British puppet and contributor to potential global nuclear holocaust.[3] An ASIO memorandum presents a useful snapshot of the industrial make-up at the range sites. Six private firms employed approximately 400 workers (mainly Australian citizens). The memo identified that a small number of British scientific employees were not subjected to Australian security vetting. Thus, security breaches at this time were only deemed possible by unpatriotic Australian workers. Discovery of two alleged communist workers at Woomera rang security alarms bells, and an immediate re-vetting of every Australian worker was ordered.[4]

Several weeks before ASIO's Woomera workforce memorandum was compiled, a communist named Elliott Johnston ran as candidate for the SA state seat of Stuart. This electorate incorporated Woomera, where Johnston attracted 110 votes (almost a quarter of the town's population) despite not applying for permission to campaign in the community because 'he had been told by the Party not to make trouble'. The federal government was outraged that so many workers had voted red, and ordered an inquiry into the ballot result.[5]

The objective of the memorandum investigating who was who at Woomera now takes on an added dimension. This surprising election result created panic in Canberra. Minister for Supply Beale had sent ASIO operatives scurrying around Woomera days after the disturbingly high communist vote emerged. But Adelaide's *Mail* reported that at a briefing, four senior security officers informed Beale of 'no Communist infiltration at Woomera'. On this basis, Beale attributed Johnston's high vote to a misunderstanding among rocket range workers about which party he represented.[6] As far as Beale was concerned, the Communist Party was definitely not that popular.

Communist front organisations

Paradoxically, many in the government believed that communists were everywhere. Some were thought to be Party members, and others were suspected as cleverly concealed within communist front organisations. Fears of these insidious groups drove ASIO operatives to compile extensive reports about who they were and what they hid. In October 1955 one such report comprehensively described what these front organisations were supposedly all about. Its content provides fascinating insight into the psyche of Australia's most alert and alarmed security operatives.

According to the ASIO report, front organisations were a means 'to forge a link between other classes and the working class...in an attempt to promote the ripening of conditions for the historical changeover from capitalism to socialism'. This alleged, sophisticated communist strategy distinguished the 'popular front' from the 'united front', whereby the former included front organisations covering 'spheres of community life stretching beyond the boundaries of the working class', or united front. In essence, the report described a form of brainwashing, whereby the non-political became the political by stealth – via organisation of the unwitting general public into a mass movement. The ASIO author of the report defined this process as Marxist 'dialectical materialism' theory. Front organisations were allegedly distribution points for communist propaganda. Respectable memberships entangling people such as Lady Jessie Street provided perfect cover for subversive activities. In this way, the Party line of the Soviet government would be slyly infiltrated into mainstream Australia.[7]

One of the sneakiest ways to disguise communist activities, according to this ASIO report, was to conceal subversives within broader humanitarian organisations. Aboriginal rights and ban-the-bomb campaigns were perfect covers for communist infiltrators. People with 'high academic qualifications' often provided a veneer of respectable authority, luring unsuspecting community members into the communistic fold of a front organisation. Once hooked, the report predicted that these pawns of Moscow would soon be succumbing to the full force of ideology. These indoctrinated recruits then easily transformed into propaganda couriers, or even spies. For ASIO, the entire concept of front organisations was insidious. Opposition by any groups to the weapons program spelt clear and present danger.[8]

So what did ASIO think these front organisations were? Communist targets were always, it was supposed, strategic. Groups such as the Eureka Youth League groomed future comrades. According to ASIO, pacifist groups attracted energetic movers and shakers hell-bent on eliminating imperialism in their quest for world peace. One ASIO report identified that there was 'very good reason to believe that the Australian Peace Council was created by the [Communist Party] in line with the current foreign policy of the Soviet Union'. It concluded that the Council was riddled with communists hiding behind the propriety of prominent citizens and clergymen.[9] Other insidious organisations named by ASIO included women's groups, student bodies and cultural societies, the 'intelligentsia'. Cunning individuals hid within film societies, theatre groups, friendship societies, and a variety of artistic bodies. Indeed, ASIO identified 'well over 500' organisations believed to be concealing subversives.[10] Those communists were everywhere.

ASIO produced a secret list of communist front organisations considered operational across Australia in September 1956. It identified Peace Councils, New Theatres and Eureka Youth Leagues in five states, Union of Australian Women branches in six states, the Realist Film Association, the Australasian Book Society, Realist Writers' Groups, and even the Association of Australian Dancers. Not surprisingly, also included in this comprehensive list were the Australian–Soviet Friendship Society and Australia–China Society.[11]

Australian security officials were clearly on high alert as the nuclear program loomed. Communists too were highly alert, but their fears were not related to state security. One sensational front-page *Tribune* headline in October 1953 left no doubt about fears for central desert Aboriginal people – 'ABORIGINES IN DANGER' [*Tribune*'s capitalisation]:

> Many Australian Aborigines will almost certainly be killed in the atom bomb tests on the Woomera Rocket Range. The bombs will be exploded in the vicinity of the Great Central Aboriginal Reserve. This utter disregard for human life emphasises the danger to all Australians of the failure to ban the atom bomb... the range passes right through the territory set aside as the inviolable right of the First Australians.

Horrific consequences were predicted:

> Even if the atom blast does not kill and mutilate a number of Aborigines, it will devastate their hunting grounds, destroy their waterholes and devastate tribal territory that is sacred to them, and to which they believe their spirits will return after death. The inevitable result will be disastrous to the tribes.[12]

One week after the *Tribune*'s sobering article went to press, the first nuclear weapon was detonated at Emu Field. Central Australia was to be subjected to a series of atomic explosions over the next twelve years.

Giles Weather Station

Adverse weather conditions and nuclear clouds are a bad combination. Mysterious diseases struck South Australian wheat, barley and wild onions in 1955, and the *Tribune* blamed radioactive dust in falling dew for destroying 'thousands of acres of crops'.[13] Communists again called for the perilous nuclear tests to be abandoned, but the government had another idea to counteract environmental concerns.

In October 1955 British scientists decided to establish a weather station at Giles (in the Rawlinson Ranges). This was nearly 1,000 kilometres north-west of Woomera, on the 'firing line'. The facility would monitor meteorological conditions during nuclear weapons experiments, identifying optimum conditions for minimal fallout spread. Native patrol officer MacDougall was alarmed, as this proposed site was a widely known water source regularly attracting tribal people. Builders, road workers and miners would also soon enter this remote area often inhabited by nomadic people. MacDougall considered this an invasion into the Aboriginal Reserve and direct threat to the extinction of tribal life. The government dismissed his concerns as overreaction and building of the station (necessitating the excision of 1,012 square kilometres from the Aboriginal Reserve) finished in May 1956.[14]

In early June 1956 Adelaide University reported that radioactive rain had fallen in South Australia. The nuclear tests referred to had been conducted at Monte Bello Islands (about 130 kilometres from the Pilbara coast). Minister for Supply Beale told parliament he was 'pretty sure that the rain was not caused by tests', but undertook to inquire into the matter.[15] A day later Beale stated his findings that the report was exaggerated, rumours of radio-active rain in New Zealand were unsubstantiated, and that all was completely safe.[16] The next nuclear weapon was detonated at the same islands on 20 June. Acting Prime Minister, Sir Arthur Fadden, assured parliament of no danger to 'life or property on the mainland or elsewhere'.[17] Beale quietly discarded radiation dangers for Aboriginal people living or moving around near the imminent Maralinga nuclear test. In response to a parliamentary question by Fred Chaney MHR about safety of 'nomadic natives', Beale reported:

> The position is that there will be no natives within the prohibited area for the atomic tests, and that will be ensured by constant

patrols by aeroplane and helicopter and on foot...we shall ensure complete safety for the native population.[18]

MacDougall's concern for 'nomadic natives' was probably not pacified by this flimsy ministerial guarantee. His reports to weapons testing authorities that numerous Aboriginal groups continued to walk through and near danger zones were treated with contempt, or completely ignored. He advocated relentlessly on behalf of the people he knew to be there, but government officials chose to look the other way. Indeed, the 1985 Royal Commission identified the government view that MacDougall's pleas for safety involved only a 'handful of natives'. True numbers of Aboriginal people in the danger area will never be known, but MacDougall documented more than 100 people in the Giles area alone.[19]

Newspaper mogul Rupert Murdoch visited the Giles Weather Station site in early 1957. He reported no possibility of contact between the ten 'weather men' and Aboriginal people. Murdoch lauded the 'extremely competent and sympathetic natives' protection officer', and Robert Macaulay's valiant 'shielding' of the natives.[20] Government claims that this facility had 'done no harm to the Aborigines' were contemptuously rejected by communists. The *Tribune* reported the absurdity of Beale's supposition that no Aboriginal people had been affected 'because his officers had not been able to find any Aborigines in that area'. It was also noted that small tribes of Aboriginal people could easily evade contact and detection by clumsy white trackers in vast arid Central Australia.[21]

This argument was to prove correct seven years later. In 1964 Walter MacDougall discovered a group of Aboriginal (Martu) women and children in the Western Desert, still completely oblivious to the existence of white man and white governance. Their isolation ended abruptly, as they were loaded onto a government truck, and then relocated to missionary care at Jigalong.[22]

MacDougall was not a communist, but his deep knowledge of the remote weapons testing region and solid understanding of its indigenous population aroused intense security interest in his activities. This is evidenced by his numerous ASIO files containing an extensive array of MacDougall's correspondence and reports. A letter from MacDougall to his Department of Supply superintendent featured feisty communication style, as he related his concern for Aboriginal people. MacDougall believed that the governmental policy of assimilation would likely cause:

> ...degeneration from self-respecting tribal communities to pathetic and useless parasites – it has happened so often before that surely we Australians must have learned our lesson...the country under discussion belongs to the tribe and is recognised as such by other tribes. However, we propose to take it away from them and give nothing in return – we might as well declare war on them and make a job of it.[23]

MacDougall identified the 'Aboriginal problem' as 'dynamite' for the government. He urged that a superintendent of 'Native Reserves' with sound knowledge of tribal customs and languages be appointed. His argument that this position demanded thorough understanding of the dangers of cultural contacts indicates that he may have coveted that job for himself. MacDougall suggested that failure to accommodate these vital prerequisites could embroil the government in a 'first-class scandal'.[24]

A report by MacDougall in August 1956 presented a valuable description of Central Reserve Aboriginal people. He estimated that there were 1,000 tribal and semi-tribal Aboriginal people scattered throughout the area. MacDougall wrote that contact generated cultural demise:

> Their beliefs can be destroyed soon after contact with whites solely by their observing the white man contravening their laws

and customs and not coming to any harm as a result…When their beliefs are gone they are left with nothing to hold on to, and it only needs the mistaken and misguided kindness of the white to turn them into the pathetic and spiritless beggars, devoid of self-respect, which has largely been the history of contacts since the white man first came to Australia.[25]

He made five recommendations intended to minimise the effects of contact with Research Establishment employees. They were designed to reduce damage he had witnessed when white encounters with Aboriginal people created relationships of dependency and cultural decay.[26] MacDougall was not the only one observing ramifications of contact. Months later, a government report created furore, as its exposé of Aboriginal Australia confronted the world.

The Grayden Report

Actual harm inflicted upon Aboriginal people near to the nuclear test sites will never be fully understood. The welfare of one affected group, however, became the subject of a government investigation. In the Laverton-Warburton Ranges area, many of the tribal Aboriginal people had been protectively relocated away from danger zones to the safety of missions. Parliamentary questions about their well-being in these new, alien living circumstances were soon to trigger controversial and polarised findings.

In 1956 a WA Parliamentary Select Committee undertook investigation of Aboriginal conditions in the Laverton-Warburton Ranges area. It was chaired by Liberal MLA William Grayden and conclusions were published in 'The Grayden Report'. Grayden later published a personal account of what he witnessed in *Adam and Atoms*. His book described visits to missions, the subsequent report, and ramifications for Aboriginal people unlucky enough to have lived and hunted within the danger zone.[27] In November the Select Committee (Grayden and four other parliamentarians) travelled to Warburton Ranges to interview missionaries, teachers, other mission staff and police at three missions: Warburton United, Mount Margaret and Cosmo Newbery. They identified 'violations' of the Reserve. A total of 1,100 square kilometres had been ceded to the Commonwealth, and Giles Weather Station had been built at an important ceremonial and water-source place. The Maralinga Testing Ground was identified as the primary cause for Aboriginal loss of lands.[28]

Grayden's findings were shocking. His Committee identified numerous complex problems affecting Warburton Ranges Aboriginal people. These included: malnutrition, blindness, disease, lack of medical or educational services, unsanitary conditions, pastoral-worker exploitation, lack of hunting grounds or game, and inadequate water supplies.

The Grayden Report highly embarrassed the federal government, and so Beale went on the offensive. In parliament he described it as grossly inaccurate, challenging the veracity of findings:

> That [Report] was one of the most unreliable documents, result-
> ing in the worst possible service to aborigines [sic], that has ever
> been promoted in any Parliament [sic] or publicly delivered.[29]

Beale's primary source of evidence was the 25-year-old owner/ editor of News Limited's *Adelaide News* (Rupert Murdoch), who had travelled to the Warburton Ranges on what Beale described as a 'special trip'. Murdoch reported that no-one was starving or sick. Beale considered this to be 'the comment of a responsible person' revealing the truth, and proving that Grayden's report was rubbish.[30]

Murdoch's articles chronicling what he saw contradicted all that Grayden and his Committee members had recorded. A few of Murdoch's comments effectively illustrate this point:

> No aborigines [sic] in the Central Australian reserves are dying of thirst or starvation – or disease...the great nation-wide consternation for these people has been unnecessary.
>
> ...these fine native people have never enjoyed better conditions...no-one is allowed to starve...
>
> The [Grayden] report [was] hopelessly exaggerated...
>
> Not one really sick person did I see. All were obviously well fed and happy and at no place was there any chronic shortage of food.[31]

These disputed details in the Grayden Report fuelled debate. Labor MHR Gordon Bryant pressed Beale about the Warburton Reserve. He wanted to know exactly how much land had been taken over for the weapons program. He also requested details about 'desecration' of waterholes, hunting grounds and sacred places, plans for compensation to traditional owners, and methods of protection for Aboriginal people in the Reserve. Beale responded with continued defence of his government's actions. He told parliament that Giles Meteorological Station was the only Commonwealth establishment within the Reserve, and 'special care' had been taken in selecting its position. Beale believed two native patrol officers were sufficient to protect and monitor Aboriginal people in the huge area. He argued that 'no tribalized aborigines [sic]' even lived in the Woomera area, and those living near Maralinga were constantly 'surveyed' while nuclear detonations occurred.[32]

Grayden's report into Aboriginal living conditions in the Laverton-Warburton Range area was presented to state parliament in December 1956.[33] The shocking and confronting findings were initially ignored by mainstream media. But a month later, the Communist Party made sure that the report's revelations became common knowledge. The *Tribune* revealed Grayden's disturbing findings in January 1957, and it is interesting to note this ardent communist endorsement of a report by a Liberal Party politician. Findings about the 'deplorable' situation at Warburton area missions were detailed, prompting interest then extensive coverage in mainstream press. The *Tribune* reported that the committee 'ripped aside the screen that has veiled the cruel plight to which our Governments [sic] condemn Australian Aborigines', with suffering occurred while:

> ...huge areas of the most favorable [sic] land are being taken from their reserves and provided for mining interests, atomic and guided missile testing grounds, and other purposes.[34]

Pastoralists in the Warburton area were also targeted in the Report. The *Tribune* detailed findings that Aboriginal station workers were 'given conditions like animals', and exploited for cheap labour. The committee found 'many instances' of Aboriginal children being trained at mission schools as pastoral and domestic workers for station owners who provided no accommodation or other facilities. The *Tribune* reported these pastoralists making 'rich fortunes for themselves [with] ostentatious wealth and extravagances', while treating Aboriginal workers abominably, 'blithely condoned by officialdom'.[35]

In the turbulent wake of the Report, state Minister for Native Welfare John Brady toured the Warburton–Laverton district, accompanied by a *West Australian* journalist. In an effort to ensure accurate reportage, Pastor Doug Nicholls accompanied two committee members (Grayden and Stan Lapham) on an independent tour of the area. Nicholls' observations (recounted in the *Tribune*) added gravity to the situation: 'the pitiable squalor, the sight of my people starving – the most shocking sight I have ever seen'. The article continued:

> Pastor Nicholls said that at Giles weather station [sic], deep in the heart of the best hunting grounds in the Warburton reserve – a region the Government had stolen as part of the Woomera range – the white people lived like kings, and the Aboriginal tribes worse than paupers...The Commonwealth has spent a fortune on Woomera, but has not even supplied a well for the Aboriginals...What is happening out there...is a blot on our vaunted civilisation.[36]

By contrast, Rupert Murdoch's reconnaissance mission into the contentious Warburton area culminated with his *Adelaide News* report describing happy, well-fed Aboriginal people who had nothing to grumble about.[37] Donald McLeod was one person who, not surprisingly, vehemently disagreed with Murdoch. After reading Grayden Report descriptions about 'widespread starvation...and suffering from extreme and pathological forms of administrative malpractice', McLeod approached the publisher. Decades later he recalled 'discussions with the newspaper publisher...Murdoch [who] agreed to give me some space in his local newspaper to draw attention to the reality of this situation'. McLeod's optimism was, however, premature. Shortly after his visit to Warburton Mission, Murdoch reneged on his pledge to McLeod and no such article was published.[38]

In the wake of Grayden's shocking findings, communists and unionists added their voices to calls for UN investigation into conditions endured by tribal Aboriginal people. The *Tribune* urged ACTU representation to the UN about the 'inhuman' treatment of Aboriginal people.[39] Australia was not a signatory to two important UN Human Rights covenants drafted in 1955, and so any appeals from the UN to Australia's government would likely have fallen on deaf ears anyway. In Melbourne, the Grayden Report prompted establishment of the Save Our Aborigines Committee. Outspoken advocate Doris Blackburn was instrumental in attracting the support of a wide range of individuals and organisations to this urgent common cause – protection of the Warburton Ranges Aboriginal people from continued harm.[40]

South Australian communists proclaimed ongoing commitment to ending the tests. Their resolution was published by the *Tribune*:

> Our Party has consistently pointed out that the atom and rocket war projects at Woomera and Maralinga not only endanger our country as a whole, but strike directly at the Aboriginal people who have been driven from their tribal lands with such dire results.[41]

Prominent communist (and Australian Railways Union Victorian branch secretary) John Brown was quoted arguing that 'if £1 million less had been spent on the rocket range and used instead to help the Aborigines, Australia would have more to be proud of'. South Australian unionists joined other Adelaide activists to rally against the Maralinga tests at a three-day conference in late 1957, hosted by the Australian Assembly for Peace (co-convened by union leader Bill Morrow).[42]

'Old Friends at New Theatre'

The *Tribune*'s headline announced New Theatre's latest production of *Rocket Range* in Sydney. Jim Crawford's powerful play was staged for new audiences in March 1957, a decade since its first performance. The *Tribune* reminded readers that 'over ten years ago this play predicted the plight of the Australian Aborigines and what removal from their tribal grounds would mean when the rocket range was built'.[43]

Despite this changed environment of fear, the reprised production's script of *Rocket Range* was not modified to incorporate new threats by nuclear weaponry (thus, identical to that presented to audiences in 1947).[44] The message remained the same although the weapons were vastly different – Aboriginal people still lived in the danger zone and government activities posed new, more extreme risks. *Rocket Range*'s season in Sydney commenced on 30 March 1957. New Theatre's advertising flier identified the production 'under the auspices of the W.W.F. Cultural Committee'; hence, a close collaboration between theatre and union: waterside workers were endorsing and sponsoring this play about weapons testing and dangers for Central Australian Aboriginal people.[45] Indeed, New Theatre was housed in WWF's Maritime Industries Theatre (in their Sussex Street building) for eight years from 1954, and managed to present plays in an extremely cramped performance space.[46]

A play such as *Rocket Range* was a very useful tool of propaganda reaching many audiences across Australia. For example, it was presented at Brisbane's New Theatre in 1948, 1950 and 1955.[47] In 1953 the *Guardian* published a report about *Rocket Range*. A CIS Officer added the newspaper's commentary about the 'famous' play to Jim Crawford's security file:

> [In *Rocket Range*]…the voice of the aboriginal [sic] people speaks
> in condemnation of the barbarity of the atomaniacs.[48]

Rocket Range reinvigorated old concerns now regarding a new form of weapons testing, but it was soon apparent that with the changing capability of weaponry came need for a wider raft of activist concerns. This was evidenced by a public lecture in February 1957 convolutedly titled: 'Atomic & Hydrogen Tests, Woomera, Aborigines & the Australian People'. ASIO identified the Communist Party and trade union movement as central protagonists linking peace and anti-nuclear campaigns with Aboriginal rights.

These 'propaganda opportunities' (according to the security organisation) provided perfect opportunity for cunning communists to take full advantage to protest when tribal lands were used as testing grounds.[49]

Other artists publicly opposed nuclear weaponry testing too. During late 1957 ten Australian writers and artists banded together in protest action. They wrote to Prime Minister Menzies, asking for immediate cessation of nuclear tests. Communist sponsors of this *Appeal from Australian Authors and Artists* included Katharine Susannah Prichard, Judah Waten, Kylie Tennant, and communist sympathiser Alan Marshall (who coordinated the appeal). Other sponsors were William Dargie, Leonard Mann, Dame Mary Gilmore, Napier Waller, Professor Walter Murdoch, and *Meanjin* editor Clem Christesen. The *Appeal* called for like-minded writers and artists to support their plea, and one copy was co-signed by communist writer and musician John Manifold.[50]

Three years earlier, Sydney's *Daily Mirror* editor had expressed derisive views about Menzies' relationship with Australian writers. Both the prime minister and Opposition Leader Evatt were Commonwealth Literary Fund Committee members, and a scathing editorial accused the body of subsidising communist propaganda through the allocation of grants. Provision of £600 for communist Judah Waten to write a book about revolutionary Industrial Workers of the World activities was noted as a prime example. The editor declared that taxpayer money was helping 'the reds' to peddle their wares, and that committee members were 'dupes of Communist propagandists'. A call was made for Menzies and Evatt to 'demand a thorough overhaul' of the committee's activities, instead of throwing a 'blank cheque to an author', who could then write subversive literature aimed to 'overthrow...the Commonwealth in favour of an alien ideology'.[51]

The Warburton Film

Film was also used to great effect. When relocation of Aboriginal people from the danger zone to missions went incredibly wrong, a film of their plight reached nationwide audiences. Doug Nicholls and William Grayden created a film in 1956. They had visited the Warburton-Laverton region together, and then returned with ministerial and medical groups. This documentary is widely recognised as *The Warburton Film* (also sometimes known as *Their Darkest Hour*). Speaker notes accompanying the colour, but silent, film briefly describe the scenes. Images of malnourished, sick and poverty-stricken Aboriginal people bombard the viewer. A mother's arm has rotted off with yaws. A blind man with one leg hobbles grotesquely on an artificial leg stuffed with furs and bandaged into an elephant-like stump. Malnourished children with huge swollen bellies stare blankly at the camera. A baby lies deathlike beside a mother too weak to walk. A sickening close-up of a toddler who fell into a fire reveals cooked flesh covered with flies. Skeletal remains of a man, dead from thirst, lie beside a dried-up waterhole. As the film concludes, his body is buried in an unmarked grave.[52]

The *Tribune* revealed details of the shocking film imagery several months later. Grayden's findings were now public knowledge, and communists were outraged when Rupert Murdoch published his incongruous version of life at Warburton Mission. In the *Tribune* his account was declared to be grossly inaccurate: for example, Murdoch had spent minimal time at the Mission, his visit happened when health services were actually offered (the Mission was closed during the hottest three months of the year), and Murdoch only saw a few Aboriginal people (thus minimal disease) because he visited in school holidays during the three-month 'walkabout'. The *Tribune* reported children spending nine months at the Mission, before returning to tribes and enduring three months of food and water shortages. Communists considered Murdoch's experience aberrant and unrepresentative of Mission life.[53] Indeed, Murdoch did not report anything like the poignant film scene described by communist Aboriginal rights activist Jack Horner. His autobiography recalled disbelief at images of children 'scavenging for food' at Laverton Hotel while the Mission was closed.[54]

The *Tribune* also identified photographs in *Adelaide News* (purportedly taken by Murdoch) as actually 5 years old and taken by Grayden himself during a 'good season…[with] the Aborigines looking very healthy'. Grayden's showing of the film at an Aborigines Advancement League meeting was reported:

> The children with skinny matchlike arms, trunks and legs, with stomachs swollen enormously from starvation, too weak even to brush the thick mass of flies from the eyes, mouths and faces. Imagine their faces – lips bleeding, dead-pan listless looking, with non-blinking eyes and gaping mouths covered with flies.[55]

The Warburton Film reached a much larger audience in Melbourne during April. Horner recalled:

> In a brilliant move, [Stan] Davey arranged for [the film] to be shown exclusively on Melbourne's GTV-9 to raise funds for [Victorian Aboriginal Advancement League]. The movie shocked people. Money poured in to help…the league and many people joined up.[56]

Another significance of the film has been identified. Television was new. Images of starving and sick Aboriginal people in *The Warburton Film* were among the first that 'mainstream' Australians had encountered. Aboriginal Australia had become far more visible.[57]

Soon after the televised event, the film was shown to 2,000 people at Sydney Town Hall. The *Tribune* reported 'cries of disgust and horror and people openly wept'. Doug Nicholls chaired the meeting organised by the Aboriginal–Australian Fellowship. One important outcome was a petition demanding a referendum 'to make Aborigine Affairs a Commonwealth responsibility – thus depriving the Commonwealth Government of the alibi it uses to excuse its past and present neglect'. A Labor MHR assured the audience that his party fully supported the meeting and its objectives. He also promised to present the petition in parliament. AWU general secretary Tom Dougherty also pledged union support.[58] Copies of the pamphlet *New Deal for Aborigines* were distributed there.[59] Don McLeod was also invited to speak. But in characteristic recalcitrant fashion, he declined the offer, refusing to share the stage with Methodist clergy. McLeod argued that the church had shanghaied control of Aboriginal rights activism, with its agenda to Christianise and civilise indigenous people.[60]

By November, the federal Minister for Territories Paul Hasluck had clearly had enough of bad press and public anger about the film – it was time to pass the buck back to its rightful owner. He informed parliament that a petition from three churches about the Warburton Ranges people should be redirected (away from his department) to the WA government. This also accorded Hasluck ideal opportunity for his timely reminder: the Commonwealth was not responsible for state-based Aboriginal welfare, and it was time for WA to deal with its own very public mess.[61]

The Aboriginal rights movement continued showing *The Warburton Film* as a powerful example of injustice and inhumanity. It was screened at meetings in Melbourne, Sydney, Canberra and country areas throughout 1957. In Tasmania, the AEU conducted a public film evening in Launceston to increase awareness and rally support for the petition.[62] Faith Bandler credited the film's powerful cinematic representation of tragedy with 'moving' Gordon Bryant to become involved with Aboriginal affairs for the next two decades.[63] In 1959 the Aboriginal-Australian Fellowship again presented the film to Sydney members, one of whom was a covert ASIO operative. He/she recorded its impact in a report:

> It is a coloured film and shows natives suffering from yaws, malnutrition, burns etc. Most of the natives shown are in a very thin and emaciated condition and it could be regarded as an indictment of the treatment of aborigines [sic] in Australia.[64]

The ASIO report concluded with an unusually emotional statement:

> ...Source states, "I was personally very shocked when I saw the film".

Such a human response by an ASIO official was rare. This emphasises the invaluable role of the film as a compelling vehicle of propaganda.

Power of *The Warburton Film* endured. When singer Paul Robeson visited Australia in 1960, unions and the Communist Party made sure that he viewed the shocking imagery. Robeson's US passport had been recently re-issued after an eight-year ban because of alleged communist activities. Since the 1930s he had supported the USSR and American Communist Party. For Robeson, communism represented invaluable international perspective embracing human values of all people, transcending race.[65] At the BWIU's invitation, Robeson sang for workers building Sydney's Opera House. This followed a welcome by communist writer Frank Hardy. He then travelled with Faith Bandler to Hardy's flat, where they viewed the film as a Party fundraising evening. Hardy's biographer described that 'Robeson sat in silence for about fifteen minutes, tears streaming down his face'.[66] Robeson's biographer also described Robeson's trip to Australia. Following the emotional Sydney experiences, he gave interviews to major newspapers in capital cities he visited about the plight of Australia's Aboriginal peoples. Robeson's overt activism added significant kudos to the Aboriginal rights movement.[67]

Doug Nicholls returned to Warburton Ranges in April 1971. It was his first visit back to the area since 1956. This later experience was disturbingly similar:

> Doug found little improvement...very little change since 1956. The Warburton Ranges Mission has existed for 80 years but the 480 Aborigines who live there still live in humpies; there is no hospital; no maternity service – women go out into the bush to have their babies – and no employment.[68]

Ramifications of the weapons tests lasted long after the program had concluded. Relocation of Aboriginal people to overcrowded and poorly resourced government and mission settlements prompted heated debates in Canberra. In 1964 Labor stalwarts such as Kim Beazley Snr, Gough Whitlam and Jim Cairns pressed the Government for urgent health and welfare assistance. Beazley identified the core issue as 'the need to protect the interests of Central Australian Aborigines induced to leave their tribal lands for inadequately prepared Government settlements'.[69]

Beazley noted that seventy-one Aboriginal people had been 'contacted' near the corner point where the borders of WA, SA and the NT meet. These contacts were instigated and undertaken by the Woomera Research Establishment. Of the seventy-one, over forty people were removed 480 kilometres away to Papunya in the NT. This example raised a number of questions which went unanswered. Did the Aboriginal people know where they were going? Were they forcibly removed? Did government workers speak Aboriginal languages? Were they free to leave Papunya and return home? Would the government transport them home? Cairns asked: 'Will you give them a ride back?'. Minister for Territories Barnes replied. He stated that, should Aboriginal people prefer to return to their homelands, they were permitted to walk back...the enormous distance they needed to cover was not an issue, because 'journeys of hundreds of miles are nothing to these people who will walk forty miles a day when hunting'.[70]

♫ This is a rainy land
This is a rainy land
No thunder in our sky
No trees stretching high
But this is a rainy land

My name is Yami Lester
I hear, I talk, I touch but I am blind
My story comes from darkness
Listen to my story now unwind
This is a rainy land

A strangeness on our skin
A soreness in our eyes like weeping fire
A pox upon our skin
A boulder on our backs all our lives

My name is Edie Milipuddie
They captured me and roughly washed me down
Then my child stopped kicking
Then they took away my old man to town
They said 'Do you speak English?'
He said 'I know that Jesus loves me I know
Because the bible tells me so ♫[71]

Australian musician Paul Kelly wrote *Maralinga (Rainy Land)* in 1986 after reading a newspaper article about Aboriginal people affected by Central Australian atomic tests during the 1950s and 1960s. Kelly met and formed a friendship with Yami Lester, one of the people reportedly affected by nuclear rain.[72]

Communist activist and ophthalmologist Fred Hollows also met Yami Lester. Some years after atomic bombs were detonated in the desert of South Australia, Hollows conducted a medical assessment of his condition. He believed Yami Lester's blindness was likely the result of radiation exposure following a nuclear test known as Totem One. This explosion occurred close to where Lester lived with his parents and around twenty other Aboriginal people near Wallatinna Station (north of Emu Field). Lester described 'the black mist' cloud to Hollows. A legal case mounted on Lester's behalf was described by Hollows as 'inconclusive', as the government blamed trachoma and measles for his extremely unusual eye disease. Hollows was more decisive, laying likely blame for Lester's blindness squarely at the feet of those responsible for the radiation cloud.[73]

Yami Lester's story was also told in a most formal setting. In 1985 the Royal Commission report about Australia's nuclear tests revealed Lester's plight, as well as detailing what happened to Kelly's other song-line character. Edie Milpuddie was with her two children and two dogs when government officials discovered their 'unexpected and untimely appearance' at a 'dirty' area in May 1957. Officers had already found her husband at the edge of one of the bomb craters. This was a mere eight months after the nuclear weapon had been detonated, while this family group continued to live in the affected desert. The Milpuddies were oblivious to the nuclear radiation contamination area they had wandered within. Pregnant Edie and her family were roughly showered by government officials, then trucked off to a mission at Yalata. Edie's baby was born dead. The dogs were shot.[74]

Conclusion

Announcement of plans to conduct the weapons program in 1946 had marked the beginning of a lengthy protest campaign involving a diverse range of activists. One of their objectives was to protect Aboriginal people living within the danger zone. As we have seen, radical-left activism manifested in all the characteristic ways, such as newspaper articles and protest meetings, but was also articulated more creatively by a talented group of artists, writers and intellectuals. As activists protested, intelligence personnel watched closely, amassing large amounts of evidence about things they thought might happen. And these government fears of communist and unionist incursion at the rocket range manifested as a forceful legislative gag, stifling activist dissent at Woomera and much more widely.

But at the heart of it all were desert people like the Milpuddies, who lost the right to walk their land. In the following chapter, the final case study about land and rights begins. Again, left-wing activists are featured participants in this northern campaign where the Aboriginal rights movement was to gain crucial new ground.

NORTHERN TERRITORY

Wave Hill Walk-Off

Chapter Seven

For the first time in over 80 years, a white man was seen chopping
his own wood at Wave Hill this week…No one comes running
when the white missus of the station rings her little bell now.[1]

Twenty years after Pilbara workers walked away, Aboriginal
workers and families left impoverished pastoral station existence
in another part of Australia. This time no singular Don McLeod
figure dominated, but communist and unionist activity was
highly evident as the campaign progressed.

The Wave Hill cattle station walk-off in the Northern Territory
has been recounted in books, documentary films and songs. On
23 August 1966 more than 200 people (mostly Gurindji) gathered
up meagre belongings and walked to Victoria River. There, in
most uncomfortable living circumstances, they sat down as 'illegal
squatters on a pastoral lease'.[2] Before moving to interpretation of
this extreme action the background needs to be considered.

Aboriginal workers and the Northern Territory cattle industry

Northern Australia is an extremely challenging place to farm cattle. Enticements to NT pastoralists, in the form of low-rent leaseholds, had been on offer since the early 1860s but the initial take-up rate was very low. Droving cattle up from South Australia (to which the NT was annexed) or over from Queensland was a costly and labour-intensive exercise, and markets were limited. The NT cattle industry did experience some growth during the 1880s as markets opened up and prices rose, but this halcyon period was short-lived. The northern cattle industry became a casualty of the 1890s international depression that overwhelmed the rest of the nation's economy as well. But with the new century came industry advancement. Cattle became more resilient to tropical diseases and insects, and sales to other states increased. Pastoralists learned how to synchronise their routines to the two (dry and wet) seasons of the tropics. However, overall economic performance of the NT cattle industry was poor, and herd management proved particularly problematic. Fences were few and far between (and so were the cattle), making the job of locating, monitoring and mustering them time and manpower intensive. The NT became an expensive and burdensome appendage that South Australia's government was relieved to hand over to the Commonwealth in 1911.[3]

Federal control of the Territory heralded infrastructure improvements. New roads and a railway line from Darwin to Katherine were built. A government deal with the newcomer 'Vestey Brothers' group facilitated the construction of meatworks at Darwin in return for (among other things) public upgrading of the city's jetty. The industry grew for several years, but by 1920 again experienced sharp decline. Prices fell, the meatworks closed, and smaller failed pastoral property leases were gobbled up by the two big company players, Vestey and Bovril (Vestey had acquired

Wave Hill cattle station a few years earlier, and its relationship with the area is explored shortly).[4]

Aboriginal labour produced Vestey's profits, and the communist press wasted no time revealing that situation. The Party had a long tradition in its short history of disseminating its truths of the NT cattle industry. Indeed, its first national article about the situation – '"Advance, Australia Fair": The Black Slaves in the Northern Territory' – had appeared on the anniversary of colonisation in 1923. Romantic imagery of intrepid frontiersmen wrestling valiantly with Australia's hostile (but tameable) native landscape was brutally confronted. Cold prose described their industrial pursuit as:

> ...wealthy squatters "obtaining" Federal Government permits that entitle them to force aboriginals [sic] to work on their holdings without any wages being paid. In return for their labour they receive some food, a few rags, and a bark gunyah. The blacks are not allowed to leave the stations, are rounded up like station cattle, and are fed on offal and other refuse...[5]

This story was published in the *Communist*, which was the second version of the Party's national newspaper, superseding *Australian Communist* (first published on 6 May 1921). *Workers' Weekly* was the next incarnation, commencing on 22 June 1923 (and the *Tribune* replaced it in 1940). In 1927 *Workers' Weekly* reported that the vast majority of Aboriginal workers did not actually receive wages in return for labour. Two stations had paid their workers during the previous two years, but the Aboriginal people did not actually touch or even see their money – it was sequestered away into 'trust funds' administered by station masters.[6] In 1932 the Communist Party actively investigated conditions in remote Aboriginal communities, with secretary Bert Moxon going 'among the aborigine [sic] in Central and Northern Australia to spread the doctrines of the party'.[7]

Aboriginal protector John Bleakley had conducted an investigation into Aboriginal pastoral worker conditions in 1929. He found that most were not receiving wages and lived in appalling circumstances. The 'Bleakley Report' concluded that the pastoral industry was 'absolutely dependent upon Aboriginal labour' and government was guilty of inadequate service provision and oversight of the industry. But unfortunately for Bleakley and the Aboriginal workers, timing of the report's release could not have been worse. His concerns were not addressed, as the global depression confronted governments with far more pressing issues.[8]

Communists and NT unionists had a frosty relationship during the 1920s and 1930s. Mainstream press reports cited in *Workers' Weekly* noted that Darwin unions were planning to draw 'the color [sic] line among the toiling masses', by boycotting bosses employing non-white workers. The Party unequivocally stated its position on Aboriginal workers – 'the correct policy is to fight for the full wage for all workers irrespective of color [sic]', because:

> The aboriginals [sic] are an oppressed people. They have been driven from their natural hunting grounds by the capitalist class… they are being absorbed into industry and there is no reason why they should not be organised with the rest of the workers in the trade unions.[9]

Aboriginal workers were not protected by the North Australian Workers' Union (NAWU) which, according to *Workers' Weekly*, viewed them as a threat to white worker comfort levels. It reported the 'plentiful supply of native workers at low rates of pay [was] a direct menace to the station workers in North Australia'.[10] NAWU members were described as 'two-faced individuals [who were] exploiters of native labor [sic]'.[11] Industrially then, Aboriginal workers were totally dependent upon flimsy 'protections' offered by the Chief Protector of Aborigines. Until the 1940s government protection in the north was scant, and pastoralists operated with impunity. Relatively recent settlement of the region meant that control and power was grasped overwhelmingly by white frontier settlers.[12]

Workers' Weekly described savage and brutal life in the north, reporting atrocities committed by colonial imperialists upon Aboriginal peoples. In one example, a group of seventeen ('old men, women and children') were reportedly 'shot down in cold blood by the police', for attempting to camp near a watering hole needed for white man's cattle. The story of these people, inconveniently in the way, was described as part of the NT 'civilising process' incorporating slaughter, rape and dispossession of land, culture and hunting grounds.[13]

In 1931 the Party released its draft 'Policy of Struggle Against Slavery'. This comprehensive Aboriginal policy included a demand for all lands in 'Central, Northern, and North West Australia' to be handed back. It proposed 'Aboriginal republics' to make treaties and operate independently of imperialism, to 'prevent Capitalism exterminating this race'.[14] Meanwhile, humanitarian groups were establishing a defence against racial discrimination. Feminist organisations, church missionary societies and anti-slavery bodies shared common views about the treatment of Aboriginal people in northern Australia. However, the NAWU continued to beat a different drum, arguing that 'full-blood' Aboriginal pastoral workers should not receive any wages.[15] Prior to 1933 there was only one small group of NT Aboriginal workers (apprentices) who actually had parity with white workers. But in that year, the federal government responded to white employer needs by ruling that Aboriginal workers were not entitled to the same rate of pay as their white counterparts (this ruling applied to apprentices who were racially categorised as 'half-caste'). This ordinance removed the only slim-picking of Aboriginal worker equality, and wage rates fell significantly.[16]

Vestey time

During the 1940s communists turned their attention to the British-owned Vestey group of companies. By 1946 the NAWU was also attempting better support for Aboriginal pastoral workers. The *Tribune* identified their 'on-tap' supply to cattle stations by NT government officials, particularly to those owned by Vestey (operating as Australian Investment Agency Pty Ltd). Aboriginal workers were still unable to be protected by NAWU as they remained outside the Award system, but now at least the union was actively attempting to gather these workers under its protective cover.[17] It applied to adjust the Commonwealth Works and Services (NT) Award so that they were no longer excluded from coverage. This application was granted and union confidence was buoyed. NAWU then attempted to vary the Cattle Station Industry (NT) Award, despite the curious situation that the union's own membership rules excluded most Aboriginal workers.[18] At that time Vestey leased eleven stations in the NT (including nearly 18,210 square kilometres at Wave Hill Station). It also owned W. Angliss and Co., described in the *Tribune* as 'Australia's largest meat monopoly'.[19] Australia's northern cattle industry was, thus, firmly in British hands.

Vestey's role in the top-end pastoral industry was clearly substantial. Indeed, Gurindji people often refer to events as occurring before, during or after 'Vestey time'. Minoru Hokari lived with this community while researching his doctoral thesis during the 1990s. He stressed the importance of this notion of time. For example, a Gurindji person may tell of a shooting which occurred 'before Vestey time'.[20] Vestey was an integral component of Gurindji life for a long time. This powerful northern cattle industry business dominated many Aboriginal workers' lives and merits a closer look.

The group of companies commenced operations in 1897 with two Vestey brothers at the helm. Their wealth grew rapidly. By

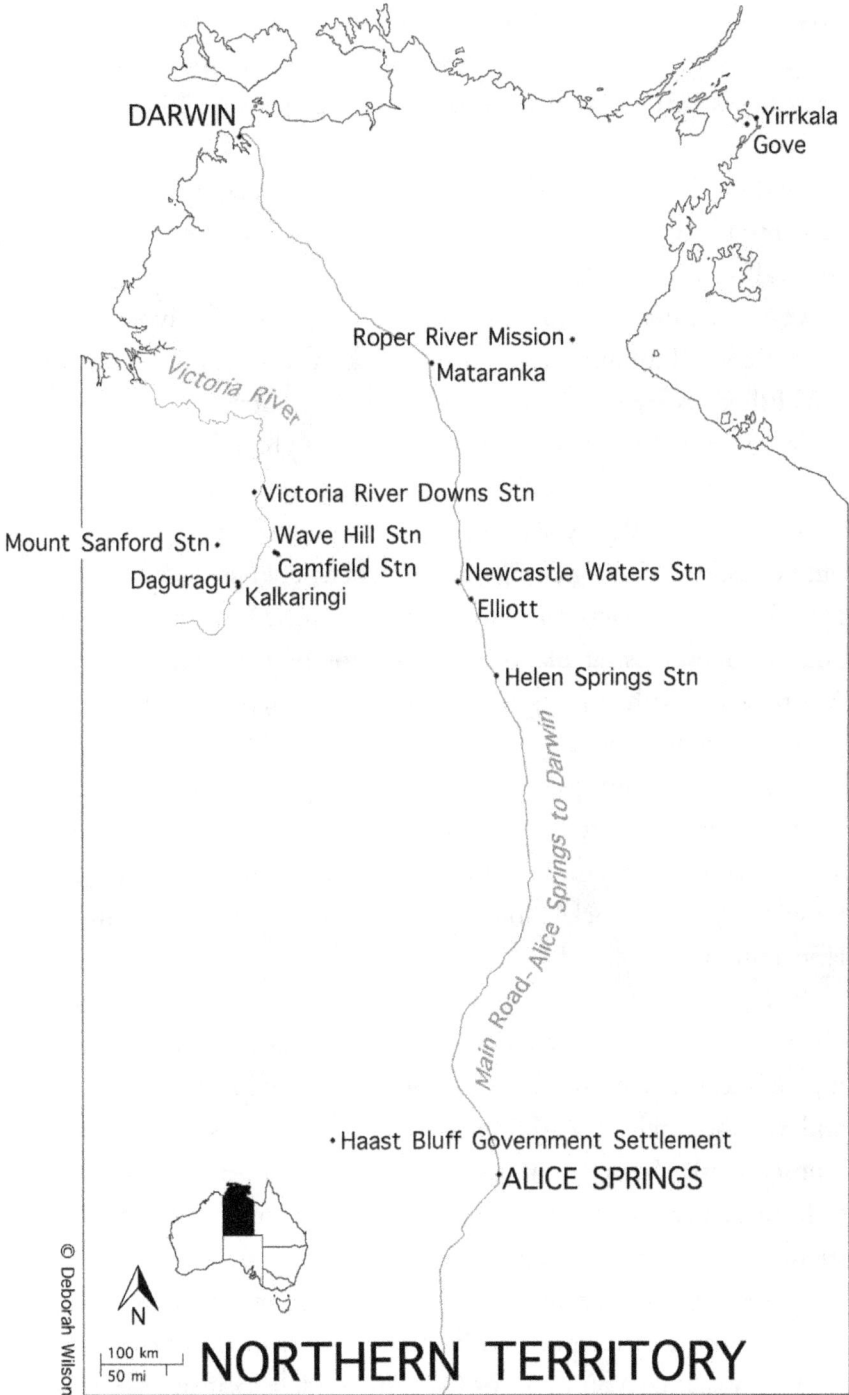

1913 Vestey was establishing processing and refrigeration plants in countries such as China, Argentina, France, Russia and Madagascar. Its first Darwin meat-processing plant was built in 1917, following purchases of 93,240 square kilometres of pastoral leases throughout NT and the East Kimberley. Thus, Vestey had already cemented a strong presence in the Territory fifty years prior to the walk-off from Wave Hill.

Vestey company wealth continued to grow. To avoid high freight costs shipping meat from Argentina to Britain, the group established its own shipping company (Blue Star Line). In 1933 Vestey bought Angliss meat businesses throughout Australia, and its new shipping line facilitated profitable exportation of chilled meat to Britain. Vestey acquisitions increased exponentially. Shipping lines, stevedoring companies, butchers, cold-storage facilities, ice-cream manufacturers, frozen and canned meat suppliers and wool processing plants were bought or established within Australia and other parts of the world. In 1935 the Australian government allowed Vestey to lease even more NT stations. The pastoral industry was now firmly in the grip of overseas interests. This situation persisted despite insipid government murmurings about lease arrangement reviews and transport infrastructure (new roads and stock routes) supposedly assisting the smaller land-lessees.[21]

In 1936 Wave Hill Station was the focus of investigation by the Chief Protector of Aborigines. Findings indicated Vestey's booming financial situation was not being shared with its employees and families, whose conditions were described as 'inadequate'. Consequently Vestey was ordered to pay Aboriginal workers 5 shillings per week.[22] However, its wages pain was short lived. In 1937 the company group discovered a loophole allowing it to earn 'income derived directly from primary production' in the NT without incurring tax. This situation remained in place until 1952. It was a halcyon time for the non-resident British lessees.[23]

Vestey commissioned Ronald and Catherine Berndt to conduct anthropological surveys of seventeen northern Australian
stations between 1944 and 1946. Their brief was to establish why
the pool of Aboriginal labour was decreasing so significantly,
but the Berndts soon discovered the company's real objective for
their work. Vestey had hired them to identify and recruit a fresh
workforce of 'bush Aborigines', to buoy dwindling numbers of
pastoral employees. Disease, malnutrition, low birth rates and
high mortality rates among station Aboriginal people had created
a labour shortage. The Berndts' response to what they witnessed
was not what Vestey expected. For example, they described the
Wave Hill Station a 'feudal situation [consisting of] an overlord,
with a circle of serfs'. Their far-reaching recommendations
included improved medical, housing, sanitation and food provision for Aboriginal workers. Vestey argued incapacity to pay
for any of these improvements, and the Berndts' report was not
released publicly. Indeed, they described their own document as
too 'hot', and politically dangerous. Their recommendations went
unmet, and the Berndts maintained their castigation of the Vestey
conglomerate decades later:

> The AIA [Australian Investment Agency, which was Vestey's
> Australian identity] was blatantly engaged in exploiting the
> natural resources of the country, including the human resources,
> for commercial profit...Our own appointment within that
> structure was an anomaly, devised as a means through which
> benefits could be obtained for the firm.[24]

Vestey activities were also monitored in federal parliament.
In August 1946 Adair Blain (Member for the NT) directed
twenty-two questions to Minister for Commerce and Agriculture
William Scully. Most pertained to Vestey operations and influence
upon the Australian government. Blain suggested that Vestey's

monopoly in the meat industry gave them a stranglehold on the booming export market, particularly to war-torn Britain. He also questioned Vestey's enormous Australian landholdings, given that Argentina had recently prohibited that company (as an exporter) from owning land there. Scully's answers to Blain's questions were scant and evasive. He refuted claims that Vestey controlled Australia's meat industry or received special government treatment, and refused Blain's request to investigate the land-ownership ban in Argentina. Scully also refused to provide information detailing acreage across Australia under Vestey control.[25] Vestey was a lucrative British-owned group of companies, and the Australian government appeared content with its presence and prosperity.

NT pastoral leases were again discussed in parliament two years later. Blain doggedly pressed the government about land lease extensions for companies such as Vestey and Bovril. Minister for the Interior Herbert Johnson revealed that Lord Vestey and company representatives had negotiated lengthened leases on huge pastoral properties such as Wave Hill until 1980. Blain was quick to point out Vestey's profitable arrangement with the government thus far, with the public purse paying for half of all Vestey improvements including fencing, water bores and windmills. The company had also been granted heavily subsidised transport costs. Blain again raised Argentina's reaction, where inappropriate pressures upon government culminated with removal of all Vestey land rights there. Blain claimed that by comparison, the Vestey NT 'racket' was 'taking the [Australian] government for a ride', and he pushed for a royal commission investigation of government dealings with the company group. Similar parliamentary sentiment in 1949 noted the poor condition of cattle on large stations, and that large station sizes should have been reduced when leases were re-negotiated two years earlier.[26]

Vestey-leased stations continued to make big profits while exploiting large Aboriginal workforces. Doris Blackburn MHR pressed Johnson about NT Aboriginal wages and conditions, and his answers present a clear picture of worker life in 1949. An industrial agreement determined Aboriginal wages, paid on a 'sliding scale' up to a maximum £3 10s per week. Most stations were obliged to provide an unspecified quality of worker accommodation, with all wages held in trust by Native Affairs officers. This was because Aboriginal workers didn't understand money and needed to be 'protected'. Johnson stressed that workers were 'not employed under duress', and food provisions were adequate.[27]

Vestey circumstances continued to improve. In parliament the Liberal Minister for Territories (Paul Hasluck) explained NT Legislative Council's limp new Crown Lands Ordinance. Vestey and other big pastoral companies could convert previous lease arrangements to fifty-year contracts. In return they had to 'surrender' 36,260 square kilometres of extremely poor quality land, and make minimal pastoral improvements.[28]

Industrial rumblings in the Northern Territory

The Pilbara disputes had alerted other Aboriginal people to new industrial possibilities. In 1947 approximately 100 Darwin workers downed tools and refused to go to work until paid more. This strike was orchestrated and driven by the workers, with subsequent support from the NAWU. The industrial action was successful, and wages increased significantly. The workers also secured a new school, compound store, and additional clothing and provisions.[29] In late 1950 around 300 Aboriginal people in the Darwin area walked away from bosses for two days, protesting low wages in government and private-employer jobs. The *Tribune* reported the strikes 'led by the natives themselves', with their strike committee issuing information to sympathetic organisations and media groups. Unions gave 'all possible assistance' to the Aboriginal-driven industrial action. NAWU provided publicity and lobbying on the workers' behalf, and pledged future nationwide union support if necessary. It also hired a lawyer to represent arrested Aboriginal activists.[30]

In 1951 Darwin workers again abandoned bosses. Government administrators believed the strike was a communist plot involving Aboriginal worker puppets.[31] The *Tribune* reported wider demands, including minimum £7 per week wages, and 'full legal and social equality and freedom of movement' throughout NT. It also emphasised governmental power to remove and relocate people to missions, deny Aboriginal travel to their homelands, and restrict people's movements to certain days, so that a simple pleasure like going to the pictures was limited to one night per week.[32]

Publicity about the Darwin strikes stimulated strong support from unions nationally, protesting 'racial discrimination' and calling for 'elementary rights and a decent standard of living'. Unions and peak national bodies in Queensland, NSW and the NT rallied to support Aboriginal workers, via official protests and collections.[33] Troublesome Darwin strikes leader Fred Waters was surreptitiously removed by Native Affairs officers to remote Haast Bluff Government Settlement, a concentration-camp-like facility in the Central Australian desert. Communists and unionists were outraged by Waters' removal from his family, for daring to stand up to oppression by instigating industrial action that white men legally undertook. In the *Tribune*, these government actions were described as 'terror tactics'.[34] NAWU lodged a High Court application for an order to return Waters from banishment, but it was refused.[35]

NAWU's backing for Aboriginal workers was, however, short-lived. Support for the Aboriginal strikes of the early 1950s was not evident again until 1961. After 1948 the union had experienced anti-communist opposition as Cold War fears spread. A new guard of racist anti-communist NAWU leaders in 1951 likely promoted the ten year hiatus in its pro-Aboriginal activities.[36]

Brian Manning (who worked as a communist Darwin wharfie during the period) endorsed this view:

> The policy of the NAWU generally reflected the policies of whoever was the Secretary. There were some real Right Wingers at times. When I arrived in Darwin in 1956, it was in the hands of the DLP.[37]

Interestingly, Manning's comments also reflect contemporaneous political machinations, given that the DLP (Democratic Labour Party) had been created as a right-wing labour party by anti-communist ALP members who had been expelled for criticising communist influence within unions.

But northern Aboriginal workers found friends in the south, and a pivotal organisation was formed. The Council for Aboriginal Rights (CAR) was established at a Melbourne public meeting organised by the Communist Party and NAWU in March 1951. Communist Shirley Andrews became secretary of this national body, working tirelessly and unpaid for many years in a personal quest to end racism and oppression. Fellow Party member Barry Christophers was also heavily involved. CAR was driven by the theory that equal wages and conditions held the key to Aboriginal advancement. Members vigorously opposed the assimilationist 1953 NT Welfare Ordinance declaring most 'full-blood' people wards of the state (the Ordinance, which became operational in 1957, was the brainchild of Minister for Territories Paul Hasluck). By creating awareness about Aboriginal workers, CAR members hoped that southern public outcry would influence governments to 'overturn the racism of the north'. Andrews and Christophers also pounced upon the Pilbara worker cooperatives' success story. Pilbara successes were circulated in national CAR bulletins, correspondence and media releases. Informative propaganda educated white readers about the potential of Aboriginal activism.

Unions were less convinced. While some rallied to support the new Council, many (in particular the AWU) did not commit.[38]

Wave Hill Aboriginal workers instigated a one-day strike against Vestey in November 1955. The *Tribune* reported this 'stirring example of spontaneous action by workers who are the most pitilessly exploited in Australia'. It also predicted future industrial turmoil at the station:

> Lacking organisation and experience, and confronted with the concerted pressure of the management, a policeman and a Native Affairs officer, the Aborigines were unable to win their strike. But that will not be the end of it. Though forced back to work, their restlessness persists. Unless something is done to improve their lot, further action by them is on the cards.[39]

Aboriginal workers also found friends overseas. When London's Anti-Slavery Society exposed conditions endured by 'Australian natives', Minister for Territories Hasluck reacted in parliament. He vociferously defended his government's record against statements made by the Society's secretary in the Melbourne *Herald* article, 'They Fight a Thriving Slave Trade'. He said the report gave 'an impression so false and injurious to the reputation of Australia' and that Aboriginal workers had freedom to 'seek and enter employment on exactly the same terms as any other member of the Australian community'. Hasluck painted a positive picture, arguing most received fair wages, with some paid even more than the minimum prescribed. The Aboriginal worker, he stated, enjoyed 'freedom of negotiation' and was 'certainly not a slave'.[40] Gordon Bryant MHR pressed about worker rights during a parliamentary question time. Hasluck stressed that the Aboriginals Regulations and Aboriginal (Pastoral Industry) Regulations represented a secure and reasonable safety net for all NT workers (the Regulations were repealed in 1958 and replaced by the NT

Wards' Employment Ordinance).[41] Aboriginal workers, according to Hasluck, were all in good shape.

Aboriginal rights in the early 1960s

A two-day Native Welfare Conference was conducted in January 1961. Hasluck presented a summary of proceedings to parliament, followed by over four hours of robust debate about policy directions. He presented the state and territory conference agreement about how assimilation should work:

> The policy of assimilation...means that all aborigines and part aborigines [sic] are expected eventually to attain the same manner of living as other Australians and to live as members of a single Australian community enjoying the same rights and privileges, accepting the same responsibilities, observing the same customs and influenced by the same beliefs, hopes and loyalties as other Australians.

Hasluck believed that conference outcomes 'demonstrated the strong and growing interest of Australian governments in aboriginal [sic] welfare'.[42] But as John Nelson (Member for the NT) was quick to point out, the conference had not addressed Aboriginal wages and conditions. He argued that unions should have participated in that golden opportunity to improve industrial rights.[43] Hasluck countered, by suggesting that station workers were, indeed, lucky:

> The easiest adjustment that the aborigines [sic] of this continent ever had was on the pastoral stations because, whether it was good or bad, living in a sort of feudal situation...where the pastoralist was something like a feudal baron with a tribe and two or three white stockmen around him, it was comparatively

easy for the native tribe...to enter into an easy new personal relationship with the new white society.[44]

Communists had other ideas. Resolutions from the nineteenth Congress (published in *The People Against Monopoly*) called for an end to persecutory and racist assimilationist government policies. This also included the CPA program to 'assist oppressed peoples', emphasising inclusion of 'mixed Aboriginal-European descent' people via removing discriminatory laws and social regulations. The communist solution was for 'these magnificent people' to have:

> ...full citizens' rights, full award wages...especially in the pastoral industry, preservation of the remaining tribal lands and provision of land for those driven off the reserves, education and training facilities, abandonment of racial discrimination...repeal of the infamous Aboriginal Protection Acts, and encouragement to the Aborigines to establish their own communities to manage their affairs.[45]

The People Against Monopoly strategy was comprehensive, and communist support for Aboriginal autonomy and equality intensified. During 1961 the Party also produced a broad document: *The Australian Aborigines in the Present World-Wide Struggle for Emancipation of the Colonial Peoples*. This spelt out fears about Menzies' assimilation policy. It noted his 'subtle form of racial chauvinism [policy] based on the assumption that white Australians are superior and that Aborigines have nothing in their lives worth preserving'. The author ('S. M.') clung to beliefs that Stalinist policy had benefitted Soviet indigenous peoples, citing the example of northern Siberian Chukchi Eskimo people rescued (then benevolently controlled) by Soviets to protect them from Western exploiters, particularly 'Americans'.[46]

Australian communists were very aware that Soviet President Khrushchev had spoken to the UN General Assembly in late 1960 about dispossession of indigenous land via colonisation. His comments sparked debate in Australia's parliament. In particular, Khrushchev raised the plight of Australian Aboriginal peoples (although mistakenly describing them as 'exterminated'). He threw down the gauntlet for Prime Minister Menzies to acknowledge the damage inflicted by his country's governments. Menzies was unperturbed, describing Khrushchev's utterances as 'fantastic accusations by a person and a State clearly on the defensive'.[47]

Australian parliamentary discussion also focused upon the NT situation. Questions were asked about Aboriginal cattle station workers. Hasluck continued to paint his picture of a fair and reasonable industrial framework, where employees were well-paid and well-treated, with nothing to complain about (indeed, similar questions were asked a year later and Hasluck's replies were almost identical).[48] Federal Council for the Advancement of Aborigines and Torres Strait Islanders (FCAATSI) activist Faith Bandler had other ideas about what was happening for Aboriginal pastoral workers at that time:

> Black men were working on cattle stations in the North and Centre from sun up to sun down seven days a week for damper and salt beef. Black women were raising white pastoralists' children and doing all the domestic chores in return for the scraps from the kitchen.[49]

So did communist journalist Helen Hambly. Upon return from a tour of NT cattle stations, the *Tribune* published her findings. Aboriginal workers, she wrote, endured:

> ...shocking conditions: they are little better than chattel slaves of the cattle companies. The Department officials "hear

complaints" by calling at a station, lining the Aborigines up, and then, with the station owner and his book keeper present, asking "Any complaints?"[50]

Federal Council for the Advancement of Aborigines and Torres Strait Islanders

FCAATSI was an important national rights body that features in later chapters. Since establishment of the Council for Aboriginal Rights (CAR) in 1951, a new era of national activism had begun. People such as Shirley Andrews and Barry Christophers worked tirelessly for many years promoting Aboriginal rights to the wider community and lobbying governments, the UN and the ILO for support and change. In 1958 national rights campaigns were then coordinated by the newly formed Federal Council for Aboriginal Advancement (FCAA). Its prominent activists (including Lady Jessie Street, Bandler, Andrews and Charles Duguid) collaborated to garner support for a national approach to Aboriginal rights campaigns.[51] FCAA was a non-partisan body, despite having known communists as members and influential executive office holders. Unions also became actively involved from 1962 when the organisation's constitution enabled affiliation.[52]

FCAA's first conference in February 1958 attracted twenty-five people. Three were Aboriginal. Delegates representing rights organisations from all states except Tasmania (NT was also unrepresented) drafted a united cooperation strategy to achieve 'equal citizenship rights' and repeal any discriminatory state or federal legislation. Members called for constitutional change to enable Commonwealth control of all Aboriginal matters. FCAA also formalised policies on equal pay and entitlements for Aboriginal workers, various health and welfare recommendations, and ending governmental assimilationist policies in favour of an 'integration' approach.[53] FCAA's name change to FCAATSI in

1964 formally acknowledged Torres Strait Islanders. Focus upon equal wages intensified the following year when delegates at its annual Easter conference called for direct trade union action to end discrimination.[54] At the FCAATSI conference a year later, unions were again urged to support Aboriginal industrial rights at arbitration level.[55]

FCAATSI was widely considered a 'leftist' organisation, thus attracting keen interest by ASIO. At its 1962 annual conference, for example, an undercover ASIO operative wrote detailed reports about proceedings, highlighting persons of interest thought to be communists or their enthusiastic (but non-committing) travelling companions. An address to the gathering by communist Secretary Shirley Andrews was scathingly reported by the spy agency as a 'tirade'.[56] In this way, it must be emphasised that the success of the national Aboriginal rights movements was all the more remarkable, given the hostile environment of Cold War politics.[57]

Constitutional change was a key FCAATSI aim. In October 1962 it launched a national petition, calling for a referendum to delete the following two constitutional clauses:

Section 51 (xxvi)   The Parliament shall...make laws for the peace, order and good Government of the Commonwealth with respect to the people of any race, other than the aboriginal [sic] race in any State, for whom it is deemed necessary to make special laws.

Section 127   In reckoning the numbers of the people of the Commonwealth or of a State, aboriginal [sic] natives shall not be counted.[58]

∞

In 1967, over 90 per cent of Australia's electorate voted to delete 'other than the aboriginal [sic] race in any State' in Section 51 (xxvi), and to repeal Section 127 altogether. This change enabled Commonwealth legislation on Aboriginal affairs that would not conflict with any state powers. Federal funds could be allocated directly to Aboriginal services (particularly in Western Australia and Queensland) where large Aboriginal populations would most benefit. All major party leaders endorsed a 'yes' vote, as evidenced in Victoria's Aboriginal Advancement League journal featuring extensive commentary urging change by Prime Minister Harold Holt, ALP Leader Gough Whitlam, Country Party Leader Doug Anthony, and DLP Leader Vincent Gair.[59]

By 1963, parliamentarians were also broaching complex issues of land rights and compensation. Kim Beazley Snr called for government creation of 'an aboriginal [sic] title to the land of the reserves of the Northern Territory', in reference to legislation sanctioning royalty payments to Gove Peninsula Aboriginal people (in return for land sliced away from their Reserve to mining companies). Beazley also moved the discussion into the global arena by reminding parliamentary colleagues that Australia was not a signatory to the ILO's Convention 107.[60]

International Labour Organization and Convention 107

The ILO was established in 1919 as a League of Nations agency, to become architect and overseer of international labour obligations and standards. Its formation was underpinned by humanitarian concern for workers and procurement of adequate entitlements to avoid mass global uprisings so soon after the conclusion of World War I. Worker unrest (or even revolution) endangered international political stability, as did an unequal labour market creating wealth in unscrupulous countries at the expense of those treating workers fairly. This social justice model drove ILO establishment of employment standards (as conventions and recommendations) to be applied internationally.

Commencing in 1936, ILO created conventions specifically targeting the rights and entitlements of indigenous peoples. Convention 107 concerned the 'Protection and Integration of Indigenous and Other Tribal and Semi-Tribal Populations in Independent Countries'. It was drafted in 1957, came into force in 1959, and by 1977 was ratified by twenty-seven countries. However, despite significant pressure from Aboriginal rights groups during the late-1950s and 1960s, Australia was never to become a signatory. One activist particularly notable in this push for government ratification was Mary Bennett, who urged fellow-FCAATSI members to lobby for abolition of the assimilation policy. Convention 107 was endorsed at FCAATSI's second conference in 1959.[61]

Convention 107 was intended to protect indigenous peoples whose 'social and economic conditions [were] at a less advanced stage' than the rest of a colonised nation's community. It specifically included 'semi-tribal' peoples 'in the process of losing their tribal characteristics [but] not yet integrated into the national community'. Article Seven stipulated that indigenous populations 'be allowed to retain their own customs and [legal] institutions', in clear dispute with Australia's staunch assimilationist position. In the most contentious section, part two concerned land rights. Article Eleven stated that:

> The right of ownership, collective or individual, of the members
> of the populations concerned over the lands which these popula-
> tions traditionally occupy shall be recognised.

Article Twelve demanded compensation for people forced to leave their land. Articles Thirteen and Fourteen established how indigenous peoples should be allocated land ownership and usage on the basis of custom.[62]

Beazley read Article Eleven in parliament. He argued that application of this 'very simple statement...should not be beyond the wit of the Government and advisers' in the creation of NT Aboriginal title, to be overseen by Aboriginal trustees.[63] A year later he repeated his call, and then added:

> Nothing can be said in defence of granting pastoral leases on tribal lands as though nobody was there.[64]

ACTU also called upon the government to adopt principles of the Universal Declaration of Human Rights and ILO Convention 107. Union solidarity culminated with their peak national body's adoption of a national policy on Aboriginal issues in 1963. ACTU Congress delegates voted to endorse the work of FCAA by fighting for equal wages, social services and worker compensation entitlements.[65] They also resolved to endorse the national petition calling for constitutional changes via referendum.[66]

∞

Between 1962 and 1966 two key events influenced the nature and timing of the Wave Hill walk-off. The first involved the establishment of an important new NT Aboriginal rights organisation. The second concerned a drawn-out industrial hearing, culminating with decisions satisfying station managers little, and Aboriginal people less.

Northern Territory Council for Aboriginal Rights

In 1962 the NT Council for Aboriginal Rights (NTCAR) was formed. It became an important and influential support body for Aboriginal pastoral workers and their families when the Wave Hill walk-off occurred four years later. NTCAR support continued over the long years that Gurindji people quietly fought for their rights and their land. This organisation was extremely unusual, in that most members were not white. Brian Manning and Terry Robinson were the only two non-Aboriginal office holders. They were both also very active Darwin-based members of the Communist Party.

In Terry Robinson's ASIO file, a report identified that one member of NTCAR would definitely not have been welcome. The organisation had only been operational for two months when an ASIO operative first reported his/her attendance at a meeting in Robinson's home, along with twenty-three Aborigines and 'several Europeans'. A similar report was compiled in July.[67]

The NAWU was sceptical about this new organisation and its communist connections, and distanced itself from the unproven group's activism. But this aversion to align with NTCAR was not common to all of this union's members. The Waterside Section soon openly supported the NTCAR in a campaign supporting

This photograph was the first taken of the newly formed NTCAR at Lee Point in 1962. Terry Robinson and Brian Manning are the non-Aboriginal men. (Image provided by Brian Manning.)

an Aboriginal man jailed in controversial circumstances. The union's support for Aboriginal workers then increased, evidenced by its appointment in early 1965 of the first Aboriginal organiser: an Allawah man named Sydney Cook. He was also an executive member of the NTCAR, indicating that hostility towards the organisation by the NAWU may have been easing by then. Dexter Daniels soon replaced Cook and became firmly entrenched as the NAWU's resolute, though often frustrated and under-resourced, Aboriginal industrial representative.[68] His contributions to the Wave Hill walk-off campaign were to be significant.

NAWU concerns about communist control of the NTCAR may have had some merit. But although most non-Aboriginal members of the rights organisation were indeed members of the Communist Party, Brian Manning refuted accusations that the body was communist-controlled:

> ...we (whites) were all CPA members but the Council was not a CPA "front". We were all passionate about the treatment of Aboriginal people at a time when it was not a popular cause for activists. We encouraged non-party people to join and a few did...The Communist Party was considered to be "subversive" and indoctrinating Aboriginals. However, although other political parties joined up "token" aboriginal [sic] members, we consciously left party politics out of the [NTCAR] organisation.[69]

Fear of communist control in the NTCAR mirrored wider beliefs about Aboriginal rights organisations. The government was intensely interested in what was going on between communists and Aboriginal people. In 1962 ASIO head Charles Spry furnished Hasluck with comprehensive documentation regarding Party 'interest and influence in aboriginal [sic] affairs'. An appendix (detailing penetration into Aboriginal activities and organisations) stated ASIO belief that communists were fostering 'growth of a militant Aboriginal "elite" in both trade unions and Aboriginal associations'. This 'united front' aimed to 'achieve political power in Australia'. ASIO believed the 'Aboriginal national minority' would integrate with Soviet international campaigns for 'national liberation struggle'.[70]

Community trepidation about communism was powerfully expressed in mainstream media. In this example, a story published by Melbourne's somewhat excitable *Truth* condemned the Party:

> A secret Soviet plot to foment trouble among Australian aboriginals [sic] has been uncovered by the United Nations. Canberra has warned all State governments...Orders to start the campaign are reported to have been sent directly from the Kremlin to Communist agents in Australia. The plot is described by the UN as part of a campaign to foment trouble among colored races...part of a plan to make democratic countries more receptive to Communist "educational" propaganda. Agents have been instructed to infiltrate every organisation working for the welfare of the aboriginals [sic]...They are told how to use respected, community-minded citizens to push their doctrines once they are inside these organisations.[71]

This article reveals so much more about the period and its edgy political environment. The NTCAR emerged with the Cold War very much alive. In the same year the Cuban missile crisis that almost enveloped the world in nuclear war was played out. Australia's government was sending soldiers to fight communist guerrillas in Vietnam. Fear of communism, and those who espoused it, meant that Aboriginal rights activism by communists and travelling companions was bound to attract adverse attention. Rumours of Soviet collaboration forced communist activists into an even more challenged position. And as will be identified, the *Truth* article was not as far-fetched as some may have believed.

ASIO operatives infiltrated deep into the heart of Aboriginal activist organisations as the Wave Hill campaign wore on into the 1970s. Its records present fascinating evidence of what went on behind the shadowy cloaks of Australia's security organisation.

Australian student activism heightened in 1964, and the US-inspired 'Freedom Ride' on a bus through rural NSW is notable. Ann Curthoys was one of the 'riders' identifying and publicising Aboriginal needs. She was also a communist. Curthoys recalled that 'just over one-third of the students were from the organised Left', including Brian Aarons, Pat Healy, Colin Bradford, Bob Gallagher, Alan Outherd and Norm Mackay. Aboriginal activist Charles Perkins and Polish-born Jim Spigelman organised the Freedom Ride, and Curthoys identified their concern that the event might have been directly linked to the Party as a communist plot.[72]

In 1964, the Party's extensive *Communist Policy on the Aborigines of Australia* recommended that Aboriginal rights 'be taken up by all progressive people, all true patriots, headed by the organised working class'. The draft was distributed for comment by unions, church and women's groups and political bodies such as FCAATSI. The predominant aim was 'to give [Aboriginal people] fraternal aid in their struggle for emancipation, not to act as paternal "benefactors"'. This policy incorporated key points of 1961 Party Congress decisions, stressing identification of Aboriginal people as a 'distinct national minority', to prevent 'the elimination of the Aborigines as a people through enforced absorption into the general population'. Industrial demands were succinct. Aboriginal workers were positioned within the generic industrial relations framework that all workers had a right to expect. It called for 'the right of all Aborigines to organise [and] trade union wage-rates and award conditions' and 'to receive and control the full amount of wages earned'.[73] The *Tribune* publicised this new policy targeting the 'oppressed national minority' telling of an 'organised, growing movement in which capable Aboriginal representatives are beginning to take leading parts' in the push for full citizenship, employment, land and human rights, and improved government services.[74]

But a week later, Melbourne communist Barry Christophers argued in the *Tribune* that a broad program building an Aboriginal 'nation' was impossible. Many different language groups across the huge Australian landmass of many tribal areas made an overriding notion of nationhood fraught. Christophers preferred Aboriginal peoples be considered 'an ethnic group possessing in varying degrees a common cultural heritage'.[75] He believed that the Communist Party's stress on Aboriginal peoples as a national minority placed 'undue emphasis [on] such things as a discussion on assimilation, integration, identity as a people, control of their own affairs, etc'. Christophers thought this approach masked the common and urgent issue of economic exploitation, which was much more able to be fixed.[76]

During 1964, the *Tribune* also published a 'Supplement for the Student of Politics' which urged support for victims of colonisation. Included was President Khrushchev's position (published in *Pravda*'s December 1963 edition) regarding imperialism and anti-colonialism by the 'newly liberated countries' of Ghana, Algeria and Burma. Khrushchev emphasised readiness to 'give all possible aid to the peoples conducting a national-liberation struggle'. The Soviets supported Algerian, Indonesian, Yemeni and Egyptian peoples by supplying arms and military training. Khrushchev reiterated willingness to support colonised peoples escaping imperialistic oppression by 'consummating the national-liberation, anti-feudal, democratic revolution'.[77] One contemporary commentator described Africa as 'increasingly covered with a network of the pink auxiliary organizations [sic] of communism...operating as a great dredger', including peak youth and union bodies in this wave of communist control.[78]

Similar fears were echoed in Australia at that time. Jesuit priest W. G. Smith believed that vulnerable Aboriginal people would be recruited to the Party unless the government took more interest in their plight.[79]

Aboriginal politics gained international attention when two NT Aboriginal men travelled to Kenya as guests of its government in early 1965. Phillip Roberts (NTCAR President) and Davis Daniels (Secretary, and brother of NAWU union organiser Dexter) called for wages parity between black and white.[80] Upon return they shared new knowledge about Kenyan cooperative farm schemes, where indigenous people bought land back from their government with profits from their farming enterprises. Daniels urged the establishment of cooperatives and land hand-back at meetings across the country and FCAATSI conferences over the next twelve months.[81]

FCAATSI also increased commitment to the NT situation. Its predominantly white membership established an Equal Wages Committee, receiving significant union support including donations of $1,200 during 1965–66.[82] The Committee supported NAWU's application to vary the Cattle Station Industry (NT) Award 1951 by deleting discriminatory clauses relating to Aboriginal workers.[83] FCAATSI member (and Postal Clerks' and Telegraphists' Union general secretary) John Baker instigated a two-cent levy on all ACTU members to support that landmark case.[84]

A statement of support for Gurindji workers issued at FCAATSI's 1965 annual Easter conference described them as 'the only people in the Australian workforce who had formed such a consistent and energetic labour force under near-slavery and degradation, and survived'.[85] FCAATSI circulated 45,000 copies of a petition demanding improvements to NT worker rights. Faith Bandler recalled that they were received 'with an amazing response from the trade unions, particularly the Seamen's Union and the Miscellaneous Workers' Union of Victoria'.[86] FCAATSI also established a strong relationship with NTCAR, which was invited to affiliate by prominent member Gordon Bryant MHR. One conference delegate was an undercover ASIO operative, whose report noted surprise at 'the absence of communist influence or strength'. One 'source comment' (in other words, a comment by the spy) about a FCAATSI delegate is particularly interesting: 'Despite his good intentions, DANIELS of N.T. could be easily swayed by the communists if they ever went to work on him'. Here, he/she is referring to either Dexter or Davis Daniels, both Darwin Aboriginal activists and prominent NTCAR members.[87]

The NAWU planned its Cattle Station Award strategy with the best-case scenario of Aboriginal parity with white workers. But this industrial activity did not end well for Aboriginal workers, with the hearing progressing to decisions that no-one was happy with.

Cattle Station Industry (NT) Award case 1965–1966

Industrial possibilities for NT Aboriginal workers had been momentarily buoyed in September 1964. A new 'Social Welfare Ordinance' replaced 'Welfare and Wards' Employment Ordinances' that had controlled Aboriginal lives in the NT since 1953. The NAWU naively assumed that Aboriginal workers would now be automatically included under standard industrial Awards (as determined by the federal Arbitration Commission). But 'specific regulations' within the new Ordinance meant that Aboriginal workers would continue to be hamstrung by special rules just for them; thus, infuriatingly cocooned from the mainstream industrial system.

In January 1965 the NAWU lodged what proved to be an incendiary log of claims in the Arbitration Commission. It sought to amend the Cattle Station Industry (NT) Award to include

Aboriginal workers in all provisions and strike out any discriminatory sections. Protestors demonstrated outside the Melbourne Commission hearing as the NAWU lodged its application for equal wages. Not surprisingly, the application was opposed by the NT Cattle Producers' Council, arguing inability to pay.[88] By February the NAWU was actively lobbying for full Aboriginal pastoral-worker Award wages. It even threatened a 'general stoppage' (with the support of many other unions), and appointment of an Aboriginal organiser was touted as proof of NAWU commitment to non-white workers.[89]

Darwin union support for Aboriginal workers soon provoked ASIO investigation. In a letter to Minister for Territories Barnes, the NT Administrator (Roger Dean) identified the troublesome 'left wing part of the N.A.W.U' plotting to call all waterfront workers out on strike 'if the decision on the aboriginal [sic] wage case is not satisfactory to them'. Dean believed this to be 'part of the communist programme to dominate the aboriginals [sic]'.[90] On that same day, ASIO speedily compiled a 'comment upon the matter raised' by Dean. But it found no evidence of any planned waterfront industrial action.[91]

ASIO may have taken some comfort in knowledge that any subversive communist scheme was going to struggle for numbers. A file-note compiled a month later presents a most interesting precis of actual communist activity in Darwin. The ASIO officer reported that the Darwin Party had been 'struggling to maintain a membership', with only twelve to fourteen members since 1962. Party meetings only attracted five or six members. However, despite such low numbers, ASIO maintained resolute (and costly) surveillance of this 'hard core of Communist activists [exerting] strong influence in the [NAWU]'.[92]

The NAWU called for a general strike to support the Aboriginal 'right to go into the market and sell their labor-power to the employer at the highest price they can obtain'. The *Tribune* urged amendment of the Cattle Station Award for 'industrial freedom'. The union's more agreeable relationship with the NTCAR was again evident in its call for that organisation and the ACTU to support the action.[93] The general strike was planned, then deferred, pending outcomes of the Commission hearing commencing in mid-July. FCAATSI appealed to Prime Minister Menzies, Opposition Leader Arthur Calwell, and the Farmers and Graziers' Association, urging them to 'use their influence' to end wage discrimination.[94]

While the Award hearing progressed in Sydney, the *Tribune* levelled accusations at media outlets in southern states. It reported newspaper, television and radio coverage about NT Aboriginal workers painting pictures of hard-done-by pastoralists with meagre profits being ravaged by drought and poor prices. According to the *Tribune*, the actual situation in the north was just the opposite – new meat processing plants had been established to cope with increasing demands, northern cattle producing areas were actually receiving above-average rainfalls, and reliance upon Aboriginal workers was far greater than mainstream media reported. Indeed, the *Tribune*'s writer argued that before any decision could be handed down, vital evidence needed to be presented about the following:

- the actual numbers of NT cattle and cattle exports over the previous twenty years;
- numbers of Aboriginal people working in that industry during that period;
- rainfall figures since 1945;
- pastoral development, mission profits and station profit histories since 1945; and
- the extent of foreign ownership in the NT pastoral industry.

Aboriginal workers were reported as valuably 'subsidising' primary producers, of whom several were blatantly racist and held powerful positions on cattle associations.[95]

This argument was vigorously supported by one observer recording what actually happened on stations. Jack Kelly had conducted northern beef surveys for the Bureau of Agricultural Economics since 1950. He argued that Aboriginal pastoral workers, as the 'backbone' of the cattle industry, endured shocking living and working conditions. Based on what he had witnessed, Kelly recommended sweeping changes to Aboriginal workers' lives, including full Award wages and conditions, adequate housing and nutrition, and vocational training. To expose true living conditions, he also advocated cessation of the permit entry system onto native reserves, because 'government officials selectively endorse visits for those most favourable to their administration'.[96] Kelly believed that he was one of the few outsiders to see the true picture on NT stations.

In late September Australia's peak union body became actively engaged in the fight for Aboriginal wage equity. ACTU Congress approved a new Aboriginal rights policy and levy to support the NAWU's case in the Award hearing. It also advocated immediate industrial reforms across all states, territories and industries to facilitate Aboriginal parity in wages and conditions. The *Tribune* emphasised calls for federal and state government provision of full social, educational, housing and medical services, plus amendment to the Commonwealth Constitution so that Aboriginal people could become equal members of the Australian community.[97]

The Cattle Station Industry (NT) Award hearing wore on. John Kerr QC was industrial advocate for the pastoralists and the *Tribune* reported his arguments that employers were unable to pay their Aboriginal workers. Kerr also suggested that payment of Award wages for Aboriginal people would be 'fraught with social risk', with workers not reliable or efficient enough to deserve full Award provisions. He shadowed his arguments with ominous warnings, for example arguing that, should Aboriginal workers be granted full Award rates, 95 per cent would lose their jobs to 'mechanisation' (in the form of helicopter mustering).[98] It was also feared that the case could create ramifications in the form of a 'money-hunger', whereby any rumours of wage parity with white workers would have 'run like wildfire' through Aboriginal pastoral worker communities, placing significant economic pressures on stations.[99]

The government exercised statutory power by providing a submission to the hearing. Minister for Territories Barnes informed parliament that the government recommendation was for equal treatment of Aboriginal workers under the Award. He warned that to do otherwise would be discriminatory.[100]

Northern Territory Cattle Station Award decided

After a hearing lasting almost nine months, the Commission handed down its determination about the Cattle Station Industry (NT) Award on 7 March 1966. The *Tribune* reported it took a mere three minutes for this momentous decision to be read. Aboriginal workers had been granted the right to earn wages at the same rate as white workers, but the sting in the tail was barbed. The decision would be implemented on 1 December 1968, delaying wages parity by another two and a half years. And, there was no provision for back-dated payments to the original decision date. Domestic workers were also excluded from the Award, leaving many Aboriginal workers (predominantly women) across the NT without industrial protection. To add insult to injury, a 'slow-worker' provision was also incorporated into the Award, whereby any workers deemed incapable of a standard day's work would be paid at a lesser rate.[101]

The *Tribune*'s editor considered the 'slow-worker' provision a loophole enabling employers to legally dodge fair pay for Aboriginal workers. His comments were blunt:

> Contrary to assertions in some quarters, the Aborigines do not go "walkabout" at the slightest excuse. They are in fact "laid off"

in the wet season after mustering. It is the white boss who goes walkabout – to Sydney or Melbourne for a luxurious holiday.

The editor deemed the overall result a 'reiteration of the employers' case' but was not overly impressed with NAWU efforts either, arguing 'it must be said that the employers went to much more trouble than the union, which did not even call witnesses'.[102]

NTCAR communist activist Brian Manning described the union's failure to call Aboriginal witnesses 'disgraceful'.[103] And Richard Kirby (one of the judges presiding over the case) emphasised the shabby union campaign: 'The NAWU's sporadic, bit-run presentation meant that we on the bench had to do a lot of thinking for the union'.[104] However, bouquets were thrown to the NAWU by Stanner, describing the union's conduct of the case a 'very confident' no-nonsense approach. He believed that the NAWU's use of 'two undecorated arguments – necessity and justice' were all

Paddy Carroll reports to an NTCAR meeting on the outcomes of the 1966 NT Cattle Station Award hearing. (Image provided by Brian Manning.)

that was required. Stanner deemed it simple logic — 'the hinge on which the judgement swung was that of industrial justice'.[105]

Despite criticism about its poor showing, the NAWU was quick to criticise the decision.[106] However, in reality, the Union's venom was weak, given the lack-lustre and half-hearted performance of its advocacy for Aboriginal workers at the hearing. Other union bodies were vocal, with quick condemnation of the decision by the NSW Labor Council as an example of 'unprincipled discrimination', calling for the ACTU to take 'urgent action'. Queensland's T&LC echoed these sentiments, calling upon its state government to immediately act to protect Aboriginal pastoral workers.[107]

Given that the hearing was conducted in Sydney by Commissioners not familiar with the nature of Aboriginal work and life on cattle stations, lack of understanding about these unusual workplaces would have compounded difficulties in their decision-making. Historian C. D. Rowley argued 'the court was obviously at a loss when it came to operate in cross-cultural area where the familiar industrial indicators were lacking'. He also apportioned a share of blame to the unions, with the hearing highlighting the movement's history of neglect for Aboriginal worker rights. The sheer need for the case to be run was a clear indicator of serious, long-term problems in the northern cattle industry, and unions needed to take responsibility for their lack of action or support for Aboriginal workers.[108]

Ramifications of the decision were discussed in parliament. Kim Beazley Snr and Gordon Bryant quizzed Minister for Territories Barnes about welfare of the workers' families, inequity for Aboriginal workers, and the three-year time lag before the new Award became operational. Barnes quickly handpassed full responsibility for the decision to the Commission, while emphasising the government's own commitment to equality and need to heed 'the umpire's decision'.[109]

∞

In 1966, five months after the contentious Cattle Station Award decision was handed down, Aboriginal people walked away from Wave Hill. Between these two events came an important step by workers on a cattle station few have even heard of. Forty years to the day after Pilbara workers abandoned their employers, pastoral employees walked away from Newcastle Waters.

Chapter Eight

The match was in the spinifex.
Right or wrong there was no road back now.[1]

Three months before the Wave Hill walk-off, workers and families at another station packed their belongings and left. A *Tribune* front-page headline described this forerunner action as 'the Aborigines' Big Step'. With support by NAWU organiser Dexter Daniels and leadership by Gurindji stockman Lupgna Giari (known also as Captain Major), the group of around eighty Newcastle Waters people walked 18 miles to set up camp at Elliott on May Day 1966. The 12-square-kilometre station was abandoned, but for two Aboriginal families. The large group which left included twelve stockmen, women, old people and about thirty children. AWU sent funds to purchase food, and a spokesman assured the *Tribune* that the walk-off was Aboriginal-driven and organised, with 'backing of the trade union movement'.[2]

'The Aborigines' Big Step'

Significant union financial support for the Newcastle Waters people was quickly evident. Sydney waterside workers collected $250 for the Elliott camp, and branches of the BWIU and Miners' Federation in NSW and Queensland sent money and telegrams of support. Darwin ship workers donated $40 and food per each ship in port. The *Tribune* again distanced the unions from any coordinating role in the walk-offs, reiterating that Aboriginal people protested the Award decision 'on their own initiative'. NAWU secretary Paddy Carroll said that Aboriginal workers from other stations:

> ...would be asked to leave the stations gradually...our recent action at Newcastle Waters is only the beginning. We have encouraged the Aborigines to leave the property to seek award employment...It is not the intention of the Union to allow a state of stagnation to exist until 1968.[3]

The following week the *Tribune* added more union emphasis to the Newcastle Waters story. NAWU's Dexter Daniels reported that 'their [strikers] confidence is being boosted by their faith in the unions'. Aboriginal workers and families at three other stations had also walked away, but were forced to return due to the remoteness of their settings and consequent unavailability of union assistance. According to Daniels, the problem was transport. Workers were keen to leave stations, but the union lacked infrastructure to get them away. With mustering season upon them, stations were keen to maintain their workforces. Daniels declared that 'station owners need the Aborigines, but the Aborigines don't need them'.[4] Melbourne's communist *Guardian* ran a similar story the next day. Its front page featured a beaming Captain Major, resplendent in spotless white stockman's outfit and dashing kerchief. The newspaper reported Newcastle Waters wages as $10 per week for stockmen and $6 for other workers.[5]

Mainstream coverage of the Newcastle Waters walk-off soon raised communist and unionist hackles. Mirroring the press war that played out during the Pilbara dispute twenty years earlier, the *Tribune* slammed southern daily newspaper reports of 'starvation' at Elliott camp. It reported the NAWU's description of contentious mainstream press articles by writer Douglas Lockwood as 'inaccurate and grossly misleading'. The article also emphasised NAWU's reassuring position that people at the camp were well-fed and supported.[6] Indeed, three weeks earlier the *Guardian* reported total union donations exceeding $2,700. And a week later, it reported another $1,000 donation for striking stockmen by the WWF federal office to the NAWU. Other Victorian union donations included $30 from the Plumbers' Union, $40 from the Boilermakers' and Blacksmiths' Society, $100 from the Amalgamated Engineering Union, and $20 from the Railways Union. A union organisation (described as the 'Equal Pay for Aborigines Committee') sent '250 pounds weight of warm clothing as the children are feeling the winter cold'.[7]

Financial support by unions enabled eighty Newcastle Waters Aboriginal people to maintain their campaign. During the next month support infrastructure for the impending, more famous Aboriginal walk-off was fine-tuned in preparation for the next big step.

Prelude to Wave Hill walk-off

NAWU and NTCAR activists were again at loggerheads one month prior to the Wave Hill walk-off. At a Rapid Creek meeting on 24 July called to revive interest in NTCAR, 200 people unanimously voted to adopt a program of reform and development. In a badly timed and inappropriate address to the meeting, NAWU secretary Paddy Carroll infuriated listeners with his assimilationist suggestion that Aboriginal people forget about their identity. The

Tribune reported his incendiary comment: 'I urge you to refer to yourselves as Australians and forget this black fellow, white fellow talk'. Carroll's words were immediately challenged by NTCAR members, saliently reminding him that the whole purpose of their organisation was, indeed, to fight for 'native rights'. They strongly recommended Carroll's ongoing support for his Aboriginal union organisers and their fight for justice.[8]

It was at this heated meeting that the *Tribune* reported the first active presence of a communist soon to become a significant character in the Wave Hill story. Renowned (and sometimes controversial) author Frank Hardy told those present that he could raise support 'in the South', from people 'anxious' to support NT Aboriginal people. Another significance of this meeting was the election of Robert Tudawali (also known as Bobby Wilson) to the position of vice-president.[9] Tudawali, best known for leading roles in the film *Jedda* and television series *Whiplash*, was to become a most valuable spokesman and emissary for the organisation when the major walk-off began. He and Hardy had met during the week before the Rapid Creek meeting. When interviewed a few months later, Hardy said that his encouragement prompted Tudawali's agreement to actively participate in the rights movement and become NTCAR vice-president.[10]

Hardy also contributed his writing skills to the NTCAR meeting. At the organisation's behest, he drafted its 'Program for Improved Living Standards for NT Aborigines'. This comprehensive document declared worker conditions a 'disgrace to Australia and a clear breach of the Charter of Human Rights'. Eleven resolutions addressed Aboriginal worker rights, women's rights, discrimination, welfare payments, housing, nutrition, education, medical facilities and legal entitlements. The final resolution established NTCAR's game plan. It aimed to 'work with the trade union movement and other interested organisations to bring this program into effect'. Importantly, the ninth resolution demanded

'That natives have full control and ownership of reserves'. This demonstrates that NTCAR had already placed land rights central to the agenda a month before the Wave Hill people left.[11] An original copy of this program (signed by Davis and Dexter Daniels) is held in an ASIO file, epitomising the keen governmental interest and observation of this very active Aboriginal rights organisation.[12]

∞

A week before the Wave Hill walk-off, Prime Minister Harold Holt received a hand-written letter from the Amalgamated Engineering Union's branch in Littleton, NSW. Members had instructed their secretary (Hallam) to protest the 'inhuman treatment' of Aboriginal people in the NT. How, Hallam asked, could Mr Holt's 'class government' allow the 'privileged few to exploit them'?[13] This profound sentiment of one small branch of one big union is evidence of so much more. The letter identified that Aboriginal worker rights in the NT were not just the concerns of big union bodies in Melbourne or Sydney. In this case, a smaller group of union members at the back of the Blue Mountains had voiced solidarity for people they would likely never meet.

'We been waiting for you fellas'

On 23 August 1966, more than 200 Aboriginal workers and their families walked away from Wave Hill Station. Communists and unionists immediately mobilised support for this large group of people. A temporary camp was established about 16 kilometres from Wave Hill homestead, in the stony Victoria River bed. Darwin-based NAWU secretary Paddy Carroll overcame initial trepidation about supporting the walk-off, and the first supply trip was organised. Unionist and communist Brian Manning transported the first load. He was accompanied by Aboriginal union official Dexter Daniels, Aboriginal actor and activist Robert Tudawali, and 14-year-old Kerry Gibbs (son of union activists and communists George and Moira Gibbs).[14]

Manning's small Bedford truck was crammed to overflowing. Half the space was frustratingly filled by three drums of fuel needed for their return journey to Darwin. The 'horror stretch' road to Wave Hill necessitated a painfully slow crawl for the overloaded vehicle and its impatient passengers. But what awaited them at the riverbed camp swept discomforts of travel away. Manning recalled the welcome:

> I will never forget the reaction to our arrival…loud and excited cheers from a swelling crowd around the truck. I could actually sense their relief in the realisation that they were no longer on their own…and the promise of support was now a reality.[15]

Victoria River camp life and first truckload of supplies in the foreground. (Image provided by Brian Manning.)

This was also Manning's first encounter with Vincent Lingiari. Manning recalled their welcome by the leader of the walk-off: 'It's good to see you. We been waiting for you fellas'.[16]

Manning offered his truck as a gift for the Wave Hill people to transport their belongings and supplies. Frank Hardy described this action: 'Such rare generosity I found to be typical of Brian Manning. If anyone – especially an Aborigine – was in need they could have anything he had'.[17] Hardy's respect for Manning was profound. In an interview a few months after the walk-off, he declared 'Brian is the white man the Aborigines trust most'.[18]

August in the Territory is dry season. The riverbed camp people needed food, and bush tucker was insufficient to feed such a big mob. Manning, George and Moira Gibbs, and other left-wing activists quickly mobilised support. Supply trucks arrived regularly to more warm welcomes.

Adults, children and dogs at the riverbed camp. (Image provided by Brian Manning.)

When interviewed many years later, Gurindji elder Mick Rangiari remembered the relief each time a truck of provisions arrived.[19] The riverbed camp was a temporary step in the walk-off journey to final destination at Wattie Creek (now known as Daguragu).[20] Strategically, the site of this first camp was a good move – close to the police station and Wave Hill Welfare Settlement.

Welfare officer Bill Jeffrey and his wife Ann were sympathetic to the Aboriginal requirements, and their Welfare Settlement provided basic provisions and all-important connections to the outside world: phone, radio, mail and telegraph. Gurindji people asked Ann Jeffrey to contact the NAWU and NTCAR for assistance. She sent the messages from Elliott Post Office, to avoid 'retribution from Welfare' for collaborating with Aboriginal people.[21] Manning recalled that the two telegrams had been pre-written and given to Vincent Lingiari. He was instructed to send them to both organisations when the walk-off occurred, to trigger mobilisation of support in Darwin. Manning explained why two were necessary:

> ...the reason we gave Vincent two telegrams to send when they walked off...was because we believed that in the previous occasion, the Union might have known about the Strike and ignored it.[22]

With wet season approaching, the Gurindji camp moved out of the riverbed and up to bare stony ground at 'Drovers' Common' (now Kalkaringi). The move to permanent settlement at Daguragu/Wattie Creek (near Seal Gorge – one of many Gurindji Dreaming sites) was made when the 'wet' ended in March 1967. Bough shelters were erected as temporary houses, until volunteers arrived to help build more permanent shelter. Regular visitor Manning described feelings at the camps:

The people felt empowered, they were elated, being able to live their lives free of the institutional poverty, servitude, shame and degradation they suffered at the hands of British cattle barons where they were virtually assigned by their Welfare Department "protectors".[23]

Communist perspectives of the walk-off

A week after the Wave Hill walk-off, the *Tribune* published details in a prominent front-page story. It reported 'employees of the giant foreign meat monopoly, Vesteys' leading the 'battle' themselves, supported by the NAWU/NTCAR Disputes Committee.[24] Manning recollected about the Gurindji support system:

> The support organisation was overseen by the Rights Council [NTCAR], with guidance by CPA, financial and practical support from Unions and many committed individuals who are largely unnamed and forgotten heroes who travelled to Wattie Creek under their own steam, interacted with the people, giving up their own time and money; some for periods up to a year, working as mentors and advisers.
>
> Philip Nitschke, Hanna[h] Middleton, Lyn Riddett, Rob Wesley-Smith, Jack Phillips, with George & Moira Gibbs from the Rights Council probably spending the next 6–7 years totally committed.[25]

The *Tribune* reported that this Aboriginal-driven 'self-reliant' action, led by Vincent Lingiari, marked 'a new and decisive stage in the long striving of the native people for wage justice, equality and dignity'. It also targeted incorrect 'daily press' reportage about low supplies and morale at the camp, emphasising that Gurindji people were indeed well-provisioned and spirits were high. The *Tribune* identified the nature of the dispute as 'paternalism and handouts' versus 'independence and the right to handle their own money'. Extreme circumstances at Wave Hill Station were detailed:

> Keep consists of handouts of working clothes, the worst cuts of meat, treacle, flour, tea, sugar. No fruit, no butter, no green vegetables, just enough to keep body and soul together. And the living conditions in native camps on the stations [are] so squalid that they have to be seen to be believed.[26]

One firsthand account of conditions at the Station is particularly notable. Hardy visited Wave Hill with Lingiari and graphically described his friend's hut:

> It was a rusty humpy no more than four feet high, eight feet deep, by perhaps five feet wide. Vincent Lingiari, the elder of the tribe, the sacred Kadijeri man, and a noble human being, had had to crawl into this dwelling, often after working from daylight to dark.[27]

The aim of this visit to Wave Hill by Hardy, Stan Davey, Dexter Daniels, Robert Tudawali, George Gibbs and a policeman was to confront manager Tom Fisher about alleged property theft from 'native camp' huts following the walk-off. Hardy described other huts they visited:

> No floors, no water taps, no toilets, no laundry facilities, no wood, no beds, no furniture – nothing except a few pathetic heaps of rags, tattered blankets and old clothes in each hut, and here and there a rusty tin plate or a picture of Jesus pasted on the wall.[28]

Hardy's eye-witness account of Wave Hill Aboriginal camp is extremely important. Manning later explained that 'Vesteys had bulldozed the aboriginal [sic] camp within days of the Gurindji walking off to avoid national press focus on housing, which could only be described as dog kennels or humpies'.[29] Thus, Hardy's published descriptions of Aboriginal housing and conditions were all that were left, because the real evidence had been conveniently destroyed.

When Gurindji people first walked away, Hardy returned briefly to Sydney. He used that time productively, meeting often with the Communist Party's national secretary. Hardy appreciated Laurie Aarons' 'valuable advice and assistance' and was impressed by his motives:

He [Aarons] seemed motivated by the moral issue – not the political expediency. This was important. I sought the same sincerity in everyone I contacted. The propensity of the Left to take up every issue likely to embarrass the established order, as

Cross-cut saws cut timber for bough shelters at Daguragu/Wattie Creek. (Image provided by Brian Manning.)

a reflex action without feeling or depth, robs the movement of spirituality and moral fibre. It can create a spiritual barrenness that is self-defeating.[30]

Communists considered the NT Aboriginal rights struggle highly important. Hardy was supported by Queensland communist leader Ted Bacon and encouraged to use his influence spreading the Gurindji story through all sectors of mainstream Australian media – even women's magazines. Another of Hardy's communist friends described his experiences in the north. Filmmaker, journalist and activist Cecil Holmes educated Hardy about the NT Aboriginal workforce, land ownership and cooperatives.[31] Hardy was thus well-briefed not only about the past, but also possibilities of the future. Holmes had been a communist for many years, but it is unclear whether he was still a member in 1966. Historian Bain Attwood suggested that he was expelled in 1958, but one of Holmes' ASIO files identified him an active Party member in 1961.[32]

ASIO perspectives

Three days after the walk-off ASIO distributed an 'Intercept Report'. This document was filled with transcript and details of tapped phone calls between several of the main communist players working hard behind the scenes. On 26 August Hardy called NAWU secretary Paddy Carroll from the national Communist Party office in Sydney. Phone-tap transcript revealed Hardy informing Carroll of attempts to contact prominent activists Barry Christophers and Stan Davey. Hardy said, 'The people down there [Melbourne] were preparing to go to any lengths to assist'. Carroll informed Hardy that everything had 'blown up', with talk of walk-offs all over the Territory. Later that day Laurie Aarons called Hardy, advising him to remain in Sydney, pending instructions. Aarons informed Hardy of stories written by mainstream journalist Douglas Lockwood, who was at Wave Hill the previous day. Hardy told Aarons that Lockwood 'had sent a story down last night but not one word had appeared in any Sydney newspaper or on the radio…the continued [mainstream media] policy of suppressing news is going to be adhered to as long as possible'.[33]

This fascinating ASIO transcript revealed communist publicity tactics. Aarons and Hardy deliberated about when to break the Gurindji story to the media. Hardy informed Aarons he had instructed 'them' in Darwin to contact the ABC, so that the news blackout in southern states would be exposed. He told Aarons of a $1000 donation from the wharfies, adding that Lockwood had told him of 300 Aboriginal people camped at 'Catfish Creek'. Aarons responded that he 'would spread it around and get someone on to it'.[34] This report is clear evidence of high Sydney communist activity in the first days of the Wave Hill walk-off.

One day after Hardy and Aarons' lamentations about the dearth of mainstream coverage, articles about the walk-offs miraculously appeared in major southern state dailies. The *Australian* reported Paddy Carroll's denial that his union had anything to do with it and that 'other people…urged the Aborigines to walk off'.[35] Three days later more articles appeared in mainstream newspapers. The *Canberra Times* reported a three-ton truck (we now know to be Manning's) delivering supplies, and 'money to help the strikers [union donations] had been subscribed from all over Australia'.[36]

Press coverage was also noted in another ASIO document. A phone-tap transcript presented Hardy informing Aarons that a 'good article' had appeared in the *Mirror* and a long article in the '*Sun*'. Hardy also told him that one of his 'native friends' said that 'a match is in the spinifex'. The ASIO official compiling the report added a personal note at this point, praising the aforementioned phrase as a 'highly original way to put it'. Hardy informed

Aarons of conversations with Manning, assuring him that all was 'in order' up north. He also flagged his intentions to bring 'Bobby' (Robert Tudawali) to Melbourne to promote the cause, and 'not some white person'.[37]

A report by Chief Welfare Officer Evans to the NT Administrator provides a clear picture of what Manning was up to at this point. On 30 August Evans and Wave Hill manager Tom Fisher met with five male Gurindji elders at the riverbed camp. In a solid example of industrial solidarity, the men informed Evans that as Lingiari, Daniels and Tudawali (their representatives) were absent, they would not negotiate. In his report, Evans described that he and Fisher proceeded to Welfare Officer Jeffrey's house and school, and were unpleasantly surprised to discover Manning there. They were further shocked to discover Manning's bold use of the government facilities for his accommodation requirements and storage of foodstuffs in the Welfare Branch shed. The report noted Jeffrey's instruction to remove Manning from the single quarters immediately.[38]

An ASIO report (written five days after the walk-off) firmly positioned responsibility for the industrial action at communist and unionist feet. It described a reconnaissance party representing the NAWU and NTCAR, dispatched to stations on 17 August. Three men – Dexter Daniels, waterfront communist Nick Pagonis, and a Darwin Aboriginal man named Matthews – visited Wave Hill and Victoria River stations, returning to Darwin on 23 August.[39] A further report on 12 September from a 'reliable contact [and] resident of this area', detailed a meeting organised by the trio with '200 [Aboriginal workers] on Wave Hill and about 400 on Victoria River Downs'. According to the local ASIO contact, workers were told to 'walk off'. This informant was clearly no fan of Jeffrey, reporting the welfare officer as 'a liar and a very able troublemaker' assisting Manning and Daniels to distribute food to Aboriginal people at the riverbank. The report identified a police request for Manning and his party to leave the area, and they departed on 3 September.[40]

One week after the walk-off the government stated its position. In federal parliament, Minister for Territories Barnes indicated no need to intervene in the dispute and that he was happy to leave it to Vestey to sort out.[41] Gordon Bryant MHR saw every need for government members to address questions about the situation. He said he was sick of the government's usual rhetoric filled with 'sycophancy, humbug and nonsense', and pressed for the exploitation of Vestey's workforce to be exposed. Bryant suggested the government apply 'simple humanity, honesty, decency and [Australian] egalitarianism' to right the wrongs in the Territory.[42]

Left-wing support intensifies

When Aboriginal people walked from Wave Hill to their temporary riverbed home, the ACTU Executive met. It forwarded a resolution to the Department of Territories, advising that industrial welfare of NT Aboriginal people could 'best be protected and advanced by the trade union movement'. It also fired a warning shot at the Communist Party:

> We wish to make it clear that the ACTU has in the past and will in the future be prepared to closely cooperate with the NAWU… in accordance with the ACTU rules. Other organisations outside the trade union movement should not interfere in industrial matters which are the concern of the NAWU and the ACTU [which] over the years has developed a comprehensive policy for the advancement of Aborigines and has taken steps to achieve this policy.[43]

The *Tribune*'s editor was not impressed with the peak union body's efforts. He noted that ACTU's Executive did not even deliver a resolution of condemnation about Vestey, the Industrial Commission or the government. Nor, he wrote, was there a 'stirring call' for national support of brave Gurindji people taking on the 'White Establishment'. But the relationship between communists and the NAWU had thawed, with the editor now full of praise for its actions. He even congratulated NAWU advocacy on behalf of Aboriginal people unable to afford that union's membership subs.[44]

As far as Manning was concerned, the NTCAR was a pivotal organisation providing essential support for the Gurindji people:

> There are people who continue to play down the role of the Rights Council…and assert that Vincent [Lingiari] acted entirely on his own. The fact is he had taken strike action some years before but was starved back. He needed no urging to walk off when he was promised support which the Rights Council delivered. The Rights Council was a unique organisation of black and white collaboration where decisions were made by the Aboriginals and the paper work and organisational work was done by whites.[45]

Lyn Riddett (who lived at Wattie Creek over several short periods) endorsed Manning's view, describing the NTCAR as 'crucial' in the organisation, promotion and support of the walk-offs.[46]

Publicity intensified. In early September Hardy wrote a two-page *Tribune* article about the walk-off.[47] The front page of the following edition featured a large photograph of Vincent Lingiari, the 'Aborigine leader'. The Federal Council of the Australasian Meat Industry Employees' Union (AMIEU) had placed bans upon the handling of any cattle or meat sourced from Vestey-owned Newcastle Waters and Wave Hill stations. The *Tribune* announced the WWF donation of $1,500 to striking workers and resolution calling for ACTU proclamation of support for Gurindji people and loud condemnation of the Arbitration Commission's decision.[48] Manning recalled that Darwin wharfies continued hands-on support, by continuously transporting supplies to the riverbed camp on a rotational basis (he credited wharfies Paul Patten, Barry Reed, Nick Pagonis, Jack Phillips and George Gibbs as the main supply volunteers).[49]

Union solidarity with Aboriginal workers and high-level political collaboration across the eastern seaboard is further evidenced in an ASIO report. Conversations between Laurie Aarons and Melbourne butchers' union communist leader George Seelaf on 19 September about possible boycotts on beef from Wave Hill and Victoria River Downs were phone-tapped, then transcribed. This discussion reveals a highly orchestrated campaign involving Seelaf, Carroll, Hardy and Aarons. Seelaf needed to know the brands on cattle 'up there' so his members could 'look out for them', and was attempting to send other union officials to Darwin from Townsville.[50]

NTCAR members Davis Daniels and Jacob Roberts 'hand-roneoing' letters seeking union support. (Image provided by Brian Manning.)

Communists continued to write passionately about the walk-off, and another *Tribune* front page lauded unanimous NAWU rejection of a new hastily created wages agreement for Aboriginal stockmen. This document had been drafted by the NT Cattle Producers' Council, then somewhat surprisingly accepted and recommended by the ACTU several days later. The *Northern Territory News* editorial was scathing:

> Quite obviously the ACTU has gone the way of many industrial union leaders in relatively affluent societies…it has lost contact with reality and real interest in its proper function.[51]

The *Tribune* reported FCAATSI secretary Stan Davey supporting NAWU's rejection of this dubious new ACTU deal. This followed news of yet another walk-off at Victoria River Downs, where conditions were described as atrocious.[52] *Northern Territory News* also reported Davey's comments that the ACTU, pastoralists and government had 'sold out' Aboriginal workers, and that the ACTU 'had cut the ground from under the strikers' feet'.[53] An ASIO informant provided further detail about Davey's position while describing a conversation between Davey and NTCAR president Phillip Roberts. Davey was staying in Paddy Carroll's Darwin home, after travelling to the Wave Hill area three days earlier with George Gibbs and Dexter Daniels. Davey voiced concerns to Roberts about the widening industrial action and his intent to persuade NTCAR to limit industrial action to the stations already on strike. It was all, thought Davey, getting too big.[54]

An ASIO informant contributed another version of Davey's NT visit. Prominent FCAATSI activist Kath Walker (now known as Oodgeroo Noonuccal) had phoned this informant, and her comments were recorded. Walker said that 'he [Davey] was most concerned at the manner in which the thing was being handled by the extreme left-wing element', naming communist George

Gibbs as a radical example. Davey had told her not to send any more FCAATSI funds to Gurindji people, as he 'was afraid that funds sent to Darwin might fall into the hands of the left-wing group, and might be used to stir up more trouble among the coloured people'.[55] NTCAR member Manning provided his perspective to views about Davey:

> I had some issues with Stan's philosophy. He approached me on one occasion in Darwin proposing Communists [sic] resign from the NTCAR as our presence was holding the organisation back from building greater support. At a subsequent executive meeting of the Council, Moira, George and myself excused ourselves from the meeting and let Stan put a proposal to the Aboriginal Members on the suggestion. After an hour, Stan could only shake his head saying, "They won't hear of it".
>
> He had a problem accepting that Communist's Philosophy was in any way relevant, preferring more passive activity.
>
> Otherwise Stan was dedicated to the Aboriginal Rights Cause.[56]

ASIO informants were spies, and one lived on a cattle station. A report named a station owner or worker, but this identity is blacked out. The reporting ASIO officer described him as 'expecting a visit' from Gibbs and Dexter Daniels, explaining that 'he expects them to try and persuade the aboriginal [sic] employees to go out on strike...He stated that if he saw them on the property he would "break their necks"'.[57]

The *Tribune* published excerpts from an NTCAR letter signed by Davis Daniels and sent to the UN. The rights organisation appealed for UN intervention in the Wave Hill dispute via negotiation with the Australian government to end discrimination and improve living conditions. The NTCAR condemned government 'failure to ensure that the Northern Territory Ordinance relating to social welfare and employment of Aborigines is observed on pastoral properties, Welfare Settlements, Missions and elsewhere', and that 'this is happening in a country that is really ours'. The letter closed with a simple request – 'Please help us'.[58]

NTCAR's letter to the UN was widely circulated. A copy was forwarded from the Union of Australian Women to the Women's International Democratic Federation (WIDF) in Berlin. WIDF acting general secretary Cecile Hugel wrote a lengthy letter to Prime Minister Holt about Aboriginal worker and family life on cattle stations, protesting the unjust conditions and discrimination. Her organisation considered the situation a violation of the UDHR, calling for Australia to end racial discrimination, and grant equal rights to its indigenous peoples soon to be recognised in the 1967 referendum.[59]

The pleas from Berlin were probably only paid lip-service. Correspondence by Department of the Interior's influential secretary George Warwick Smith indicates continuation of the government's hard-line position. He advised the NT Administrator to instruct welfare officers in the Territory to actively endorse the ACTU position, and encourage Aboriginal acceptance of the contentious new industrial agreement's benefits. 'In this way', he wrote, 'it is hoped to prevent the Aborigines taking action which might associate them with undesirable political elements [possibly] detrimental to their future employment in the cattle industry'. Warwick Smith believed Aboriginal workers should realise that the agreement formulated by the ACTU, pastoralists and government provided the only possibilities of future work. This was a clever tactic. By promoting a collaborative agreement devised by such diametrically opposed parties, he aimed to eradicate communist influences altogether, thus preventing another Wave Hill–like 'wrong way to do a thing'.[60]

More walk-offs and support widens

In late September Aboriginal workers walked away from two other Vestey stations. Stockmen at Mount Sanford and Helen's Springs had not been paid their $6 per week salary for four months. The *Tribune* reported that when NTCAR representatives George Gibbs and 'Clancy' (probably Phillip) Roberts attempted negotiation with a station manager, they were menaced with a gun and told to get off the property.[61] Gibbs was used to this kind of treatment. He had been an NAWU organiser since 1949 (establishing branches in Tennant Creek and Alice Springs) and his discoveries of atrocious conditions for Aboriginal workers drove lifelong commitment to Aboriginal rights.[62] In federal parliament Gordon Bryant asked questions about reports from 'recent visitors' (probably Gibbs and Roberts) to Wave Hill and Mount Sanford stations. Minister for Health Jim Forbes answered that Department of Health officers had inspected both sites and indeed, 'a number of improvements [were] required'.[63]

Aboriginal union organiser Dexter Daniels and stockman Lupgna Giari embarked upon a well-publicised fundraising tour to Sydney, Melbourne and Brisbane. The trip was sponsored by Actors' Equity, BWIU and FCAATSI.[64] Anthropologist Hannah Middleton (who later lived with the Gurindji community) described this five-week trip as 'one of the most influential events organised by the trade unions'. She identified that between 1966 and the end of 1968, 42 per cent of the Gurindji Fighting Fund was raised by unions. Another 33 per cent came from FCAATSI, with part of that contribution including more union donations funnelled through its coffers.[65]

Hardy's role at this point was important. He had convinced FCAATSI's Stan Davey and Barry Christophers to support Daniels and Giari's tour, and negotiated with Actors' Equity secretary Hal Alexander to sponsor Robert Tudawali.[66] The Aboriginal actor had planned to accompany the two men, but was hospitalised with tuberculosis. Tudawali, who worked doggedly for NTCAR and workers' rights, spent the next five months in hospital (and in August 1967, passed away after suffering horrific burns at Bagot Aboriginal Settlement in Darwin). The *Tribune* reported Daniels and Giari, 'of quiet courage and simple dignity', speaking with workers while collecting donations for Aboriginal people overwhelmed by 'cruelties and privations'. At one meeting of 300 workers at Sydney's Australia Square building project, their powerful words elicited quick reaction. All present agreed to an immediate levy of $2, and then $1 per pay until the strike was over.[67] At another meeting a few weeks later, 800 workers pledged $1 'per man'. By mid-November the tour had reportedly raised over $15,000.[68] Queensland unionists were similarly inspired by the visits of Daniels and Giari, with meatworkers, seamen and wharfies all imposing immediate levies too.[69]

ASIO followed the Aboriginal men's tour as well. A phone-tap transcription report detailed conversation between two Melbourne persons of interest. Nancy Marks and Dave Davies discussed a meeting being held at Monash University with the 'Aboriginal stockmen'. Marks told Davies of the two men 'now attending a stop work meeting at the Seamen's Union', whom she had asked to arrive at Monash a little earlier if possible.[70] This report indicates that suspected communist Marks was an organiser of this leg of Giari and Daniels' tour, as the campaign reached out to students as well as unionists.

In the NT, Aboriginal workers were meeting further resistance, but this time it came not from station managers, but rather governmental bureaucrats. Thirty-eight stockmen were officially sacked from their Wave Hill jobs after applying for unemployment benefits when Davey and Gibbs registered them for the 'dole'. Hardy recounted the puzzled Gurindji view of this process: 'The white fella is funny: you don't want to work for him, he sacks you, then offers you twice as much money as when you worked'.[71] But the seemingly legitimate applications for the dole were refused by the Holt government. According to the *Northern Territory News*, a government representative provided the official explanation about the denial of social security payments: 'the system was not devised for this sort of customer'.[72]

The *Tribune* published disturbing revelations about Aboriginal child labour on Vestey stations. A 12-year-old boy named Billy had already worked on Mount Sanford Station for several years, maintaining horses for stockmen and doing general stockwork. He worked from dawn to dusk, and had never been to school. The *Tribune* reported Vestey profits swelling while the 'Welfare Branch turns a blind eye and denies knowledge of their [child workers] existence'.[73] Hardy revealed in *The Unlucky Australians* that he had written the story, after finding the boy during a journey with Dexter Daniels to collect disgruntled stockmen from stations.[74]

The fledgling community of Aboriginal people who had walked off stations were slowly improving their circumstances. The camp moved to higher ground at 'Drovers' Common' (now Kalkaringi) before the wet season commenced in late 1966. Using pension money, they purchased a second-hand truck to collect provisions and built a sturdy storehouse. However their determination was tested, with the *Tribune* reporting deliberately obstructionist tactics by the Welfare Department. In November Davis Daniels (brother of Dexter) alleged that the Department had refused the use of one of their buildings to store food during the wet season (which was due to persist until March).[75] However, NTCAR's newsletter reported Monash University 'friends' were undeterred by Welfare's stance, collecting 'over two tons of food and clothing...brought to Darwin by Seamen's Union members on the H.V. Baralga'.[76] These supplies were transported in part by Gibbs, who was described by ASIO as highly active, and 'making trouble at Wave Hill Ration Station [during his] regular trips... with supplies for the striking stockmen'.[77]

Bare, stony ground at 'Drovers' Common', circa late 1966/early 1967. Union organiser George Gibbs talking with Aboriginal organiser Dexter Daniels and mechanic Norm Philpott. (Image provided by Brian Manning.)

By January 1967 the walk-off community entered its fifth month of action. Wave Hill management had not shifted position, but two privately owned stations (Camfield and Montejinni) set a competitive precedent by negotiating with Lingiari and NTCAR to employ Wave Hill stockmen at Award rates of about $50 per fortnight plus keep. The *Tribune* reported this Camfield Station agreement for ten men as 'a major breakthrough', heralding 'the beginning of the end' to 'starvation-wages'. Improved living conditions at Camfield also raised the bar higher, with workers provided 'electric lights, showers, toilets and good food'.[78]

Perspectives of a more neutral observer

Economist Frank Stevens conducted surveys of Aboriginal workers on NT stations during 1965 and 1966, with his second round of visits marked by change. Workers at Wave Hill Station had recently walked away, and counterparts on other stations were now keen to join the industrial action.

The industrial environment encountered by Stevens in 1966 was very different. His 1965 field trip had been cautiously welcomed by white station managers, but the second trip was actively resisted by their peak body. The NT Pastoral Lessees' Association viewed his visits to stations as problematic and destabilising. Stevens was only able to visit ten stations, and requests to enter Aboriginal workers' camps were met with fearful, suspicious and often negative responses. In a strategic countermove, he established his own camps in 'no man's land' settings – neither close to the white homesteads nor the Aboriginal workers' camps. Ironically, this strategy resulted in significant data collection from not only Aboriginal workers but also white workers, whose hesitation to speak may have lessened at this interview site (and away from anxious eyes and ears of management).[79] During Stevens' meetings with Aboriginal workers, he was surprised to discover universal 'warmth of disposition' and detailed knowledge of 'the Union'. He found that Aboriginal workers were now very aware of the potential advantage of trade unions for them, despite their discriminatory lack of coverage under the Cattle Station Industry (NT) Award. Indeed, Stevens asked (most validly) why the Union 'had not bothered about the Territory's most depressed workforce' since the Award became operational in 1951. Stevens interviewed a white 'ringer' who described differences between white and black stockmen. His admiration and respect for Aboriginal workers is notable – 'They're good. My bloody hell, they're good!'.[80]

ASIO suspected that Stevens was a communist, and a substantial file was accumulated about his activities. In 2004 he wrote a scathing draft manuscript titled *ASIO and I*, filled with bitter recriminations about the spy organisation's treatment of him.[81] Stevens claimed never to have been a member of the Communist

Party and that his ASIO file was filled with trivia and rubbish. He also alleged that the existence of this file compromised his career. By way of protest, Stevens provided the National Archives of Australia with notes to correct his file, and these are included with the draft manuscript. He believed that the 'detritus of a dirty system [filled with] dishonest people and politicians' had driven ASIO's compilation of the damaging file about him.

Stevens' ASIO file contains numerous reports about his alleged associations with communism. From as early as 1952 until the 1970s, he was linked to the Party and reported to hold various positions as a functionary. Stevens was alleged to be close to a number of communist organisations and 'persons of interest'. In his manuscript he attempts to clear his name by exposing the corruption and ineptitude within 'Australia's Police State'. Steven's powerful argument is compelling – that ASIO's alleged manipulation of truth and errors, over a long period of time, permanently and irreparably cast him as a dangerous subversive.

∞

In the next chapter, the campaign for Gurindji worker rights is overwhelmed by what may have been the real intention all along. Land rights emerge as the ultimate goal, and the campaign shifts to accommodate changed demands.

Postscript

Two months after Gurindji people walked away, a piece by well-known communist poet Wilma Hedley was published in the *Tribune*. Her words typify the passionate communist advocacy that would endure throughout the campaign:

Man to the North[82]

I not paid
wage of a whiteman –
yet white judge purr like snake as he say:
No discrimination,
squatter all great men.

Man from south
same colour as me,
he bring message written in sand:
Soon I get wage
same as other man.

Since young feller I work
breaking in horse,
and south man ask: Who get profit this way?
Not horse,
not you, he say.

I get
smashed foot
cracked head, few bob, chunk of beef,
white flour
and plenty sour.

I see
boss man
in big house, many car, plenty tucker –
what price blackman,
what price sucker!

Man from south
he talk good talk.
Tell how whiteman union in city,
buy him overcoat,
fight who cut our throat.

When south man go,
I ask boss more money.
Boss man laugh, he think it funny.
Then pride of tribe
take hold of me –

and boss man roar
as he chain me to tree.
Chain that bind, I remember south man say:
Black and white together,
we tear it away.

Chapter Nine

Much has been made of this affair at Wave Hill.[1]

The affair at Wave Hill had indeed stirred great interest. Support for this fledgling, far-north Aboriginal settlement was now widely articulated. Australians from all walks of life donated money, food and goods. And, land rights emerged as the primary campaign objective.

Daguragu land occupation

The course of the battle altered considerably in April 1967. Aboriginal activists moved from their temporary Drovers' Common/Kalkaringi camp to establish permanent settlement at Wattie Creek/Daguragu.[2] The *Tribune*'s front page reported this event as Aboriginal occupation of 1,295 square kilometres within the Vestey lease area. It also compared their actions with the first Pilbara Aboriginal co-op established in 1947. Frank Hardy attributed this latest move and enterprise to Lupgna Giari (or Captain Major). Eighteen men and six women had walked to the new site. The official Daguragu station 'homestead' was then surreptitiously built, unbeknown to visiting Vestey officials at Wave Hill. Timing of this clandestine action was significant. Mustering season was about to begin, and Vestey needed contract white workers to drive cattle across 12,950 square kilometres of rough country to the yards at Wave Hill. Collective lifetimes of Gurindji experience and knowledge had facilitated mustering seasons since cattle were first introduced in the Territory, and the Aboriginal presence would be sorely missed. The *Tribune* reported that Vestey officials were acutely aware of the invaluable skill base they had lost.[3]

Hardy was staying with Welfare Officer Bill Jeffrey when this new land occupation took place, and ASIO reported his activities. Upon arrival in Darwin on 24 February, Hardy was treated like a celebrity (including his stay as a guest of the management at Hotel Darwin). On 15 March he travelled to Wave Hill on a flight that had been chartered by the NT Administration to transport government personnel, then he stayed with Jeffrey. ASIO's Regional Director described his host 'an undesirable Welfare Officer who, under instructions from the Administrator, Mr. R. L. Dean, is to be transferred in the near future'. ASIO was right, and Jeffrey's dismissal is discussed later. Hardy left Wave Hill for Darwin on 28 March, after what was described as a quarrel with Jeffrey. In an unusual instance, an ASIO informant's identity is revealed in this report: 'William Moyle' was ensconced within the Communist Party, working closely with George Gibbs.[4]

Hardy felt responsible for the bold Aboriginal actions. In *The Unlucky Australians*, he declared, 'I had started it and now could not stop it'. During discussions with Gurindji activists during his visit, land quickly became the central focus of demands.[5] Indeed, two months after the walk-off, he described a pivotal camp-fire conversation with Lingiari:

> We talked earnestly. I discovered that wages was not the only, perhaps not even the main, issue for them. They were concerned about their women, about the children going to school, about housing, about dignity, self-respect — and recovering tribal lands from Vesteys.

According to Hardy, this need to recover lands was not new. Lingiari told him that Gurindji people had, for 'longa time', planned to reacquire their tribal areas, and Welfare Officer Jeffrey confirmed these long-term goals. Jeffrey told Hardy that prior to the walk-offs, Gurindji elders had often spoken of the need to remove Vestey and return lands to Aboriginal ownership and control.[6] Hardy's public support for the campaign was soon demonstrated in extensive articles and press interviews. His actions were viewed with suspicion by ASIO, identifying him 'responsible for a group of natives there to start building a fence around a 500 acre patch of scrub that "had been taken from them by the white man"'. One ASIO comment about Hardy is particularly interesting to note:

> One rather disturbing item that the [NT] Administrator passed on in confidence was that he has received information from an old friend of his that HARDY has been wired funds for his work from the Australian Broadcasting Commission.[7]

Thus, in this instance, even the government broadcaster had been gilded with suspicion.

Only two months after the walk-off, Aboriginal interest in land was clearly articulated. Gordon Bryant MHR received a lengthy letter from Gurindji people (in his capacity as FCAATSI Vice-President) who requested it be read in parliament. Clearly stated requirements included the following:

> ...our earnest demand [is to] regain tenure of our tribal lands in the Wave Hill-Limbunya area...of which we were forcibly dispossessed....we feel that morally, if not legally, the land is ours and should be returned to us...we would not want [the land] as another "Aboriginal Reserve", but as a leasehold...run co-operatively as a cattle station by the Gurindji.[8]

The agenda had been set in a letter 'written down for us by our undersigned white friends'. Bryant acknowledged the signatories to the letter (Vincent Lingiari, Pincher Manguari, Gerry Ngalgar-dji and Long-Johnny Kitgnaari), but failed to identify the 'white

A bough shelter at Daguragu – these were temporary 'houses' until volunteers arrived to build more permanent structures. (Image provided by Brian Manning.)

friends' in parliament (perhaps because one of them – Hardy – was widely known to be a communist).

Daguragu people petitioned Governor-General Casey in an attempt to receive official sanction for their land occupation. This letter was very similar to that written to Bryant, and signed by the same four Gurindji men. They asked for leasehold to run a mining and cattle station co-op, with a map indicating land boundaries surrounding 'sacred places of our dreaming [sic]'.[9] Their wishes had 'been written down for us by our undersigned white friends [Hardy and Jeffrey], as we have had no opportunity to learn to write English'. While we can only surmise about Gurindji comprehension of such an important piece of correspondence, their objective was obvious.

Existence of the petition prompted the government to speedily reinforce rules about Crown land. When asked by Labor MHR Tom Uren about the Gurindji letter to the Governor-General, Minister for Territories Barnes (obviously bypassed and unconsulted in this bid for land) responded cautiously, suggesting that 'the proposal will have to be looked at very carefully'.[10] The petition to the Crown was rejected two months later, with Governor-General Casey reinforcing the validity of Vestey's lease until 2004.[11]

One month earlier, a landmark referendum result saw Australians overwhelmingly vote in favour of Aboriginal people being counted in the census, and for federal legislative control of Aboriginal affairs. FCAATSI condemned the government refusal to excise a parcel of land from the Vestey lease. It released a statement highlighting proactive Gurindji attempts to create self-sufficient enterprise, and identified government strategies trampling any actions born of such initiative. It also emphasised government's moral duty to recognise Aboriginal land rights because it was 'time Australians made amends'.[12]

Was land the original objective?

The Gurindji land claim has been examined by later commentators. Anthropologist Deborah Bird Rose argued that wages were the first step in a much more intricate long-term strategy positioning land rights as the end-point objective. The need to 'find powerful allies' was part of a bigger plan to gain control of Gurindji lives and land.[13] Her position is backed up by other scholars contending that unions were convenient conduits facilitating Gurindji engagement in a white man's world.[14] Historian Bain Attwood argued an alternative position: that the walk-off was not the first stage of a deliberate and calculated strategy, and Gurindji activities were driven by a mish-mash of aims and needs, evolving as circumstances altered. He viewed the Gurindji walk-off and aftermath as an ad hoc and serendipitous human rights dispute, producing unforeseen change and opportunity.[15] Historian C. D. Rowley had earlier argued similarly, but although considering the action 'spontaneous', he also deemed it 'well-judged' and 'ready made for the Communist Party'. For Rowley the communists were the helpers, not controllers.[16]

One commentator was a recent Daguragu visitor. Minoru Hokari lived with the Gurindji community while conducting doctoral research during the late 1990s. He was convinced that the demand for land was not a new idea. Indeed, elders informed Hokari that right from the beginning of the walk-off, the 'main purpose was consistently "to get their land back"'. In this way, he rejected contentions that the walk-off was a strike. Hokari argued that land was always the ultimate objective, and Gurindji plans to recover this tribal area were discussed well in advance of any action:

> ...ideas of getting their land back and running the cattle station by themselves were formulated by Sandy Moray and had been in the Gurindji people's consciousness long before the actual walk-off occurred.

Elders described Moray to Hokari as 'the founder of the walk-off'. Moray had worked as a stockman in Queensland and WA (where conditions were much better than in the NT). Gurindji elders told Hokari that Moray had the idea to repossess land and run a cattle station at Wave Hill – it was his plan. Hokari contended that Moray's enlightened position may have been enhanced by experiences with 'white man's ideas and practices' – he 'may have met unionists in Qld and learned how to fight'. Hokari related that as Moray was 'too old' to lead the battle, he handed responsibility to Vincent Lingiari.[17]

Hokari argued that targeting white supporters was a very deliberate strategy. They held the key to Gurindji success. The people *from outside* [his italics] would 'know how to deal with white agencies such as Vestey, the government and the Australian media'. Hardy, of course, was an outsider fitting this selection criterion perfectly. Indeed, Hokari described Hardy and Dexter Daniels as the catalysts: 'the *external conditions* [his italics] which ignited the Gurindji's long-awaited project'.[18] According to Hokari, the walk-off was undoubtedly an orchestrated land-centric campaign, and sophisticated approach saw a broad range of supporters attracted to the cause. Gurindji people understood that 'equal wages' was one thing that unions could readily understand and respond to with industrial action and monetary support. Once the unions came on board, Hokari argued that Gurindji people were well-positioned to divulge 'the real purpose of their action', which was land.[19]

Gurindji campaign intensifies

Union support for the land occupation and Gurindji business aspirations increased. At a NSW Labor Council meeting, Darwin waterfront union leader Bill Donnelly urged worker support for this new Aboriginal cooperative venture. The WWF federal council had already called upon all unionists and 'Australians of good will' to support the Gurindji community. Donnelly's calls were supported by federal BWIU general secretary Frank Purse, urging the entire trade union movement to 'back the stand' for Aboriginal rights.[20] Indeed, thirteen peak union bodies were official FCAATSI affiliates by 1967, including federal councils of the BWIU, Miscellaneous Workers and Seamen's Unions, as well as Queensland's T&LC.[21]

In 1967 Australia's communists consolidated their position on Aboriginal rights in the progressive *Full Human Rights for Aborigines and Torres Strait Islanders*. This program was published as a booklet and reproduced with some amendments in the *Tribune*.[22] It urged a move from old government assimilation policies to ones encouraging integration of Aboriginal peoples and cultural heritage into modern Australia, 'without losing their identities'.[23] Communists were charged to give 'fraternal aid in their struggle for emancipation, not to act as paternal "benefactors"'. The Party called for full citizenship and industrial rights, land rights, compensation for 'alienated' lands, equal legal rights, self-control of Aboriginal affairs at governmental level, and removal of discriminatory rules and government services overseen by state and federal agencies.[24]

Things in the NT were improving. In the *Tribune*, Brian Manning reported that Aboriginal station workers were all now being paid more, with almost half paid at Award rate. Manning and Dexter Daniels toured NT stations in mid-1967. They found the situation better for many workers, but conditions for Aboriginal women were still abhorrent, with shockingly long hours and meagre pay. They also identified a number of stations with defiant workers abandoning bosses who refused to improve conditions, then walking away in the footsteps of Wave Hill and other station workers.[25] Manning was acutely aware of Daniels' vulnerability as a black union organiser confronting 'hostile' station managers.

He considered his own presence at stations vitally important, both for Daniels' safety and as a reminder of industrial solidarity.[26]

Communists weren't the only ones monitoring Manning's tour around the stations. ASIO reported Manning and Daniels presenting the 'NAWU attitude to the station managers and stockmen' while collecting statistics about Aboriginal worker wages. The report identified nine station visits (including Ord River and Nicholson in WA). It also acknowledged Gurindji community ownership of two trucks. One was reportedly sold to them by Jeffrey for $100, with the other 'a bit the worse for wear' (likely the old war-horse Manning donated to the community).[27]

Daguragu camp resident Peter Gilgi turning out bread cooked in an iron 'Bedourie' oven covered with hot coals in a trench protected by a wind-break. Manning reminisced that Peter the baker 'cooked for the whole camp and his bread was as good as any I have eaten' (personal communication, 9 April 2010). (Image provided by Brian Manning.)

Manning was also annoying others. In parliament, conservative member for the NT Stephen 'Sam' Calder identified him as
'a ticketed communist' stirring up Aboriginal workers and instigating strike action. The NT member's angst extended to another
communist he twice named (much to the amusement of Labor
members) as 'Frank Harvey'. Calder's gaffe is notable:

> ...on the Wave Hill station...the Aboriginals have staked a
> claim... Who was out there organising this? It was Frank
> Harvey, a ticketed communist. Honourable members opposite
> may laugh, but there is nothing to laugh about. This is a very
> serious situation.[28]

Calder's frustration with Manning and Hardy's activities was
likely heightened by walk-off pressures upon the other side of
his life. Six years later, Calder informed parliament that during
the mid- to late 1960s, he 'was running a cattle station' of around
5,180 square kilometres, and we can presume that his workforce
included a high proportion of Aboriginal workers.[29]

Gurindji people faced another governmental hurdle hamper-
ing efforts for self-sufficiency. The *Tribune* reported a retributive
'strike-breaker' move to cease Social Services payments to anyone
deemed to have refused a job. It also reported Welfare Officer
Jeffrey's politically driven transfer to another posting, validating
ASIO's prediction in the aforementioned report, four months
earlier. And, as the *Tribune*'s writer pointed out, these new manip-
ulative moves occurred at the height of mustering season – right
when Aboriginal workers were most needed.[30]

Animosity towards Vestey grew as financial arrangements with
the federal government became public knowledge. In October
the *Tribune* published lease-agreement details on a number of
their NT stations. It revealed that Vestey paid only fifty-five cents
per square mile for control of over 6,000 square miles (15,540

square kilometres) at Wave Hill, capable of carrying 50,000 cattle. Rent figures for other stations varied between forty cents and seventy-five cents, depending on land quality and cattle-carrying capacity. In return for these very generous rent agreements, Vestey was obligated to erect fencing and establish water holes. The *Tribune* deemed these lease conditions 'ridiculously light', with the actual land-improvement requirement laughable in terms of the land area concerned: it was a case of 'rich land...dirt cheap'.[31]

NAWU official Dexter Daniels continually caught the wary official eyes while touring NT stations and encouraging Aboriginal workers to leave. This attention by police vividly contrasts with the experiences of Pilbara Aboriginal activists Clancy McKenna and Dooley Bin Bin twenty years earlier. In December 1967, Daniels was arrested and Hardy rushed from Sydney to support his mate.[32] In what the *Tribune's* front page described 'a trumped up vagrancy charge', Daniels was jailed then bailed following nationwide union protests. Police had reportedly handcuffed and relocated him from Roper River Mission (where he was encouraging people to walk-off) to Mataranka jail. Daniels was arrested for vagrancy after Mission staff called police, even though he had $8, a miner's right and crocodile hunting licence in his pocket. A Communist Party press release condemned the actions by officials and the witch-hunt victimising Daniels. It called upon NT and federal governments to immediately rectify the situation.[33] Indeed, four months later, Daniels threatened to sue Territory police for wrongful arrest after he successfully appealed against the conviction.[34]

Campaign donations were significant. An accountant's letter itemising the NAWU's 'Aboriginal Fund' identified that between September 1966 and June 1967, nearly $15,000 had been received. Union contributors included the WWF, BLF, engine drivers and firemen, railways, engineers, meatworkers, shipwrights and boat builders, seamen, plasterers, tramways and omnibus employees, painters and decorators, boilermakers and blacksmiths, plumbers and gasfitters, liquor and allied employees, sheet metal workers, miscellaneous workers, architects, engineers and surveyors, bank officials, miners, and T&LCs across the country.[35]

Support intensified during 1968. In May a large group including students, Aboriginal people and several politicians protested at Parliament House in Canberra. The *Tribune* reported this action organised by Aboriginal Scholarship Society (ABSCHOL), the Aboriginal Committee of the National Union of Students and FCAATSI.[36] The article highlighted increased student activism, with capital city vigils protesting the government's stand against land rights claims. Dexter Daniels spoke to protesters at a Melbourne event during his trade-union-organised tour in three states. He was shortly to leave for the World Youth Festival in Bulgaria as an Australian delegate. Daniels was sponsored by Hardy, Hal Alexander (Secretary of Actors' Equity), and the Assistant BWIU Federal Secretary.[37] His speaking tour had paid handsome dividends, with Sydney and Melbourne WWF members plus Melbourne meatworkers' unions contributing significant sums to fund Daniels' European trip.[38]

Federal land offer 1968

Minister for the Interior Peter Nixon presented an interdepartmental submission to Cabinet colleagues in May 1968. Under consideration was proposed excision of 20 square kilometres from the Wave Hill lease. The submission contained an ominous warning that the 'valuable social experiment' was a precedent that would 'need to be carefully watched'. Unsurprisingly, the submission cited objections to this initiative by cattle producers, farmers' councils and the Wave Hill Pastoral Company.[39]

Nixon's submission flagged potential national and international backlash if some land was not given to the Daguragu community. It included a useful attachment describing the Wave Hill area population. In April 1968 thirty-seven Aboriginal people were identified as living at Daguragu (twenty-three were Gurindji, eight Walibri, and six were 'other' tribes). Seventy-nine Aboriginal people were living at Wave Hill Station, with eighty-two at the Wave Hill Centre (Kalkaringi).[40] Given that these figures were calculated in the dry season when mustering was in full swing, it is likely that numbers at Daguragu increased significantly during down-time in the wet.

One month earlier, pastoralist concerns were identified in two lengthy letters to Nixon. NT Cattle Producers' Council secretary W. E. L. de Vos insisted that 'communist influences' at Wave Hill drove the land rights campaign. He viewed any government capitulation as 'surrender to communist pressure tactics' encouraging land rights claims elsewhere. In the second letter, De Vos' urgency to prohibit land rights was evident. He warned that 'the Gurindji, and the communists…cannot be swept under the Wattie Creek carpet with a new broom', with the granting of land rights a 'pre-emptive action' prejudicing future negotiations. De Vos considered that this rushed and ill-conceived 'experiment' would trap his members within a 'defensive position of communist choice with no options'.[41]

In July the *Tribune* reported what the government had decided to do. It would grant Gurindji people a mere 1½ square miles (4 square kilometres) of land. This fell nearly 500 square miles (1,295 square kilometres) short of the original Gurindji claim.[42] The next edition's front page ominously predicted 'more militant action' by Aboriginal people and unions. The *Tribune* deemed the Cabinet decision (offering residential and land-use rights at Drovers' Common Welfare Centre near the Gurindji camp) a paternalistic proposal made on behalf of big business, particularly Vestey. BWIU urged the ACTU to take decisive protest action against the government. Ex–Welfare Officer Jeffrey described the decision 'unintelligent, vicious and disgusting', and Hardy suggested a more global approach to the problem (via appeal to the International Court and UN).[43]

The government land offer was conveyed to the people it affected by a communist. NTCAR member George Gibbs announced the details during his visit to Daguragu ten days after the decision was made in Canberra.[44] This was one issue where mainstream media agreed with the radicals, and reports of the situation were scathing. The *Age*'s editorial (entitled 'Shameful Farce') declared that the government's offer:

> ...has all the marks of a determined denial of elementary justice and a disregard of popular opinion...All the Government has done is hand the Gurindjis a catalogue of public facilities and social services already available to them...The Government is now showing a pronounced taste for farce.[45]

Similar sentiments were expressed in the *Canberra Times*, the *Australian* and the *Sydney Morning Herald* editorials.[46] These newspapers also included other articles about the Gurindji land decision, indicating the heightened importance now attributed to the issue.

Activist reactions to land offer

Protest actions grew larger and spread wider. In Melbourne 1,000 people marched, as did hundreds of students in Adelaide. At Melbourne's demonstration (organised by ABSCHOL) outside Parliament House, a peaceful protest crowd was addressed by Hardy, Aboriginal activist Harry Penrith, and Victoria's Opposition Leader Clive Holding, who undertook to bring the meeting to federal Opposition Leader Gough Whitlam's attention. Prominent banners were carried by the BWIU and AMIEU, student groups and church bodies.[47]

In Queensland the T&LC endorsed the struggle as 'a landmark in the history of the Australian trade union movement...one of the most important industrial issues ever fought in Australia...a struggle not only for wages, but for wide social reforms'.[48] Communists were also now clearly stating what the Gurindji campaign had become. A front-page *Tribune* article clearly delineated the older industrial campaign roots from the now-dominant land campaign: 'The movement is now quite separate from the original Wave Hill strike for pay rights...Aborigines are now walking off entirely on the basic claim for land'. This statement was clear and unequivocal. The Party lodged formal protest with the Minister for Aboriginal Affairs about the decision to hand over what was considered a paltry parcel of land. The *Tribune* also promoted FCAATSI's call for unions and churches to appeal to their respective world councils. It endorsed this global strategy as a means to attract further international condemnation and support for Gurindji demands.[49]

Community anger towards Vestey grew, as publicity about government rejection of the land claim intensified. The *Tribune* compared the meagre request for 500 square miles (1,295 square kilometres) of tribal land with the 10½ million acres (42,500 square kilometres) of NT land that Vestey continued to ostensibly 'own'. Vestey was described as the government's 'favourite sons', with 1950s leases extending to 2004 and requirement to pay only $9,500 per annum for the entire area. The *Tribune* calculated this as equating to under one-tenth of a cent per acre per year. Vestey was not the only company under fire. Together with British corporation Borthwick and US counterpart Swift, the trio was described as 'the Big Three of the Australian meat industry'. Indeed, the *Tribune* reported that the powerful North American company controlled 'over half the area in the Top End'.[50]

As protests continued throughout 1968, Gurindji people stayed put at Daguragu. Community representatives were regularly sent on speaking tours, informing eastern states about their situation.

The *Tribune* reported Mick Rangiari's appearances at a number of Sydney meetings, publicising his community's cause. It also promoted FCAATSI's new appeal for funds. The sponsoring committee included union leaders from WWF, Actors' Equity, Boilermakers and Blacksmiths Society of Australia, BWIU, and Postal Clerks' and Telegraphists'. Two weeks later Queensland's T&LC also issued a resolution of support.[51]

Support for Gurindji people was also voiced by overseas visitors. In August the campaign received a celebrity boost, when visiting US singer Mary Travers (of the outspoken left-wing trio 'Peter, Paul and Mary') appeared in a large photograph on the *Tribune*'s front page. The story 'Singers Give to Gurindji' congratulated the group's $500 donation towards a new truck for the Daguragu community.[52]

The paltry government land offer continued to elicit angry responses. NTCAR president (and the Territory's FCAATSI representative) Phillip Roberts issued a press release, responding to a statement about land rights by Nixon publicised on the *Australian*'s front page on 10 August. The *Tribune* reported Roberts' meeting with the Minister, where land lease was offered, but Aboriginal land title was declared impossible. Roberts rebuked allegedly spurious government arguments that Aboriginal people could not cope with land ownership responsibilities, and that living standards would drop due to inadequate government and mission services. He highlighted failures of the 'segregation' policy, graphically describing cattle station and welfare settlement conditions. Despite Nixon's assertion that one-fifth of the NT had been set aside by reservation for Aboriginal use, Roberts asserted that this area was still government-owned and controlled. The land could be leased to mining companies, for example, without any consultation with Aboriginal communities who lived there. According to Roberts, Daguragu was the litmus test for other NT groups wanting to maintain identity and culture.[53]

Roberts' relationship with communists was examined in ASIO's report about FCAATSI's 1968 annual conference in Canberra. In a private conversation, an informant asked Roberts about communist infiltration in NTCAR. Roberts' response was recorded:

> We in the Northern Territory are not encouraging communists to take a leading part in any of our activity. We know there are some who want to use us to further the C.P.A. We are not as silly as they think. We will use them but they will not use us.[54]

Union support continued as Gurindji representative Mick Rangiari continued his publicity tour in the eastern states. In Brisbane, he spoke at a meeting organised by FCAATSI and unions. Queensland wharfies immediately responded by pledging $1,000 to the Gurindji fund. In a collaborative effort the Miscellaneous Workers and Seamen's Unions, Sheetmetal Workers'

Gurindji stockmen and bough shelter at Daguragu. (Image provided by Brian Manning.)

Union, Postal Clerks' and Telegraphists' Union, Australian Railways Union, Federated Ship Painters and Dockers Union and WWF unions presented Ray Peckham (the Territory's FCAATSI convenor and unionist) with a new Volkswagen Beetle. The *Tribune* reported the vehicle's purpose to enable union 'organising work in Northern Australia',[55] but how a Beetle coped with those corrugated red-dust roads is difficult to imagine. With Christmas approaching, Brisbane meat workers contributed three large cases of toys, food and clothes for Gurindji children. Woolworths donated some of the toys and a freight company transported the goods north free of charge.[56]

FCAATSI's close relationships with left-wing activists continued to attract ASIO attention. One report detailed personal information about numerous key players in the organisation (including Faith Bandler, Kathleen Walker, Dulcie Flower, Joe McGinness, Shirley Andrews, Barrie Pittock, and Barry Christophers). Political affiliations of all executive members and other active members were described in mini-biographies about each person. Past and present connections, suspect relationships and potential to subvert were clearly spelt out in this comprehensive ASIO document. It also included mini-dossiers on 'Other nominated persons active in Aboriginal affairs' (including Jeffrey, Hardy, Cecil and Elsa Holmes, Dexter Daniels, Ray Peckham, Terry Robinson and Phillip Roberts).[57]

∽

On 1 December 1968 the long-awaited changes to the Cattle Station Industry (NT) Award took effect. Two and a half years after the original decision was handed down, Aboriginal industrial rights improved at last. Some Gurindji people returned to work at Wave Hill under the new provisions that improved wages, but also freely enabled managers to categorise (therefore penalise) their workers as 'slow'. NTCAR hailed the workers' lengthy strike action and return to work in victorious fashion as a positive example, as Gurindji people led the way for other Aboriginal groups across Australia. NAWU also endorsed the workers' position, pledging to closely monitor the full implementation of Award conditions.[58]

By the 1970s, industrial possibilities encouraged wider activity. At Arnhem Land's Roper River Welfare Settlement, around 400 Aboriginal Welfare Branch workers downed tools, demanding land rights for tribal areas rich with mineral resources being targeted by mining companies. ACTU supported this action, with president Bob Hawke announcing a new 'Trade Union Committee on Aboriginal Affairs' to vigorously pursue fair wages and conditions for all Aboriginal workers. Land value in the area escalated as the Nabalco aluminium consortium scrambled to secure rights.[59] Dexter Daniels travelled to Melbourne seeking financial and moral support for Roper River people to establish a grazing cooperative on 260 square kilometres of Crown land leased by the mission. Darwin wharfies provided immediate campaign support, with a $1 per member levy. Brian Manning (their representative in the NAWU) compared this new situation with Gurindji and Yolngu land battles: '[NT] Aborigines continue to lay bare the Australian Government's policy of suppression of the demands of indigenous peoples in order to forward the interests of foreign and Australian monopoly companies'.[60] Daniels also travelled to the annual Communist Party Congress, where his powerful speech prompted $300 in donations for the Roper River people.[61]

Black Power

Since the late 1960s, Australia's Aboriginal movement had moved closer to the Black Power activism model dominant in the US civil rights movement. Communists embraced its empowering self-determination principles, and the *Tribune* increasingly reported this new version of militant activism. When the 'Tribal Council' of Victoria's Aboriginal Advancement League (AAL) determined that Aboriginal people run and staff the organisation, the *Tribune* published excerpts from its annual report:

> Since the end of World War 2, many…colored [sic] peoples who lived under white colonial rule have gained their independence… colored [sic] minorities in multi-racial nations are claiming the right to determine the course of their own affairs in contradiction to the inferior state under which they had lived.
> That is black power.[62]

A few weeks later, an explanation of 'Black Power' by a League representative at a Sydney FCAATSI conference was reported:

> [Black Power is]…not one single style of action. It does not necessarily mean violence or black supremacy, although in some expressions it has used violence and black supremacy. Those expressions have gained publicity because of their dramatic nature.[63]

Of course, there was a fundamental difference between the Black Power model in the United States and the Australian indigenous rights campaign, and this point must be emphasised. In the USA, the desired outcomes of equal civil rights for African Americans meant that equality closely resembled assimilation. The rights campaign in Australia compared more appropriately with issues tied to the retrieval of land by the Native American population. The Australian land rights movement, however, was relatively new and the critical ingredient of tribal identification was yet to assume prominence in future Native Title land claims in this country.

Black Power assumed powerful new form at FCAATSI's 1970 conference. The *Tribune* reported a Melbourne group (comprising Aboriginal people and students) pushing reform to exclude non-Aboriginal office bearers. Aboriginal delegates Joe McGinness (president) and Dexter Daniels urged solidarity of all affiliated bodies, as the conference broke into two factions.[64] FCAATSI then imploded with an acrimonious split between black and white. Seemingly, white FCAATSI members hadn't gauged the changing political climate, as separate identity became the new goal of indigenous rights activism. Indeed, for many Aboriginal activists, collaboration between black and white was no longer necessary.

In early 1970, Anti-Slavery Society secretary Patrick Montgomery visited Australia, later publishing a short report about Australian Aboriginal people.[65] He also documented personal impressions about the trip. Montgomery witnessed people living in 'dependent poverty', and very high levels of 'illiteracy, malnutrition, disease, infant mortality, broken families, parental deprivation, emotional disturbance, institutional living, unemployment, drunkenness, gambling, idleness and crime'. He identified messy crossovers of federal and state responsibilities for Aboriginal affairs, facilitating 'procrastination and evasion of that responsibility'. Montgomery argued that Black Power activists and communists created larger problems while 'seeking to exploit the Aboriginal situation for their own ends'. He believed that the lack of Aboriginal voices in policy formulation meant continued paternalism. Montgomery identified lack of tribal land title as a violation of human rights and basic international law.[66]

More international eyes turned towards Australia. Victorian AAL director Bruce McGuinness appealed for UN assistance:

On behalf of the Aborigine people of Australia, I am urgently pleading to the United Nations to intercede on our behalf. It is vitally essential that the Australian Government be subjected to outside pressure re: Aborigine land rights.[67]

A week later Minister for Aboriginal Affairs Bill Wentworth wrote to Minister for External Affairs William McMahon, flagging 'possible repercussions in the United Nations' from the developing Aboriginal situation. Referring to McGuinness' press release and similar actions in other states, Wentworth warned:

> In view of the fact that the Federal Opposition and probably 75% of the Australian voters would support Aboriginal claims to some land rights there is a potentially dangerous situation here…you should be flexible here in order to avoid these dangers of confrontation.[68]

Two months later Wentworth was more worried. He again wrote to McMahon, conveying apprehension 'about the possibilities of all Aboriginal affairs (and particularly Aboriginal land rights) being raised in the United Nations'. He identified communists who 'fostered' agitation, adopting 'a cause…considered noteworthy by a substantial section of the Electorate'. Wentworth also feared the USSR would embrace the Australian Aboriginal situation in the UN for their nefarious purposes as well. And, he reminded McMahon, the Anti-Slavery Society report was now tabled in the UN too. And the press were asking more and more questions about Aboriginal rights.[69] It was clearly a most delicate time for the government.

Wentworth had every reason to be worried about Australia's reputation at the UN. On 7 October, a petition that had been tabled in the UN was received by Australia's Consulate General in New York. It contained an 'urgent plea of several hundred thousand so-called "Aboriginies [sic]"' for UN help to secure land rights and compensation (and referring particularly to UN's Item 55 that targeted racial discrimination and ILO Convention 107). Signatories to the petition were the AAL in Victoria, Aboriginal Advancement Council of WA, and National Council of Aborigines and Islanders.[70]

In an attempt to improve Australia's image, Wentworth speedily produced an eleven-page Cabinet submission about assistance for Gurindji people. Wave Hill township improvements had failed to draw people away from the growing settlement at Wattie Creek, so Wentworth recommended government provision of various goods and services for the activist community. These included basic housing, a water bore and windmill, fencing, establishment of new economic ventures, and access to Aborigines Benefits Trust Fund monies. Wentworth also recommended government assistance to develop a self-governing community model, and endorsed any move by Vestey to sub-lease land directly to Gurindji people.[71]

Statistics in Wentworth's submission provide a useful snapshot of the Wattie Creek/Daguragu community in 1970. The population of 121 included the following: thirty Gurindji families, six Bilinara families (described as a 'sub-group closely linked with the Gurindji'), one Walibri family, and one Jaminjung family. The population of Wave Hill township was ninety-nine. Houses cost $18,000 each, whereas 'less elaborate' houses at Daguragu cost $2,000 to $3,000. Wentworth urged Cabinet colleagues to embrace this second option, most especially because volunteer labourers from the south (such as students and communists) were providing most useful free labour.[72]

A few days after his Cabinet submission, a clearly rattled Wentworth again wrote to McMahon. This was an off-the-record letter marked 'Personal' and began with 'Dear Billy'. This time, his fears about a communist-country-led revolt against Australia in the UN were palpable. Embarrassing international scrutiny of Aboriginal truths prompted Wentworth to absolve himself of all responsibility for the ongoing dilemma. His contempt for parliamentary colleagues was obvious:

From my point of view the whole thing is a tragedy which need never have occurred. Proper handling of this would have obviated all this trouble. I would regard the policy laid down by Cabinet as both stupid and provocative.[73]

Here, Wentworth conveniently transferred responsibility for the mess in his own portfolio to his Cabinet associates. On that same day, Wentworth also wrote an on-the-record letter to McMahon. In it, his ignorance of ILO Convention 107 is notable:

The text [of the petition from Aboriginal rights groups to the UN] makes mention of articles 11 and 12 of the International Labour Conference Convention 107. What is the status, if any, of this document?[74]

Five months after his flurry of correspondence with McMahon, Wentworth was asked a series of parliamentary questions about the UN petition by Labor MHR Les Johnson. Wentworth's knowledge of Convention 107 had improved – he was now able to provide details about what it was and who had signed on to it. He confirmed Australia's non-signatory status, blaming 'some difficulties [arising] through lack of uniformity among the Australian states'. As only Victoria, NSW and SA had agreed to ratify the Convention, Wentworth attributed blame for this situation to the dissonance among the other states.[75]

Southern activism for land rights

Quiet occupation of Daguragu by Gurindji people continued as they waited for land to be granted. Down south, however, it was much noisier. After a relatively subdued period, southern state activists stepped up protest supporting Gurindji land rights. But this time they took a very different tack. The *Tribune* reported a fiery Sydney public meeting convened by Hardy, with calls for public boycott of Vestey meat products. The campaign was now more sophisticated, with a committee nominated to coordinate the boycotts, demonstrations, publicity and direct assistance to Gurindji people. Hardy made it very clear to the 250-strong group that land was the key issue, and flagged the Daguragu experiment as a 'watershed' in future negotiations.[76]

Boycotts of Vestey products began with gusto. Large demonstrations were held outside the company's Sydney offices, and one group of protestors invaded the building. Another protest strategy was quite mischievous. Teams of activists (including prominent communists such as Alan Outhred and Brian Aarons) travelled around to supermarkets that stocked Vestey products.[77] At peak-shopping times, trolleys full of Vestey goods were 'parked' in checkout aisles by activists pretending to shop, thus blocking movement. Spokespeople then addressed everyone in the store – the literally captive audience – about the 'evils' of Vestey, and pro-Gurindji pamphlets were distributed to shoppers. The *Tribune* published a how-to list of meddlesome activist tactics. These included writing over Vestey product labels, scribbling 'Boycott Vesteys' graffiti on store walls, phoning stores to protest stocking of Vestey products, and letter-writing to Vestey and their subsidiary companies. The newspaper also published a comprehensive list of goods and services owned or controlled by Vestey in Australia, calling for comprehensive boycotts. Among these were meatworks, an itemised list of smallgoods and canned products, Blue Star Line Shipping, Villawool, various store outlets, and the W. Angliss group (Vestey's large meat business with outlets in most states).[78]

Supermarket boycotts intensified. The *Tribune* featured a large front-page photograph of an activist speaking, with police moving in from behind to arrest him. Another showed Dexter Daniels speaking to a group at another Sydney supermarket.[79] The *Tribune* had earlier published a full-page story about the main Vestey group players. The international conglomerate was controlled by the Vestey family, and 28-year-old Lord Vestey was identified as the key family spokesman regarding the Gurindji land claim: 'their lives are very remote from those of Aborigines working in a type of peonage on north Australia's baked land, looking after the cattle that help to keep the Vestey family in opulence'.[80] The *Tribune's* editor identified the denial of land rights as a capitalist plot:

> Why this rigid denial of land rights? The answer lies in the basic character of the capitalist system itself, which requires private monopoly of the land, the right of capital to dispose of the land and determine [its use]...Vast tracts of Australia...are being assessed and slated for exploitation by big modern capitalist concerns whose sole function is to gain maximum profit.

Protests and boycotts against Vestey were described as 'an important movement of solidarity with the freedom struggles of our Aboriginal and island brothers'.[81]

Union support continued. A Sydney 'Aborigines in Industry' seminar (organised by the Trade Union Education and Research Centre and Aboriginal Co-operative College) attracted representatives from ten unions and many other organisations. Participants voted unanimously to support Gurindji people, and urged unions to lobby for more structured ACTU Aboriginal rights programs and policy. Like other Aboriginal-rights activism organisations, unions were moving away from the old paternalistic model of support, to a modern way for Aboriginal people to negotiate change. The new ACTU Committee on Aboriginal Affairs urged union discussion with Aboriginal representatives, to facilitate more productive participation in union activities and leadership.[82]

Aboriginal people were much more visible in southern states activism for Gurindji rights now. The *Tribune's* front page featured a large photograph of Aboriginal activists leading a Sydney protest march and being arrested in Redfern. The story emphasised

Aboriginal organisation, describing the mixed mob of protestors as 'Aboriginal-white', with 'participation of Aborigines [marking] a new development in the militant, direct-action campaign of solidarity with the Gurindji'.[83]

This Sydney demonstration was a relatively ad hoc event. Aboriginal activists Paul Coe and Dexter Daniels (and Frank Hardy) had been in the Redfern Hotel earlier that afternoon, speaking to patrons. Their stirring call to protest buoyed numbers, and marchers proceeded to the city Vestey building, where the *Tribune* reported a police presence numbering 'hundreds', indicating high governmental priority to quell public demonstration against this powerful company. Forty-five people (including national Communist Party secretary Laurie Aarons) were swiftly arrested, as police moved in a reportedly 'sudden, unprovoked attack'. The *Tribune* reported that extreme actions by the large police contingent 'suggested that the multi-million dollar company [Vestey] has demanded State Government action to defend it against the campaign of exposure'. Bail conditions were reportedly dubious, with amounts increasing substantially for 'fictitious charges' allegedly aiming at 'stifling political dissent'.[84]

A 'Save the Gurindji Committee' appeal (launched a week later in Sydney) targeted $50,000 for building works at Daguragu. Establishment of a permanent, unmoveable Gurindji settlement had become an urgent priority. Sydney unionists announced formation of their Aboriginal Rights Committee and a Vesteys Boycott Action Committee. They also endorsed a new book (*The Vestey Story*), produced by the Victorian Meat Industries Employees' Union to expose Vestey 'truths'.[85]

Forty-five protestors who had been arrested during the Redfern march appeared in court two weeks later, and the *Tribune* reported their grand theatrical performance. Activists dressed in colonial guard uniforms led others (made-up as Aboriginal people) into the court by neck ropes. This black pantomime featured an effigy of Lord Vestey, three ironic cheers for the Queen, and a proliferation of Australian flags displaying swastikas instead of stars. A number of communists appeared before the court, including Brian and Pat Aarons, Alan Outhred and the *Tribune* journalist Denis Freney.[86]

Handling of any Vestey goods was banned by the NAWU. Large Melbourne and Sydney meetings urged ACTU boycott support, and Vestey appeared to be shifting their position. The *Tribune* reported rumours of company willingness to hand over land to Gurindji people, provided that Australia's government facilitate the process. Three Daguragu representatives were elected to travel 'down south' for negotiations. But the government continued to hold its line. Nixon (Minister for the Interior) doggedly maintained that traditional ownership of land was not government policy, and Vestey handover of land not permissible. In a statement, Nixon said that land would need to be handed back to the government, which would then choose a suitable party to offer a lease to.[87] Vestey was thus unable to rid itself of an awkward situation due to the powerful Department of the Interior bureaucracy – perhaps appropriately described as the 'villains' of the piece.[88]

Land tenure information (as disclosed in parliament) was reported in the *Tribune*. More than 199,500 square kilometres of NT land was held under forty-three pastoral leases by overseas companies. Vestey held six leases (totalling nearly 44,000 square kilometres) that were not due to expire until 2004.[89]

During September 1970, Joe McGinness travelled 6,500 kilometres around the Northern Territory. The FCAATSI leader's tour was sponsored by WWF's Sydney branch, and the *Tribune* published his full report. McGinness recommended government training of Aboriginal people for mining, agriculture and marine industry opportunities developing in the NT. He stayed at Daguragu for a week. Gurindji people told McGinness they had no intention of moving to Welfare houses built by the government on 'desolate, barren, treeless and grassless' Drovers' Common (Kalkaringi) at Wave Hill. McGinness' observations of Daguragu were remarkably similar to those of Jessie Street during her Pilbara visit twenty years earlier. He described lush vegetable gardens tended by work parties, job allocation systems, and organised routines of camp life and duties. McGinness' comments about advocacy for NT Aboriginal people were far less glowing. He reported that the 'almost defunct Rights Council [NTCAR]' had lost its ability to represent Aboriginal people, because it 'had its leadership curtailed and put into welfare jobs where their work has no real value in helping the cause'.[90]

Global attention increasingly focused upon racial equality and human rights. The year of 1971 was declared by the UN to be the 'International Year for Action to Combat Racism and Racial Discrimination'. In Australia, a union conference urged members to lobby the ACTU for a dual boycott of the South African Rugby tour and bans on Vestey and Nabalco products (Nabalco was the company mining bauxite in the Gove Peninsula, where an application for land by Yolngu people at Yirrkala had recently been rejected in the NT Supreme Court). Three key unions called for ACTU bans on construction projects and companies adversely affecting Aboriginal people. The Amalgamated Engineering Union, Boilermakers and Blacksmiths Society and Sheetmetal Workers' Union also demanded full land rights, and tighter legislative control over racist discrimination. They proposed Aboriginal Rights Councils within each state union body to provide educational material and advisory services about Aboriginal rights campaigns. Unions were also urged to employ Aboriginal organisers. Frank Hardy, however, continued to antagonise the union movement by again publicly bemoaning its inactivity in the Gurindji fight.[91]

Dogged anti-apartheid protest culminated with cancellation of South Africa's cricket tour in Australia. One *Tribune* writer used this example to highlight Australia's own record of treatment towards indigenous peoples. Denis Freney blasted previous activist organisation attempts to improve Aboriginal rights: 'they have got virtually nowhere, except for the abolition of the more blatantly, apartheidist [sic] laws'. He identified paternalism as 'deadly to any development of black cultural self-identity and militancy'. Freney believed that a black 'revolutionary party' was vital, and urged communists to contribute financially to this cause.[92]

Not long after Freney's impassioned article, a revolutionary Aboriginal rights party was formed. The Australian Black Panther Party organised a protest march in Sydney, with 500 activists calling for land rights and abolition of Queensland's discriminatory anti-Aboriginal legislation. Queensland Black Panthers leader Denis Walker gave an impassioned and inflammatory speech. This disturbing excerpt is indicative: 'Everything was taken off you with a gun, the only way you are going to get it back is with a gun'.[93] In a *Tribune* interview, Walker explained why his group had formed. He believed that the 'system' had co-opted Aboriginal 'puppets' such as Charlie Perkins, Kath Walker and Neville Bonner. Denis Walker argued that Aboriginal people needed to stop employing 'acceptable' and 'respectable' methods to engage with the white system. A 'revolutionary' approach was necessary to overthrow it, and 'whites' were welcome to 'come in and assist' if they wanted.[94]

Hopes for resolution to the Gurindji stand-off were temporarily buoyed when Council for Aboriginal Affairs chair 'Nugget' Coombs requested a meeting with a Daguragu delegation. Hardy, Eva Jago (the Gurindji campaign treasurer), Vincent Lingiari and Donald Nangiari (another Gurindji man) visited Coombs' Sydney office on 21 May. When asked what they urgently needed at Daguragu, they requested a mustering plant, bore, and homes for 'old people'. The reportedly heated meeting ended with Hardy and Coombs in a stand-off. Despite this unsatisfying stalemate, the *Tribune* reported Hardy's 'abrasive approach' once again 'demonstrat[ing] his sincerity towards the Gurindji cause'.[95]

In November the WWF donated $10,000 for Daguragu 'with no strings attached'. The *Tribune*'s front page featured a large photograph of the union's general secretary Charlie Fitzgibbon and Gurindji elder Mick Rangiari drinking a toast. Rangiari said that the money would be used to build 145 kilometres of fencing around the 1,295 square kilometres the Gurindji people were claiming. Fitzgibbon noted the WWF's 'real and serious sympathy for the return of rights to a people who have been dispossessed'. The *Tribune* acknowledged the union's staunch support for Aboriginal campaigns, with 'thousands of dollars' previously contributed. It also reported government and Vestey contempt for the significant donation, and their accusations that the union was 'stirring trouble' for people not capable of achieving success without white guidance.[96]

Aboriginal political action

In 1972 the political environment changed markedly, as Black Power gained momentum and the government changed hands. Early that year, one pivotal event in Canberra stimulated quick parliamentary discussion that included the following:

> Has the Minister noticed a series of tents pitched on a public lawn in front of Parliament House? Is this area of public lawn open for anyone to camp on at will?

John Gorton MHR asked these unusual parliamentary questions on 23 February 1972. Ralph Hunt MHR (the Liberal Minister for the Interior) responded that he was, 'of course, well aware', of this new development. His explanation seemed relaxed: 'The people concerned are Aborigines who are demonstrating in a peaceful way for a case in which they believe'.[97] This small group had established an embassy made of tents. Their case was sovereign rights over lands taken from their ancestors.

The Tent Embassy symbolised change. Australia's white-and-black-together model of activism had been essentially shunned, and was replaced by the new more militant Black Power order. Aboriginal voices now called for land rights, housing, education, health and welfare services, legal representation, cultural protections and national recognition. The calls now emanated from the people the campaigns supported.

Previous attempts by Aboriginal activists to organise and lobby for change had struggled to endure. Aboriginal people in southern states formed protest groups during the late 1920s and 1930s (notably the Australian Aborigines' League led by Aboriginal activist William Cooper). However, until the late 1960s most activists were non-Aboriginal supporters, but their contributions added firm foundations to a strong movement for change, providing optimal conditions for Aboriginal people to take control of their own affairs. The Tent Embassy epitomised new guard, with Aboriginal people now assuming control of activist platforms. This new assertion of Aboriginal power changed forever the way that the rights movement functioned.

The Aboriginal rights movement planned an event to showcase its solidarity for land rights and self-determination. The *Tribune* reported the 'Moratorium for Black Rights' on National Aborigines' Day (14 July 1972) as a show of 'valuable solidarity [by] white radical and militant workers and students', welcomed by the new guard of black rights campaigners. It endorsed this 'beginning of a continuing mass mobilisation in solidarity with Black struggles'.[98]

The Tent Embassy attracted international interest. The McMahon government reacted by threatening to pull it down. The *Tribune* reported 'big articles' about the front lawn activism in the *London Times*, the London *Guardian*, the *New York Times*, Paris' *Le Figaro*, Asian newspapers, a Jamaican publication, and even Norway's the *Way of the World*. The *Tribune* also noted extensive coverage by the BBC, Westinghouse Radio in the USA, and a Japanese documentary film crew. Gifts were sent to the Tent Embassy from Kenya and the Irish Republican Army. Embassy representatives visiting the Aboriginal activists included Canadians, Maltese, Ghanaians and Soviets.[99]

Despite the Minister's casual response to the question in parliament, Canberra police moved in and removed the Tent Embassy in mid-July 1972. Activists attempting to re-erect tents two days later were beaten by officers, and the *Tribune* published a long list of people injured at the scene or in the cells. A week after this disturbing day a *Tribune* article predicted what would happen: 'One thing is certain. Black Australia and White Australia will never be the same after the moving and militant events of July 1972'.[100] The Tent Embassy was re-established for a few hours in September, then again removed by police following the rushed passing of legislation aimed at banning its presence permanently. Aboriginal activist (and former Tent Embassy secretary) Pat Eatock stood as a 'Black Rights' candidate in the federal December election, and she committed to re-establish the Embassy.[101]

∞

Resolute Aboriginal activists rebuilt their Embassy in 1973. Since that time, it has been pulled down and put back up a number of times in several locations. The Embassy has been in its current (the original) place on lawns outside Old Parliament House in Canberra since 1992. The Federation of Aboriginal Sovereign Nations continues to demand Aboriginal sovereignty in the form of land rights and compensation.

Tent Embassy Canberra, 6 March 2012. (Author's photo.)

'Some sort of deep, dark, Red Plot'

A Ministerial statement about land rights pre-empted lengthy debate on 23 February 1972. A proposal for an Aboriginal fifty-year leasehold arrangement by Minister for Aboriginal Affairs Peter Howson was described by Opposition Leader Whitlam as 'patronising'. To emphasise his point, Whitlam was granted leave to incorporate sections of ILO Convention 107 into Hansard, as a reminder of the 'international obligation' concerning 'occupancy' of tribal lands. He reiterated Labor's intent to establish land trusts to administer hand backs and protect sacred sites from mining companies and the like. Whitlam acknowledged the legal mine-field that lay ahead, but undertook to systematically unravel 200 years of British and Australian tenure. He proposed a commission of inquiry to identify the facts.[102]

Minister for the Interior Hunt responded to Whitlam's speech. He described the Aboriginal rights situation as a 'political football' that communists and unionists planned to turn into militant revolution, 'using...Aborigines as a launching pad for their own motives'. Hunt also claimed that Whitlam's support for Aboriginal rights was a strategic pre-election sweetener that would disappear should he win power. Labor member Gordon Bryant described Hunt's 'red baiting' diatribe (that coloured support of Aboriginal rights as 'some sort of deep, dark, Red plot') to be 'disgraceful' and 'unbecoming'.[103]

Communists articulated their position on Aboriginal rights a few months later. Their 1972 policy objectives included land rights, national self-determination, self-governing areas, full compensation for stolen lands, and an end to discrimination by governments. The Party also explicitly aligned itself to the Black Power movement.[104]

In March the *Tribune* reported pressure upon Minister for Labour Phillip Lynch to reveal government inspection details at Wave Hill and Victoria Downs stations. Lynch admitted that workers' food and accommodation were well below standards required in the Cattle Station Industry (NT) Award, but unless Aboriginal workers were NAWU members, he was powerless to intervene, and that responsibility lay with station owners.[105] The *Tribune* slammed the lack of solidarity and inaction of some unions. An aggressive article pinpointed AWU and the Federated Miscellaneous Workers' Union (FMWU) as two of the worst offenders. At the LJ Hooker–owned Victoria River Downs (VRD) Station, 150 Aboriginal workers and families had recently walked away to join the Daguragu settlement, and the FMWU was particularly singled out for its lack of financial or other support.[106]

To counter this perceived inertia, Brian Manning wrote a full-page *Tribune* article imploring unions to become more active and aggressive for Aboriginal rights and land. A few weeks earlier, rumours abounded that white 'scab' workers had been moved onto VRD to replace absent Gurindji workers.[107] Manning argued that unions were ineffectual. NAWU had failed to recruit or represent Aboriginal worker interests (the NAWU had amalgamated with FMWU in 1972 – Northern Territory workers then became NT branch members of the FMWU, thus allying them to a larger, more powerful national labour organisation with far greater potential industrial muscle). Manning believed that 1,500 Aboriginal workers should have been recruited to the union. This large membership hole meant that Aboriginal issues were unheard or paid flimsy lip-service. Manning believed that 'any real effort to organise Aboriginals would radically change the character of this union'. Aboriginal in/ability to pay union subs was a main reason why the NAWU chose to look the other way, instead of getting involved in the fight. Manning was quite scathing about NAWU operation:

> The union was run in a bureaucratic way in the past – the handpicked executive rarely met except to endorse leadership decisions. The controlling body, the Central Council, met annually, composed of delegates from selected pockets of union members with, in practice, little or no rank and file control... The NAWU has not been democratised since amalgamation with the MWU.[108]

He also identified a 'deliberate strategy', whereby canny station owners actually orchestrated walk-offs. Manning believed that by not stopping (and perhaps even encouraging) Aboriginal workers to walk away, stations were then able to pick and choose the workforce who might return. In this way, young and fit men would be accepted back. Responsibility for old people and children would no longer be an issue. Manning also flagged changing employment requirements. Stations modernising their herds replaced shorthorn cattle with smaller mobs of larger breeds (such as Santa Gertrudis and Brahmans). Fencing and better pasture management meant the cattle grazed closer to homesteads. Technological changes such as helicopter mustering decreased the number of Aboriginal workers required to manage stock. In other words, high numbers of Aboriginal station employees were no longer necessary – they were becoming redundant. And their families were absolute liabilities for station owners. Manning believed that pastoralists had even provoked one particular walk-off 'to get rid of the families'. He argued FMWU obligation to sign up as many Aboriginal workers as possible, and fight tenaciously for them. Manning urged the ACTU to step up and provide an organiser for this purpose, as well as imposing national sanctions on companies such as LJ Hooker.[109]

It's time for change

In 1967 anthropologist Bill Stanner had identified the 'quickening of aboriginal [sic] political acumen', and 'the simple fact...that the people as well as the times have changed. One cannot any longer put off the aborigines [sic] with make-believe'.[110] Five years later, the Council for Aboriginal Affairs submitted papers and a recommendation about Gurindji land rights to the Cabinet Committee on Aboriginal Affairs. This influential government advisory group had formed in 1967, when Prime Minister Holt invited Stanner, 'Nugget' Coombs and senior public servant Barry Dexter to establish the new body. In light of a report released to government four months earlier, they submitted formal recommendation to Cabinet:

The offer of Lord Vestey to make available land for Aboriginal purposes from the Wave Hill property still stands and the Council for Aboriginal Affairs therefore recommends that the

Commonwealth acquires, in terms of the procedures for the acquisitions of properties off reserves, a viable area of up to 1500 square miles from the Wave Hill Pastoral Lease for the economic and social benefit of the Wattie Creek community.[111]

The Cabinet Committee on Aboriginal Affairs did not agree. It released an alternative decision, agreeing that Vestey's offer to surrender 35 square miles (90 square kilometres) be accepted. And it rejected the Council's recommendation of 1,500 square miles (3,885 square kilometres) for the Gurindji community as 'not practicable and should not be pursued'. The Committee recommended that their unpalatable decision needed to be publicised in 'low key' fashion.[112]

On 2 December 1972 Australia elected its first Labor Party government since 1949. Soon after, Gough Whitlam's administration created the Ministry for Aboriginal Affairs, and long-time Aboriginal rights movement stalwart Gordon Bryant was appointed first Minister (the accompanying Department had been established in 1971 by the McMahon government). Aboriginal program funding increased exponentially during 1973, after more than doubling between 1971–72 and 1972–73 to more than $60 million. This was a direct (although belated) consequence of the move to federal control over Aboriginal people in the states following the 1967 referendum. Two important federally funded bodies were established: the Aboriginal Legal and Medical services. And a new consultative body formed to advise the government about Aboriginal policy and direction – the National Aboriginal Consultative Committee.[113]

When the Whitlam government came to power, ACTU Congress quickly released a comprehensive Aboriginal Affairs policy urging increased funding for Aboriginal programs and infrastructure. It also recommended government-sponsored legal advice for groups pursuing land rights, and called for a National Commission on Aboriginal Land Rights.[114] In August 1973 Bryant announced in parliament that a new Aboriginal Land Rights Commission would be headed by Justice Edward Woodward. Two NT land rights committees were proposed, and various Aboriginal communities and groups became incorporated entities. These foundation steps underpinned future policy direction when the final Commission report was handed down the following year.

The land rights campaign was famously dramatised on 16 August 1975 when Prime Minister Whitlam poured a symbolic handful of sand through Vincent Lingiari's fingers. The *Aboriginal Land Rights (Northern Territory) Act 1976* was passed by the Fraser Liberal government in 1976, enabling claims on reserves as well as other land. The Gurindji land rights claim for Daguragu, however, was not finalised until 1981.[115]

∞

In the final chapter, we take a closer look at a number of participants whose support for the Gurindji community was direct and personal. In this way, campaign activists feature in focus, in a fitting closure to this case study about Aboriginal rights in the Northern Territory.

Chapter Ten

They are only confusing the Aboriginals. They are not really helping the situation at all, even though they may possibly be sincere.[1]

Member for the NT Sam Calder was clearly no fan of people who
were helping out at Daguragu. This final chapter about the Gurindji
campaign presents closer examination of several key personalities
and visitors at Daguragu – the very people Calder (who was also
a station manager) did not appreciate. It begins with a firsthand
account of Wave Hill conditions by a disgruntled ex-welfare officer.

Bill Jeffrey's *Tribune* story

In late 1967 the *Tribune* published three lengthy articles by Bill
Jeffrey, who claimed to have been sacked as Wave Hill's welfare
officer a few months earlier. Jeffrey believed this to be punishment

for his public criticism about the 'inhuman treatment' of Aboriginal people by government and private employers. As identified earlier, ASIO had been aware of the Administrator's intention to remove Jeffrey several months prior to his dismissal. The *Tribune*'s publication of Jeffrey's story in three (two-page) feature articles presented compelling evidence by this whistle-blower who was not a comrade.

Jeffrey's damning descriptions of Wave Hill explain the keenness of government and Vestey to move him on. He identified leg irons that 'weren't used on white stockmen' hanging in station manager Tom Fisher's office. Jeffrey witnessed people living in 'huts like dog kennels that scorched in the summer and froze in the winter'. He alleged that reports by welfare officers detailing these shocking conditions were submitted to superiors, but then mysteriously disappeared. On one occasion, Jeffrey was warned by his department to 'lay off because he was kicking uphill by having a go at Vesteys'. He insisted that his failure to heed that advice necessitated his speedy removal. He knew too much and talked too loudly.[2]

Jeffrey described a tactic involving Social Service payments. When Wave Hill people walked away to Daguragu, four welfare officers arrived via chartered plane. They witnessed conversations between Aboriginal workers and a Victoria River Downs station manager. One ex–Wave Hill stockman named Peter Gillguy was offered a job there, but refused. According to Jeffrey, his refusal to accept employment meant that Gillguy lost his social security payment. Jeffrey viewed this incident as trickery: in knocking back work, the powerless Aboriginal worker fell victim to a 'snide and bullying approach' by corrupt government officials. Gillguy's brave attempt at industrial action was publicly punished as an example to others.[3]

Jeffrey's second *Tribune* article further described Wave Hill conditions. When several people at the Daguragu camp became ill, Jeffrey took them 16 kilometres up to the homestead for treatment. There, a nurse had been employed by the Welfare Department to live at Wave Hill and care for Aboriginal residents. Pharmaceuticals from the government were also provided expressly for Aboriginal workers and families. Tom Fisher ordered the 'black bastards' off the property and refused any care. When Jeffrey returned with another welfare officer (as a witness), Fisher responded by denying medical aid and refusing permission for the government nurse to go down to the camp. Jeffrey claimed it took several months to arrange alternative medical care. During that time, four people and one baby passed away, 'because they were denied medical attention':

> There were 250 Aborigines in that camp and Tom Fisher was withholding medical supplies, while some of them were dying. And what did Welfare do about it? Nothing.[4]

Indeed, Daguragu's tenuous medical situation forced a crucial cultural change for Gurindji people at their new settlement place. When an old lady passed away, a dilemma arose about where to bury her. The traditional burial ground where people went with their ancestors was on Wave Hill Station. Jeffrey described how Vincent Lingiari informed him of the new decision about burials: 'Nobody, even when they finish up, ever go back to Wave Hill. We make new burial ground here'.[5] The walk-off from Wave Hill had, thus, created irreversible cultural change. Gurindji determination to escape Vestey shackles was so fierce that even their immensely important ancient burial tradition was adapted in the name of freedom and justice.

In his final *Tribune* article, Jeffrey advocated abolition of the Aboriginal Welfare Department, and replacement with an Aboriginal-run organisation. He also vehemently endorsed land rights, with any available land to be 'legally tied up as permanently

[Gurindji] lands, on which they should have full self-determination'. And he took aim at the union movement: 'Unions should take more interest in the Aborigines than they do…Here is a new army waiting to be recruited to unionism. This is what they need, not welfare'.[6] Jeffrey hailed a recent NT Legislative Council committee report condemning 'the social and moral suffering of the Aborigines' and lauding Daguragu's community organisation and solidarity. He believed the report identified 'strong moral ground' for Gurindji people to resume possession of land they 'considered from time immemorial' to be theirs.[7]

Even though Jeffrey had submitted his trilogy of articles to the *Tribune*, Brian Manning was pretty sure he was not a communist:

> Although Bill and Ann Jeffrey were on good terms with Frank Hardy and their support for the Gurindji played a crucial role in the early days of the walk-off, I don't think they were Party People. I believe they had links with the Unitarian church in Melbourne.[8]

Manning was an active communist interacting closely with the Jeffrey couple, and so his knowledge of them is probably accurate. Jeffrey's sacking was not a retributive governmental reaction to communist status. He was removed because he blew too many whistles. Jeffrey's support for the Gurindji people was not choreographed by the Party – his motivation was driven by what he witnessed. His *Tribune* contributions most likely tapped into a reliable conduit, so that his firsthand account of the real story could reach southern readers.

Jeffrey's dismissal was also reported in mainstream press. The *Australian* published revealing details he provided in an interview, and this article was raised in parliament by Tom Uren MHR. He then pressed the government for answers about Wave Hill. Minister for Territories Barnes immediately identified Uren as 'an associate of Frank Hardy', suggesting that the Communist Party was using Aboriginal people for political purposes. Uren defended Hardy's motives at Wave Hill, arguing that he and any other Australian had every right to protest, associate freely and criticise the government. And Jeffrey, he said, was equally entitled to criticise 'a government that looks after only the wealthy foreign monopolies and the wealthy section of our community'.[9]

Daguragu visitors

People visited Daguragu in many roles including volunteers, researchers, activists, missionaries and government officials. Ted Egan was an official. He had worked for the Northern Territory's Department of Native Affairs since the early 1950s as a teacher, then officer. In 1971 Egan visited Wave Hill with a Vestey representative to assess the situation. One incident during that visit provides another perspective to the relationship between white station workers and Aboriginal stockmen. Egan was present during an encounter between Wave Hill's embattled station manager and Lingiari. The manager pleaded for Gurindji help moving cattle to new water so they would not die of thirst. Egan recalled Lingiari's immediate organisation of stockmen to help, and his rationale for this assistance: 'Yeah...we gotta look after the whitefellas in this country'.[10]

Two notable songs have been written about the Gurindji walk-off. In a recent example, Paul Kelly and Aboriginal songwriter Kev Carmody collaborated to tell the story as 'From Little Things Big Things Grow'.[11] The other piece was penned by Native Affairs officer Ted Egan, who was also a songwriter. In early August 1968 Minister for the Interior Nixon had released a contentious statement proposing that if Aboriginal people wanted land tenure, they should save up and buy it as other Australians would do. 'Gurindji Blues' was Egan's fierce musical protest about Nixon's comments. When the song was released, Nixon demanded Egan's dismissal. But Egan recalled that Minister for Aboriginal Affairs Wentworth said 'he rather liked the song', and kept him on.[12] This verse is indicative of the content:

> ♫ Poor bugger me, Gurindji
> Man called Vincent Lingiari,
> Talk long allabout Gurindji
> 'Daguragu place for we
> Home for we, Gurindji'.
> But poor bugger blackfeller, Gurindji
> Government boss him talk long we
> 'We'll build you house with electricity
> But at Wave Hill, for can't you see
> Wattie Creek belong to Lord Vestey'.
> Oh poor bugger me.♫

Egan sang 'Gurindji Blues' for Daguragu community members during a 1971 visit. He described Vincent Lingiari's reaction to the powerful lyrics – 'The old bloke laughed, then cried'.[13]

Joan Williams also went to Daguragu. Her activities as a *Workers Star* journalist covering the Pilbara story during 1946 were noted in earlier chapters. By 1972 the feisty communist was writing for the Party's national newspaper. Williams reported rock-solid determination by the Gurindji community to acquire land. Conditions at the settlement had steadily improved and she observed solid clay-block houses on cement slabs. Young Aboriginal workers were training as plumbers and carpenters. Citrus trees and vegetable gardens were providing healthy produce for Gurindji people.[14]

Williams was one of many visitors to the developing Daguragu community. Some stayed a few days, some a few weeks or months, and some a few years. Brian Manning recalled that there were up to ten 'southerners' at Daguragu at any one time.[15] They travelled to this remote place for a variety of reasons. Some came to help or study and some, according to ASIO, came with more nefarious agendas. Several of the people who lived and worked with the Gurindji community are introduced next. Their commonality was a fierce desire to support Gurindji rights.

Visitors to Daguragu were not welcomed by everyone. Sam Calder (the Member for the NT and station manager we met at the beginning of this chapter) aired his rather strong views in parliament:

> Most of the people who rush up to the Territory and lay a few bricks, as Abschol representatives or university students did last month, are the sort of persons who spend a week or so in the Territory and then spend the next year or so writing about it and probably talking about it down here. They are only confusing the Aboriginals. They are not really helping the situation at all, even though they may possibly be sincere.[16]

Roderick Williams was one of those visitors who would not have impressed Calder. He arrived at Daguragu as an ABSCHOL volunteer who laid bricks, then later wrote and talked about his experiences. He and eleven others travelled from southern states to help build the first permanent houses at the settlement. ABSCHOL was established during the 1960s to provide schol-arships for Aboriginal university students, and its broader pressure–group activities drew accusations that ABSCHOL was a communist front organisation.

Williams' descriptions of life in the Gurindji community were published in the *Tribune*. He was part of an ABSCHOL work team providing guidance and manpower to construct permanent dwellings. ABSCHOL provided a brick-making machine and Williams' team arrived to discover enough bricks already made to erect three houses. He described brick and mortar constructions, with iron roofs and verandahs. Flat river stones were mortared together to create floors. A Melbourne architect member of the team ensured that construction was sound. At that time, around fifty people (mainly elders) lived at Daguragu. Williams explained that the population on nearby stations was about 200, with most returning to Daguragu during the wet season. He warmly described Gurindji characteristics of 'keenness', 'adaptability', 'strength and determination' and found them to be 'peaceful', 'tolerant', 'open-hearted', 'outstandingly proud' and 'brave' people.[17]

Williams was probably not aware that his trip to Daguragu was also recorded by others. An ASIO phone-tap identified Sid Mounsey informing Lorraine Salmon (both communists) that Williams and 'some fellows' were going up 'with the truck and taking Sean (FOLEY) with him and some cement'.[18]

> ♫ Poor bugger me, Gurindji
> Up come Mr. Frank Hardy
> ABSCHOL too and talk long we
> Givit hand long Gurindji
> Buildim house and plantim tree
> Longa Wattie Creek for Gurindji♫[19]

Paul Fox was another ABSCHOL visitor, and he described a very different scenario. Fox had observed the arrest of four Aboriginal stockmen, who were taken to Wave Hill police station from Limbunya Station. According to Fox, the station owner and police had fabricated alleged crimes of horse theft and general 'troublemaking' as retaliatory punishment for their industrial action. The Aboriginal stockmen (and the white workers) had refused to labour any longer under oppressive conditions. Fox considered the situation to be a clear example of victimisation. The Limbunya Aboriginal workers and families had been refused sale of food at the station store for over a week. The manager controlled the store, and Fox identified this blatant strategy to starve workers back to their jobs. He also accused Wave Hill welfare officer Richardson of ignoring their pleas for assistance. Indeed, Fox recalled Richardson daring him to go to Limbunya, as the 'managers around here were fed up with all these strikes and were itching to punchup these Southern stirrers'. Richardson told him of instructions by 'Welfare not to touch the situation'. He also revealed that Vestey flew in new stockmen from Wyndam (in WA), to replace workers who walked away following total negotiation breakdown. Fox described the 'attempt to starve strikers back to work' by both government and employer as an 'incredible' example of corrupt dealings in the north.[20]

Another visitor reported more positive happenings at Daguragu. Hannah Middleton was an anthropology student and also a member of the British Communist Party. She had written to the Daguragu community from Berlin, asking permission to visit. Middleton came to Australia and was invited into the tribe, 'given a skin', and became a member of a family. She lived with the Gurindji community on and off for a total of six months. In the *Tribune*, Middleton described the impressive building works, roofed toilet and shower block, orchard and fencing. She reported that visitor help from ABSCHOL, unions, the Communist Party, FCAATSI and other groups was most appreciated. Middleton also identified Gurindji focus upon self-sufficiency while establishing their own cattle station and associated business enterprises. She reported their plans for a school, ongoing housing development, a health clinic and an administrative office staffed by two of their young women.[21]

Middleton became ensconced in the community while gathering anthropological data. She assumed the extremely important role as reader and writer of letters on Gurindji behalf. Middleton also spoke as a representative when requested, and became immersed in cultural life. She described the warm embrace by the small community:

> My explanation that I wanted to learn about and then write about their strike, their ideas about the land, their relationship with white Australia and their plans for the future, was not only accepted but was approved of and I was actively encouraged, supported and assisted, especially by the senior men.[22]

Middleton was a communist. But as a mid-1970 government document proves, Daguragu was in no danger of being over-run with subversives. A Cabinet submission by Minister for Aboriginal Affairs Wentworth identified a total of 'only two white people living at Wattie Creek', namely Middleton and Roderick Williams.[23]

Middleton described her role as 'shuttling from white observer to Gurindji daughter'. She was, however, acutely aware of what happened to one communist anthropologist who cohabited with Aboriginal groups. Fred Rose lived and worked in Arnhem Land communities during the 1930s and 1940s. He had been a member of the Communist Party since 1942. Middleton noted his ban from Groote Eylandt Aboriginal Reserve in 1968, due to alleged 'treachery' and 'prostitution'. This ban irreparably damaged Rose's reputation. Middleton highlighted his subsequent fall from governmental grace and unwanted renown as punishment for being (according to the government) a communist disguised as anthropologist.[24]

Correspondence from the Director General of Security to the Department of the Interior highlighted ASIO belief that Rose was a spy. Charles Spry recommended, 'on security grounds', that Rose be banned from any Aboriginal reserves. He was 'certain' that Rose would 'supply the East German government with information which could be used as a basis of communist attacks on Australian Government policies towards the Aborigines'.[25] Correspondence one week later between the Department of Territories and Prime Minister's Department also discussed Cabinet's decision to ban Rose from Groote Eylandt. The letter included advice about how best for the prime minister and other ministers to spin this story and avoid public condemnation. Formulaic comment was provided for politicians to spout upon demand:

> Rose is a declared communist who has for many years been living and working in East Germany. The Government is not satisfied that the implications of the presence of Rose in the Aboriginal Reserve for a period of some months would be limited to objective academic research.[26]

Not surprisingly, this letter was marked 'SECRET'. In parliament several weeks later, Gordon Bryant asked Minister for the Interior Nixon why Rose's permit had been denied. His scripted response was short: 'The reason is that Professor Rose is a Communist'.[27] Any uneasiness felt by communist anthropologist Middleton, while living and working with the Gurindji community in that climate of fear and retribution, becomes very understandable.

Another visitor, Lyn Riddett (then Lyn Raper), spent a total of thirteen months living at Daguragu between 1970 and 1973. A speech by Frank Hardy at a protest rally had inspired her involvement. Her experiences at Daguragu were unique:

> To enter the land rights fight at Wattie Creek was to enter another world, and to meet there people...who had been experiencing life in two separate worlds since cattle had first come onto their land in the 1880s.

Riddett delineated two distinct groups of white participants or observers at Daguragu as the 'union mob' (good people) and the 'white Europeans' ('the enemy'). As she noted, to be a member of the 'union mob' did not necessarily mean that you were a unionist. This was much more of a blanket term describing people who came to help. On the other hand, the 'white Europeans' were either those who owned and/or lived on cattle stations, or the government people in Darwin – the squattocracy and the bureaucracy.[28] As evidenced in interviews with elders conducted by Minoru Hokari between 1999 and 2001 (while researching for his PhD thesis), the term 'union mob' was still being used many years later to describe those who assisted the Gurindji cause. One Gurindji elder named Jimmy Mangayarri described the relationships to Hokari like this:

> Union mob and Captain Cook different country...He [union mob] help people. Put land back...Tommy Vincent [Lingiari], union mob all right law...English man nomo [never] longa yunmi [you and me].[29]

Hence, the 'union mob' comprised those supporting the struggle for land rights. The 'English man', in the form of pastoral companies, government officers and politicians, was never to be included as part of the community or as a Gurindji ally.

Deborah Bird Rose also identified the 'union mob' in her anthropological study about three stations (including Wave Hill). She identified this diverse group of white supporters as the 'major non-Aboriginal protagonist in the struggle for equality'. Rose also acknowledged Aboriginal faith in this 'not morally bankrupt' group of people as a crucial ingredient normalising the status of black/white collaboration. Aboriginal pastoral workers now had a support group of white Australians fully committed to their struggle for justice and land. This relationship involved strong elements of trust, and enabled white supporters to move into the light, no longer part of 'a hidden history'.[30]

The 'union mob' did not have things easy in the early 1970s. Riddett described the kinds of impediments or 'harassments' (created by station administrators and government officials) to make life for the 'good people' as hard as possible. Volunteers, students, academics, church members, teachers, linguists, tradespeople, and anyone else venturing to Daguragu to lend a hand, were constantly hampered. Food and provisions from the local store were denied to these trespassers on 'pastoral leasehold land', radio and telephone access was denied, mail was opened or confiscated, and even toilets were declared off-limits at times.[31]

'Union mob' activities were many and varied. Volunteers made bricks, built houses, looked after children, fixed cars, taught languages, made gardens, planted trees. Riddett explained that these welcome visitors stayed in the 'bough-shade' guest area, or camped with Gurindji families. Everyone was situated within the 'traditional kinship classificatory system', thus experiencing what Riddett termed a 'genuine cross-cultural situation'. This also facilitated an extremely useful reciprocal relationship, whereby Gurindji people who travelled 'down south' for political or perhaps medical reasons always had a bed somewhere.[32]

The 'union mob' was not positively perceived by the 'white Europeans'. According to Riddett, Daguragu volunteers were viewed by pastoralists and government bods as 'southern do-gooders', 'shit-stirrers', or 'nigger lovers'. Riddett also recalled relations between volunteer factions as often tenuous, with pro-communist and socialist-left activists strongly influencing some discussions with their 'charged political aspect'. Riddett saw a clear clash of interests here, with rhetoric-driven propaganda of left-wing participants at odds with the 'modest aspirations of the Gurindji' to achieve their goals 'a little bit at a time'.[33] The long-term Gurindji timetable dictated no need for political avalanches.

Riddett's association with the Communist Party is unclear. ASIO compiled a small file between 1970 and 1972. An officer's report described her as a 'NSW Identity and Gurindji Supporter' living at Wattie Creek with her children in late 1971.[34] On 27 May that year Frank Hardy met with Party leader Laurie Aarons in Sydney, and an ASIO report of that bugged meeting linked Hardy and Raper (now Riddett). Aarons reportedly said 'the C.P.A. was content to let HARDY run the show', and that 'HARDY occasionally told him [Aarons] of the reports he (HARDY) was receiving from Mrs. Lyn RAPER at Wattie Creek'. In another document, Raper was acknowledged as 'a close associate of Frank HARDY'.[35]

A further ASIO file-note identified Raper and two others as the only non-Aboriginal people at Daguragu in June 1971. One was Alan Thorpe, an ABSCHOL supporter helping to build mud-brick houses. The other was Jean Culley, a nursing sister described as a 'Victorian Identity'. In a particularly tenuous link, Culley was suspected of 'feeding' information to ACTU president Bob Hawke. She had previously complained about poor water supply and the need to sink a better bore. Hawke raised this issue in the press, and the ASIO agent leapt automatically from Culley's comments to Hawke's public condemnation.[36] Detailed text within the agent's file-note indicates that he/she was a close associate (probably friend) of Raper and Thorpe. Indeed, this document is a clear example of successful ASIO infiltration into the Gurindji support network.

Alan Thorpe's experiences at Daguragu were not all positive, and his concerns were aired in print and higher places. In parliament Sam Calder MHR read an *NT News* article published on 3 December 1971, headed 'Claim Gurindjis "Political Football"'. Thorpe had provided a series of allegations to the newspaper, which Calder quoted at length. Thorpe alleged that unions and other organisations claiming to support the land rights case were, in fact, using Gurindji people for their own political gain. Here, Thorpe was biting the very hand that fed him. He revealed in the article that ten national unions had sponsored his thirty-week stay (that began in March) at Daguragu. Each union donated $150, which Thorpe said paid his wage of $50 per week. He had been appointed an honorary NAWU organiser, but unions had criticised his lack of militancy. Thorpe claimed that his wages had been suspended since the end of April, but he continued his volunteer activities for the Gurindji community. He also believed that the Aboriginal desire to acquire a 500-square-mile (1,295-square-kilometre) lease of land at Wave Hill was being sabotaged by 'southern organisations' dictating what should happen.[37]

Calder's reading of the article in parliament continued. In it, Thorpe targeted two NT identities whose Gurindji campaign contributions he believed were inappropriate. He accused NT Legislative Council member Dr Goc Letts and communist Brian Manning of completely misunderstanding the problem. Thorpe believed both men to be out of touch with the issue and living in the past. Calder sought and was granted leave to incorporate the entire article into Hansard.[38]

Observations of a neutral visitor

When Lyn Riddett departed Daguragu in 1973, her path crossed briefly with a newcomer. His recollections provide a very different version of community life, and confirm that the community was definitely no hotbed of communist subversives. Philip Nitschke lived with Gurindji people for eighteen months.[39] He was inspired to action at a Flinders University meeting (organised by engineering workshop head Don Atkinson), where Gurindji men powerfully told their story. This leg of Captain Major and Mick Rangiari's national speaking tour had brought them to the South Australian university in 1971, where Nitschke was completing his doctorate in physics. Atkinson's efforts were rewarded when more than 200 people packed into an auditorium to hear the Gurindji story. Nitschke was deeply moved by what he heard, and decided to support the people at Daguragu.

Following that meeting the university's 'post-grad' student association raised significant funds. An argument about how best to use this money was resolved when Nitschke raised his hand to go live at Daguragu. His original designated role was as the new gardener (the skills of which he was entirely deficient), but his role evolved into something entirely different.

Nitschke and his girlfriend arrived at Daguragu during the oppressive build-up to the wet season of 1973. The non-Aboriginal welcoming committee contingent comprised Lyn Raper (now Riddett) and David Quinn. Quinn had been the extremely important Gurindji community 'reader and writer' over about three years, and it is likely he took over that role from Hannah Middleton. As Nitschke quickly learnt, Raper and Quinn had established a relationship, and when he arrived they departed post-haste. The community needed an immediate replacement to fill Quinn's vital role, and Nitschke agreed. Handy practical skills were always welcomed at Daguragu, so Nitschke's job description soon incorporated those of his too, as community mechanic.

Nitschke recalled his home there. The couple lived in a bough shelter clad in corrugated iron. He remembered it as one of the fancier sheds, featuring a floor of mortared river stones. Their home was basic – rain streamed through during the wet, and the couple shared their quarters with giant cockroaches. Nitschke lived in the community for a wet, a dry and another wet. He was responsible for reading aloud correspondence that came in for the Gurindji people. He then wrote replies or initiated new correspondence. Nitschke also wrote letters on behalf of the community to newspapers. This position was clearly extremely important and potentially powerful. In the wrong hands these tasks were, indeed, vulnerable to manipulation or corruption.

Frank Hardy was obviously still a powerful personality (perhaps hero) for the community. Nitschke recalled Gurindji people constantly asking him to write to Hardy, requesting his return. He remembered writing 'hundreds of letters' to Hardy, who did not visit during the eighteen months Nitschke was there. Indeed, Hardy rarely replied, but the few letters he did write were read out to the captivated community.

Nitschke's role was financed by the community's Murramulla Gurindji Company. This organisation was based in Darwin, where the finances were administered. Money donated to the new community by organisations such as unions was allocated through the company to expense areas. Nitschke often found this process frustrating, with funds strictly tied to budget allocations, and no flexibility to shift monies about. Fencing money, for example, could not be channelled into health care or education.

The political environment (or lack of) at Daguragu during this period is particularly pertinent. According to Nitschke, there was no evidence of activity by any political group. He was not a member of a political body so, in theory, was a prime candidate to be wooed by communists. But at no time does he recall any communist presence in the community, nor was he ever contacted by the Party. He recalled that people floating in and out tended to be attached to organisations such as ABSCHOL. Jean Culley (the freelance nurse practitioner of ASIO 'interest' mentioned earlier) was still coming into the community for extended periods. She was not a government worker, but rather travelled independently from Victoria, providing an alternative health service for Gurindji people. Communist Hannah Middleton also visited during Nitschke's time there, as an anthropologist and not agitator.

Nitschke recalled that by the time he left Daguragu (after eighteen months) the community was well organised. It had registered its own brand – 'GDT' – and all cattle were branded accordingly. Ten Aboriginal stockmen were employed, and the water bore was clean and efficient. Nitschke returned briefly to Adelaide, before moving to Melbourne to work as a tram conductor. He later qualified as a medical doctor and is now a leading advocate for euthanasia. He returned to Daguragu in 2006 for celebrations marking the fortieth anniversary of the walk-off, and plans to attend the fiftieth.[40]

Fred Hollows

Ophthalmologist and long-time communist Fred Hollows visited Daguragu in the late 1960s. He had learnt of the grave situation up north at a Sydney public meeting, hosted by the Teachers' Federation, where Hardy spoke passionately about the Gurindji walk-off (this event stimulated Hollows' ongoing commitment to eye-disease eradication in Aboriginal communities). A week later Hollows examined Gurindji visitors to Sydney, Vincent Lingiari and Donald Nangiari. He discovered both men had major eye diseases. Hollows was offered (and immediately accepted) an invitation to travel to Daguragu with the men. There, he examined around thirty men with a range of eye conditions. It was then that he witnessed the ravages of 'trachoma' in very concentrated numbers for the first time:

> It was a shock to me...It was like something out of the medical history books – eye diseases of a kind and degree that hadn't been seen in western society for generations! The neglect this implied, the suffering and wasted quality of human life were appalling.

Trachoma is a disease affecting the mucous membrane lining the inside of the eyelids and the front of the eyeball (except the cornea). If left untreated, trachoma can lead to blindness. Hollows demanded that the government send doctors to Daguragu. One doctor was provided, and he refused to consult with Gurindji patients unless they attended the Wave Hill Station clinic. Hollows described health care being used as a lever to force people back to the station. He noted the Gurindji reaction to the aggressive, uncaring medic:

> When someone starts shouting at a Gurindji he just turns away, and that's what they did then – quietly turned their backs on this fucking idiot and left him there talking to himself.

Hollows examined 150 Gurindji people. He found 'the amount of disease you'd need to look at a million and a half whites to discover'.[41]

Back in Sydney, Hollows and his wife were visited by ASIO men. Hollows was livid: 'I hadn't incited rebellion or anything, and here they were setting the bloody ASIO dogs on me'. These experiences inspired more action, with Hollows soon helping Aboriginal activists such as Gordon Briscoe, Shirley 'Mumshirl' Smith and Gary Foley to establish Redfern Aboriginal Medical Service (where he later worked). His next recognisance trip to Bourke (in remote north-west NSW) revealed trachoma among the entire Aboriginal population, including children. But he did not identify one case of the disease in Bourke's white population.[42] Hollows instigated a trial of treatment at an Aboriginal settlement named Ergonnia, near Bourke. His later Australia-wide trachoma program was based upon the lessons of that initial trial.

∞

Hollows first learned about the Gurindji situation during that speech by Frank Hardy. The chapter concludes with closer scrutiny of this important participant in the Gurindji campaign.

Frank Hardy

Hardy's participation at the first public NTCAR meeting in July 1966 epitomised his keen interest in Aboriginal rights. But this was by no means the communist's first foray into that political campaign. In 1952 the *Tribune* published Hardy's commentary about racial discrimination. This took the form of a short story examining the obstacles for a young Aboriginal man travelling to the Berlin Youth Festival. In Hardy's narrative, the Party funded the fictitious trip. His story contrasted the young man's warm welcome in Germany and the USSR with Australia's cold indifference and rejection. Once back home, Hardy's Aboriginal character toured trade union meetings, proudly pleading for collaboration between black and white to overcome imperialist and capitalist oppressors.[43]

This short piece of Hardy's fiction is important. It clearly identifies his commitment as a communist activist for Aboriginal rights. In 1952 Hardy was fully immersed in Party rhetoric and utopian ideals (he joined the Party in 1939), and his outrage about Aboriginal conditions was obvious. Another well-known communist, Katharine Susannah Prichard, wrote a letter endorsing Hardy's 1955 federal election candidacy. She identified his intense belief in communism as the hallmark of this 'courageous and honest man'. Prichard and Hardy shared the view that communism stood 'first and foremost...for the welfare of the Australian people'.[44]

Hardy's biographer (Jenny Hocking) identified him as the facilitator of mainstream media coverage about the Gurindji walk-off. She credited his many newspaper articles and *The Unlucky Australians* with 'catapulting' the story and wider discussion about land rights 'to the forefront of white urban consideration'. Hocking described him as 'pivotal...as the bridge through which the struggle could be conveyed'.[45]

But it seems Hardy was damned if he did and damned if he didn't. Some communists viewed *The Unlucky Australians* as unfair criticism of Party attitudes to the Gurindji situation. Hocking identified Hardy's 'sincerity...motivation and his self-proclaimed secondary agency' as 'stridently questioned' by the Party. She contended that some Aboriginal activists also viewed the roles of communists such as Hardy as 'unfortunate and damaging to the likely success of the claim'.[46]

Not surprisingly, *The Unlucky Australians* was well received by the *Tribune*. It validated Hardy's compelling first-hand prose:

> After all, Hardy was there. He ate, talked and slept with the Gurindji and was gripped by them. He travelled up and down, a man of few means, battled around and did much to unroll the public campaign...and he is still setting a tireless example, writing, speaking and demonstrating for them and teaching young people about them...Being a communist has basically prepared him for it.[47]

Hokari echoed this sentiment, describing Hardy's book 'the most significant report' of the walk-offs. Having lived within the Daguragu community, Hokari fully appreciated the insightful value of Hardy's personal relationships with Aboriginal people. He also lauded Hardy's 'restraint' in 'conscientiously resisting paternalism'. For Hokari, the book was a valuable first-hand documentary of events. Hokari did, however, make it very clear that *The Unlucky Australians* was not the definitive account of the walk-offs, as the circumstances prior to (and after the walk-off) will continue to be told in different ways. According to Hokari, Hardy's version was one of many valid perspectives.[48]

Hardy's publicity of the Gurindji situation was significantly hindered in June 1968. The Australian Broadcasting Commission (ABC) took the bold step of banning his appearance on a radio program called *People*. Hardy had been invited to discuss *The Unlucky Australians*, after appearing on the television version of the program discussing the book. The *Tribune* reported ABC's general manager cancelling Hardy's appearance 'at the last minute', because 'powerful pastoral interests' wanting any land claims to disappear had 'strong support within the Gorton Government'. Hardy was reported to say:

> I have no basic quarrel with the ABC, which retains the services of some outstanding Australians. However, it is self-evident that the ban on my radio interview was not unconnected with the controversy raging in Canberra about the land claim.[49]

Indeed, a week earlier Hardy's ABC track record had been discussed in parliament. Labor member Samuel Benson asked Minister for Aboriginal Affairs Wentworth whether accusations about the Gurindji situation made by Hardy during the television interview with presenter Bob Sanders had any substance. Wentworth acknowledged there were problems, but insisted that government programs were making things better. Hardy's radio ban came only a few days after this parliamentary discussion, thus explaining the *Tribune*'s reference to his tenuous relationship with the Gorton government.[50]

Two weeks later, the *Tribune* featured an important photograph. Gurindji men and Hardy stood proudly and defiantly behind a new sign announcing their 'GURINDJI Mining Lease AND Cattle Station' [original capitalisation]. At a Sydney public meeting, Hardy urged greater union involvement with the struggle, and leadership by example. Attendees decisively endorsed a resolution supporting land rights and compensation.[51]

The *Tribune*'s coverage of Hardy's speech invoked harsh response to the editor from one union official attendee. Jack Mundey (NSW Builders' Labourers' Federation secretary) berated Hardy's 'imbalance' at the meeting:

> ...I believe that instead of lashing all white unionists and sneeringly making remarks about our racist tendencies, Mr

Hardy would be better served acknowledging the fact that there is a growing consciousness amongst the Australian people for full and equal rights for our first people, and unions are playing a part.[52]

He argued that 'metropolitan unions' were leading the way supporting Aboriginal rights, referring to the many union publications, journals and documents regularly circulated to city and country members promoting Aboriginal issues. Another reader wrote to the *Tribune*'s editor in similar fashion. Ray Clarke noted that 'many trade unionists who attended the meeting were seriously disturbed by some of [Hardy's] one-sided views'. Clarke thought Hardy's position was that all Australians were racist, and guilt for Aboriginal circumstances therefore rested with all Australians. He quoted Hardy's comment that the 'great white father trade unions' had done nothing to assist rights campaigns. Clarke emphasised that the meeting where Hardy rudely castigated the union movement had, in fact, been organised and sponsored by fourteen prominent unions, and chaired by prominent Aboriginal unionist Ray Peckham. He highlighted Hardy's failure to even mention the significant and ongoing union support for NT Aboriginal workers who had walked off.[53]

During an interview in 1993, Hardy was asked about his commitment to Aboriginal rights. He clarified his position and motives:

Something was very simple for me. Stand with the betrayed. Stand with the dispossessed. The utterly dispossessed. The black against the white…In fact, it was my disenchantment and sense of betrayal and to reach down to those who had not been involved in this Stalin thing, but who had been oppressed by this system to a degree that every white Australian should still be ashamed that they have let it happen.[54]

Criticisms from communist comrades, union heavies and Black Power activists had failed to dampen his enthusiasm and commitment to Aboriginal rights. Hocking believed that Hardy's writing transcended his politics as he publicised the realities of life up north. She believed *The Unlucky Australians* enhanced the credibility of the Wave Hill Aboriginal struggle because the storyteller was a known and respected writer (a 1969 film version of the book was released by a British television company in 1974, but has never been screened in Australia).[55] But as (expelled) communist and filmmaker Cecil Holmes pointed out, *The Unlucky Australians* was a flop at the bookshop. Holmes revealed Hardy's thoughts about its failure to sell: 'He remarked to me bitterly that white Australians don't want to know about their shame'.[56]

Reviews for Hardy's book were not all glowing. Donald Denoon, a Ugandan visitor to Australia in 1968, regarded *The Unlucky Australians* as a condescending white interpretation of a

Brian Manning took this photo of Frank Hardy – 'he was intrigued to see a disused train stop at Stapleton near Adelaide River...I took a shot of him there'. (Brian Manning, personal communication to author, 17 September 2012.)

story best told by Aboriginal people. Denoon considered Hardy's motivations largely self-absorbed and paternalistic, and believed he used the Gurindji people to embark on a rant about racism in Australia.[57] In his PhD thesis, Bernie Bryan noted people who disputed Hardy's factual accuracies in the book. He argued that some Darwin communists had 'complained of its inaccuracies', and identified that Paddy Carroll's wife described it as 'lies from start to finish'. However, Brian Manning believed otherwise, stating that Hardy's account in *The Unlucky Australians* was 'spot on'.[58]

Hardy's love-hate relationship with the Communist Party endured. Hocking argued that the seeds of doubt about the utopian claims of communism had been planted during his Soviet Union visit in 1951. His 1968 articles about disillusionment with the Party were perhaps cathartic, or ways of 'coming clean', about his doubts and regrets. Hardy was, however, to pay the price for his comments. By making public his disenchantment with the Soviets, Hardy destroyed his relationship with the Party and many comrades forever.[59]

Frank Hardy died in Melbourne on 28 January 1994. His coffin was adorned with the Aboriginal and Eureka flags. Many people from all walks of life attended the funeral. However, despite such long association with the Party, no ex–Communist Party comrades spoke a eulogy for him. He was however honoured by Daguragu elder Mick Rangiari, whose words indicated warm regard and honour for the white man and his solidarity with the Gurindji community all those years ago:

> To dear Frank Hardy,
> Frank Hardy old friend you have gone away
> We share with friends and family the sorrow, grief and pain
> The passing happened so suddenly in your home far away from
>   here

We the Gurindji tribe write this especially for you
In our hearts you are alive
From us here at Daguragu
To the family and friends of Frank Hardy today
We the Gurindji share with you
To us he was the first link up to the outside world
He gave us his support in our struggle for wage and food in
    1966
He made many friends among our people
And will be remembered always
As you know old man we have what we all fought for now
And thank you to our dear friend
You will be sadly missed
From all your friends out at Daguragu and Kalkaringi[60]

Conclusion

When Frank Hardy died in 1994, the radical world he had known so intimately had changed significantly. The Cold War had ended with collapse of the Soviet Union, culminating with its dissolution in 1991. The pursuit of Aboriginal land rights had moved into a very different arena in 1992, when the long-fought-for Mabo decision in the High Court created the key precedent facilitating claims for land on the basis of native title. The consequent National Native Title Tribunal was established a year later. These advancements contrast so vividly with the immediate post–World War II period, when Pilbara people needed to fight so hard just to achieve a basic human right like equal pay, or even pay at all. But from then on, possibilities of land rights moved closer as campaigns became bigger and more widely known. Contributions of left-wing activists such as Hardy greatly enhanced the positive steps that Australia's Aboriginal rights movement would continue to take.

Conclusion

Supporters of the Aboriginal community at Daguragu (discussed in the previous chapter) represented a broad cross-section of the Australian community. Commitment to reform united them in common cause. This group of purposeful visitors mirrored the wider diversity of people campaigning for Aboriginal rights in the Pilbara and central desert region decades earlier. Left-wing activists fought doggedly alongside a fascinating mix of groups and individuals from all over Australia. Unionists and communists campaigned in tandem with pacifists, feminists and Christians. Also active in this movement were anthropologists, scientists, artists, writers, musicians and students. These activists employed an array of tactics. They marched, penned letters and articles, appealed to governments and international bodies, produced films, organised demonstrations and protest actions, lived and worked in Aboriginal communities, broke laws and got arrested, raised money, and more generally, committed enormous time and resources to the cause.

The objective here was not to focus upon the three Aboriginal rights campaigns in minute detail, but rather to create a more expansive and creative picture of activism over time. Thus, the period of investigation (ranging from 1946 until the early 1970s) resulted in a somewhat longitudinal examination. This work also featured the intentional incorporation of a range of artistic representation of activist thought. Communists, in particular, were a quirkily creative group and their art and writing has added wonderful colour and vitality to this study. This aspect of activism has been usually omitted from relevant scholarship. Its inclusion here is timely.

It is important to acknowledge that the campaigns under scrutiny occurred during an exceptional period in Australian political history. Between 1941 and 1949, the country was governed by a most progressive Labor Party. This left-wing triumph occurred at a time when union power was at its zenith. The union movement's rise to its greatest level of strength (following the end of World War II) coincided with growth of the wider Aboriginal rights movement. The fact that these advancements were contemporaneous helps to explain the solidarity so often displayed by left-wing activists for Aboriginal reform. The key issues became increasingly prominent, with mounting pressure upon governments and pastoralists from this eclectic protest body. The union movement and Communist Party (with often overlapping memberships) presented a formidable activist front for the campaigns. Communist membership was also at its highest at the end of the war, and sheer numbers exerted considerable influence in the union movement. This was a period when Marxism remained a powerful influence upon intellectuals, and Stalin was still an admired popular leader. Communists continued to ride a wave of euphoria following Red Army triumphs during the war, and were enthusiastically leading the vanguard with high hopes of revolution. And despite the onset of the Cold War after 1947, there were still large numbers in the wider community willing to work with communists, and not frightened off by growing criticism of public collaborations. These shifting coalitions continued to be important right up to the 1960s when the central focus of campaigns moved from broader human rights to land-centric campaigns for Aboriginal people, as the rights movement evolved from one being driven by white to one orchestrated by black.

Another important feature of the period examined here was the growing demands by Aboriginal people for self-determination. With the rising body of research focused upon the Aboriginal-resistance political movement has come a much better understanding and appreciation of the path to that ultimate goal.[1] From the late 1930s, Aboriginal people had gradually assumed increasing levels of responsibility for their own cause. In 1936, Torres Strait Islanders organised their own maritime strike, and Yorta Yorta people walked away from Cumeragunja Mission on the Murray River in 1939, epitomising this changing political landscape. Pioneer Aboriginal activists such as William Cooper, Jack Patten, Pearl Gibbs, Herbert Groves, Bill Onus and Bill Ferguson devoted enormous time and energy during this period in the cause of advancement and consolidation.

These internal developments need to be placed alongside the even greater changes that were taking place internationally. The period of investigation featured landmark examples of indigenous policy advancement and decolonisation at a global level. In August 1941 one goal of the Atlantic Treaty charter (for the post-war environment) between Britain and the United States declared that self-government be restored to peoples deprived of this right. This development was widely reported in Australia, and with the end of the war, demands for self-determination grew rapidly. Each step in Aboriginal advancement was mirrored in the deep wave of decolonisation. This prominent, articulated goal heightened hopes in colonised countries that self-determination (as a concept now supported by the world's two political powerhouses) was achievable. The Philippines, for example, achieved final independence from the United States in 1946. And India's struggle for independence from British rule culminated with partition into two states in 1947 (as Pilbara people in Australia were entering the second year of their own campaign for rights and recognition). Aboriginal advancement proceeded as colonised peoples in Asia and Africa gradually regained their own rights to land and liberty. The process of decolonisation occurring during the period investigated in this book accelerated much faster than anyone had anticipated, and these changes were crucially reinforced by the widely endorsed international conventions being established during the same period by the UN. Of particular importance to Australia were the great human rights documents established at this time, including the Universal Declaration of Human Rights in 1948 and draft International Covenants on Human Rights in 1961. The ILO was also a major player, taking up the cause of Aboriginal rights at an international level.

What happened in Australia during those remarkable decades was greatly influenced by these progressive international developments. The slow but persistent development of State-based Aboriginal rights organisations was consolidated with the establishment of the Federal Council for Aboriginal Advancement (later FCAATSI) in 1958. This development was stimulated by the understanding that only a national body could be accredited to appear before committees at the UN. Prominent activist Lady Jessie Street was particularly aware of the importance of appearing before these committees. International influences affecting the development of Australia's Aboriginal rights movement were clearly evident in the national body's policy development. For example, the highly influential ideas of Street and Mary Bennett were, in turn, strongly influenced by ideas inherent in the UDHR, ILO Convention 107 and the London Anti-Slavery Society. It is also important to note another international aspect of particular relevance here. As FCAATSI went about its business, the pervasiveness of the Cold War shadowed much of its activities, with suspicions cast upon its communist members, and relentless government surveillance so very evident in the copious ASIO files we can now access.

These were dramas in which it was possible to view developments in the starkest terms as black and white. Radical activists viewed employers and government officials as cruel and inhumane controllers of Aboriginal lives. The opponents of these activists had an even more distorted view of the radicals. These perceptions produced situations where protagonists held highly dramatic views of each other. Indeed, the wide range of people focused upon in this book was regarded as heroes and villains, depending upon the point of view of the observer. That is, Aboriginal rights in the Pilbara, central deserts and northern Australia had been callously disregarded and abused by paternalistic 'villains' – pastoralists, governments and officials. Left-wing activists, as the 'heroes', orchestrated formidable campaigns in support of Aboriginal people.

This robust support ensured the continuation of campaigns, particularly in the Pilbara and Northern Territory. The scale of left-wing support varied according to the nature of the issues, but the pastoral disputes are distinctly comparable in terms of direct assistance the Aboriginal people received. Given that the Pilbara and Gurindji peoples moved from pastoral stations to camps and then established brand new communities, immediate support in terms of donated money, food and equipment was vital. In both of these cases, the evidence clearly shows that donations from communist and unionist bodies (in cash and kind) enabled the Aboriginal groups to maintain their solidarity in the face of mounting pressures from pastoralists and governments. And in both cases, no evidence has been located to indicate that Aboriginal workers and their families were forced to accept these donations in return for any form of commitment to the radical left organisations. Indeed, the evidence indicates that the arrangements were based on a much simpler premise: Aboriginal people needed to eat and be housed, and the 'different white people' acted to meet those needs.

Left-wing activists supporting the three campaigns were joined by numerous influential advocates. Among the most prominent were Lady Jessie Street and Presbyterian Church moderator in South Australia, Charles Duguid. Other well-known individuals joined forces with left and right to fight for Aboriginal advancement. Some of the more visible activists involved in the campaigns investigated in this book forged (or reinforced) their credentials as staunch advocates for Aboriginal rights. They included writers such as Dorothy Hewett, Katharine Susannah Prichard and Frank Hardy. Other notable activists were Donald Thomson, Alex Jolly, Fred Rose, Doris Blackburn, Noel Counihan, Stan Davey, Fred Hollows, Philip Nitschke and Ted Egan. High profile overseas visitors such as communist Paul Robeson and musical trio 'Peter, Paul and Mary' also contributed to campaigns. Their public protests often catapulted events in remote Australian regions into the international spotlight. And several of the participants transferred their experiences into scholarship, including Hannah Middleton and Lyn Riddett.

I have found one aspect of this research project to be particularly compelling and constant. Radical left support for Aboriginal rights during the campaigns involved an exceptional generation of Australian activists. Communists (in particular) maintained resolute determination to improve Aboriginal people's lives. Aboriginal rights inspired a large number of people to do so much. Communists and unionists not only worked behind the scenes during campaigns, but also devoted their own time and money by travelling to Aboriginal communities and helping out. That support endured despite immense Cold War pressures that contributed to a drastic reduction of Communist Party members. Even during the 1960s, when the Vietnam War presented such a strong competitor for limited activist energy, communists and unionists maintained an effective and united campaign for the new community at Daguragu.

Australian government security operatives closely observed left-wing activists during the three campaigns. In an ironic twist, although surveillance was undoubtedly irritating for those activists at the time, this relentless gathering of evidence by security officers and spies has proven invaluable here, with materials generated by ASIO (and its predecessors) greatly enhancing accounts in this book. Security files are a treasure trove of fine detail about people's movements, government responses, protest actions and activist strategies. They also contain government and private documents that have proven difficult to source elsewhere. These security files have facilitated much richer interpretation of the campaigns, and are recommended as extremely useful (although often painstakingly tedious) research tools.

Interpretations of left-wing motivations have varied widely. A diverse array of communist, unionist, government and security organisation documentation identified over the course of this research has offered a variety of possible explanations. As far as the government and its security organisations were concerned, most left-wing activities were a manifestation of deep ideological commitment to the cause of revolution. Officials and spies were convinced that Aboriginal people caught up in worker and human rights disputes would become easy targets to indoctrinate, to incite to industrial mayhem and civil disobedience, and to recruit to the dark forces of communism and unionism. Governments and agencies placed very little (if any) credence on the possibility that left-wing supporters of Aboriginal rights acted on any other basis. The overwhelming impression given by the vast literature of security organisations was that little, if any, credence was given to humanitarian motives. Thus, there was a lack of deeper understanding about what drove these associations to act. In philosophical terms, communists saw the Aboriginal peoples in two ways. Firstly, there was long recognition that they were a national minority deserving self-determination. Secondly (particularly during the pastoral disputes), Aboriginal peoples were viewed as victims of international capitalist oppression. Communists believed that they were working to improve the world, and the cause of Aboriginal rights fitted neatly into two of their ideological positions.

There is also a more plausible explanation about left-wing motivation. The evidence suggests that radical activism can be interpreted in much more human terms, minus the need to invoke conspiracy theories or political imperatives. Communists and unionists fought tenaciously for Aboriginal rights, and this unwavering support manifested in a wide range of protest and support activities. Motivation to help was driven, in large part, by humanitarian desire to improve Aboriginal life in Australia. Notwithstanding that these radical activists were influenced by such hard-line political philosophies, their actions were motivated by humanitarian concern and a need to create optimum conditions for change. Don McLeod and Brian Manning epitomise this mentality, whereby their relentless work within Aboriginal communities grew into close and long-standing personal relationships with the people they were there to help. Indeed, Don McLeod's humanitarian concern is by far the most conspicuous aspect of his activism for Pilbara people.

Moreover, the radical activists identified throughout this work shared many characteristics. The ones in the frontline such as McLeod, Manning or Hardy devoted enormous energy and time to the campaigns. Their commitment was ongoing and, in the case of Brian Manning, continued until he passed away in 2013. Their endeavours were heartily supported in material ways by the left-wing movements concentrated in the eastern states, which included many individuals who donated money and goods to peoples they were never likely to meet or culturally understand. The efforts of people peripheral to this study such as Doris Blackburn and Jessie Street featured over and over again in the left-wing press and archival materials, epitomising the kinds of people who embraced this movement and committed long-term to the cause. While I am sure that, as with any activist movement, some supporters came and went with varying levels of commitment, it is clear that the leading left-wing participants in these rights campaigns were fiercely dedicated to the cause. This is evidenced by the high number who continued in supportive roles as organisations like FCAATSI were established and flourished.

∞

In this book, left-wing supporters of Aboriginal rights – the 'different white people' – have been promoted into prominence within the wider story about Australia's evolving rights movement. For Australia to reach some form of conciliation with its original peoples, it is imperative that the broader narrative of interaction between black and white incorporate more optimistic accounts of the history. This book is my attempt to do just that. The bleak and disturbing genesis of this colonial relationship must never be omitted, but in order to move forward, the focus needs to shift. And in the case of this book, a new look at the support of radical activists for the rights of Aboriginal people is added to the literature as a positive example of this change.

NOTES

Notes to the Introduction

1 D. Wilson, 'Whitefellas telling blackfella stories: musical messages of non-indigenous Australia 1945–1990', Honours thesis, University of Tasmania, 2008.

2 Australian Building Construction Employees' and Builders' Labourers' Federation, *Builders' Labourers' Song Book*, Widescope, Melbourne, 1975.

3 D. Wilson, 'Different White People: communists, unionists and Aboriginal rights, 1946–1972', PhD thesis, University of Tasmania, 2013.

Notes to Chapter One

1 H. Brody, *The Other Side of Eden: Hunters, Gatherers and the Shaping of the World*, North Point Press, New York, 2000, pp. 27, 133–41, 196–7.

2 H. Reynolds, *The Law of the Land*, Penguin, Melbourne, 2003, p. 248; H. Reynolds, *The Other Side of the Frontier: Aboriginal Resistance to the European Invasion of Australia*, Penguin, Melbourne, 1995, pp. 42–5.

3 N. J. B. Plomley (ed.), *Friendly Mission: The Tasmanian Journals and Papers of George Augustus Robinson 1829–1934*, Tasmanian Historical Research Association, Hobart, 1966; *Jorgen Jorgensen and the Aborigines of Van Diemen's Land*, Blubber Head Press, Hobart, 1991.

4 H. Reynolds, *This Whispering In Our Hearts*, Allen & Unwin, Sydney, 1998.

5 M. Lake, 'White man's country: the trans-national history of a national project', *Australian Historical Studies*, vol. 34, 2003, pp. 346–63.

6 H. Reynolds, *Nowhere People*, Penguin, Camberwell, Victoria, 2005, pp. 16–22; *This Whispering In Our Hearts*, pp. 22–9; L. Ryan, *The Aboriginal Tasmanians*, Allen & Unwin, Sydney, 1996, p. 85.

7 H. Reynolds, *Dispossession: Black Australians and White Invaders*, Allen & Unwin, Sydney, 1989, pp. 76, 183; *The Law of the Land*, pp. 99–110.

8 Reynolds, *Dispossession*, pp. 205–6; *Nowhere People*, pp. 18–32.

9 Lake, 'White man's country', pp. 352–3; Reynolds, *Nowhere People*, pp. 115–29.

10 Lake, 'White man's country', pp. 354–5; M. Lake & H. Reynolds, *Drawing the Colour Line: White Men's Countries and the Question of Racial Equality*, Melbourne University Publishing, 2008, pp. 138, 159; J. Martinez, 'Plural Australia: Aboriginal and Asian labour in tropical White Australia, Darwin, 1911–1940', PhD thesis, Wollongong University, 1999, pp. 68–82.

11 K. Blackburn, 'White agitation for an Aboriginal state in Australia (1925–1929)', *The Australian Journal of Politics and History*, vol. 45, no. 2, 1999, pp. 157–80; S. Taffe, *Black and White Together: FCAATSI: The Federal Council for the Advancement of Aborigines and Torres Strait Islanders 1958–1973*, UQ Press, Brisbane, 2005, p. 4. See also B. Attwood & A. Markus, *Thinking Black: William Cooper and the Australian Aborigines' League*, Aboriginal Studies Press, Canberra, 2004; J. Maynard, *Fight for Liberty and Freedom: The Origins of Australian Aboriginal Activism*, Aboriginal Studies Press, Canberra, 2007.

12 G. Gray, *A Cautious Silence: The Politics of Australian Anthropology*, Aboriginal Studies Press, Canberra, 2007, pp. 1–13.

13 R. M. Berndt & C. H. Berndt, 'A.P. Elkin – the man and the anthropologist', in R. M. Berndt & C. H. Berndt (eds.), *Aboriginal Man in Australia: Essays in Honour of Emeritus Professor A.P. Elkin*, Angus & Robertson, Sydney, 1965, p. 14.

14 See, for example, D. Thomson, *Donald Thomson in Arnhem Land*, The Miegunyah Press, Melbourne, 2006.

15 J. Pickering, 'Stirring burden of our song', in N. Brown et al (eds.), *One Hand on the Manuscript: Music in Australian Cultural History 1930–1960*, ANU, Canberra, 1995, p. 156; D. Symons, 'The Jindyworobak connection in Australian music, c. 1940–1960', *Context*, issue 23, 2002, pp. 33–47.

16 Lake & Reynolds, *Drawing the Colour Line*, pp. 291–3, 297–301.

17 ILO, *Conventions and Regulations: Adopted by the International Labour Conference 1919–1966*, International Labour Office, Geneva, 1966, particularly pp. 301–9, 421–34.

18 J. Elton, 'Comrades or competition? Union relations with Aboriginal workers in the South Australian and Northern Territory pastoral industries, 1878–1957', PhD thesis, Flinders University, Adelaide, 2007, p. 106; *Workers' Weekly*, 16 May 1930, p. 5.

19 Elton, 'Comrades or competition?', p. 364; A. Markus, 'Talka longa mouth: Aborigines and the labour movement 1890–1970', *Labour History*, no. 35, 1978 [edition titled 'Who are our enemies? Racism and the Australian working class', edited by A. Curthoys & A. Markus], pp. 141–4.

20 T. Wright, *New Deal for the Aborigines*, Forward Press, Sydney, 1939.

21 S. Macintyre, *The Reds: The Communist Party of Australia From Origins to Illegality*, Allen & Unwin, St Leonards, 1998, p. 266. See also J. Marcus, 'The beauty, simplicity and honour of truth: Olive Pink in the 1940s', in J. Marcus (ed.), *First in Their Field: Women and Australian Anthropology*, Melbourne University Press, Melbourne, 1993, pp. 133–4.

22 *Tribune*, 23 April 1940, p. 4.

23 Wright, *New Deal for the Aborigines*, pp. 10–12.

24   M. Hearn & H. Knowles, *One Big Union: A History of the Australian Workers' Union 1886–1994*, Cambridge University Press, Melbourne, 1996, pp. 207–10; Elton, 'Comrades or competition?', chapters 7 & 8.

25   D. May, *Aboriginal Labour and the Cattle Industry: Queensland from White Settlement to the Present*, Cambridge University Press, Melbourne, 1994, pp. 160–2.

26   Elton, 'Comrades or competition?', p. 368.

27   Macintyre, *The Reds*, pp. 4, 14.

28   Macintyre, *The Reds*, pp. 144–255.

29   Macintyre, *The Reds*, pp. 288–351.

30   Macintyre, *The Reds*, p. 52.

31   *Australian Communist*, 18 March 1921, p. 2.

32   J. Stalin, 'Concerning the presentation of the national question', *Pravda*, 2 May 1921, in J. Stalin, *Marxism and the National-Colonial Question: A Collection of Articles and Speeches*, Proletarian Publishers, San Francisco, 1975 [originally published in 1934], p. 171.

33   J. Stalin, 'The national question', extract from 'The foundations of Leninism: in a series of lectures on the foundations of Leninism delivered at the Sverdlov University', April 1924, in Stalin, *Marxism and the National-Colonial Question*, pp. 282–6.

34   '"Advance Australia Fair": the black slaves in the Northern Territory', *Communist*, 26 January 1923, p. 1.

35   Good examples of these articles include: *Workers' Weekly*, 1 July, 1927, p. 4; *Workers' Weekly*, 9 December, 1927, p. 3; *Workers' Weekly*, 13 April, 1928, p. 4.

36   *Workers' Weekly*, 23 November 1928, p. 1.

37   R. de Costa, *A Higher Authority: Indigenous Transnationalism and Australia*, UNSW Press, Sydney, 2006, p. 51.

38   *Workers' Weekly*, 24 September 1931, p. 2.

39   *Workers' Weekly*, 9 October 1931, p. 4.

40   ibid.

41   *Workers' Weekly*, 2 September, 1932, p. 2. Similar pro-Soviet rhetoric in article on 9 June 1933, p. 3.

42   *Workers' Weekly*, 13 October 1933, p. 3.

43   *Workers' Weekly*, 3 August 1934, p. 3.

44   *Workers' Weekly*, 4 January 1938, p. 4. Similar rhetoric in article on 19 August 1938, with an Eskimo 'in charge of a wireless station at Wrangel Island' cited as proof of successful Soviet policy.

45   M. Lynch, *Stalin and Khrushchev: the USSR, 1924–64*, Hodder & Stoughton, London, 1990, pp. 52–6.

46   B. Nahaylo & V. Swoboda, *Soviet Disunion: A History of the Nationalities Problem in the USSR*, Hamish Hamilton, London, 1990.

47   D. Hewett, 'The Hidden Journey', in *Windmill Country*, Overland (in conjunction with Peter Leyden Publishing House), Melbourne, 1968, pp. 71–5.

48   J. Hocking, *Frank Hardy: Politics, Literature, Life*, Lothian, Melbourne, 2005, p. 182.

49   R. Gollan, *Revolutionaries and Reformists: Communism and the Australian Labour Movement, 1920–1955*, Allen & Unwin, Canberra, 1975, p. 171.

50   F. Hardy, 'The heirs of Stalin', *Sunday Times*, 8 December 1968, p. 13.

51   Lynch, *Stalin and Khrushchev*, pp. 99–100, 113–14.

52   A. Davidson, *The Communist Party of Australia: A Short History*, Hoover Institution Press, Stanford, 1969, pp. 83–4, 108, 126–8; Gollan, *Revolutionaries and Reformists*, p. 130.

53   N. Cowper, 'Action against communism', *Australian Quarterly*, vol. 22, no. 1, 1950, pp. 5–12.

54   S. Alomes, M. Dober & D. Hellier, 'The social context of postwar conservatism', in A. Curthoys & J. Merritt (eds.), *Australia's First Cold War 1945–1953*, Allen & Unwin, Sydney, 1984, pp. 10–11.

55   Davidson, *The Communist Party of Australia*, pp. 112–18, 147–59. See also A. B. Davidson, 'The effects of the Sino-Soviet dispute on the Australian Communist Party', *Australian Quarterly*, vol. 36, no. 3, 1964, pp. 56–68.

56   Lake & Reynolds, *Drawing the Global Colour Line*, pp. 335–56.

57   A. Devereux, *Australia and the Birth of the International Bill of Human Rights 1946–1966*, Federation Press, Sydney, 2005, p. 73.

58   Devereux, *Australia and the Birth of the International Bill of Human Rights*, pp. 74–5, 132–3.

Notes to Chapter Two

1   D. Hewett, interviewed on ABC Radio National's 'Hindsight' series [entitled 'Blackfellers' Eureka'] in July 1995, in B. Bunbury, *It's Not The Money It's The Land: Aboriginal Stockmen and the Equal Wages Case*, Fremantle Arts Centre Press, 2002, p. 53.

2   D. Hewett, in preface to M. Brown's *The Black Eureka*, Australasian Book Society, Sydney, 1976.

3   Understanding of language groups in the Pilbara varies. Katrin Wilson (who conducted field studies with husband John during the 1950s and 1960s) believed there were 'thirteen different tribal groups' of desert and coastal people in the Pilbara region – 'Pindan: a preliminary comment', in A. P. Pilling & R. A. Waterman (eds.), *Diprotodon to Detribalization: Studies of Change Among Australian Aborigines*, Michigan State University Press, Michigan, 1970, p. 333. However, in 2010 the Pilbara Aboriginal Language Centre identified twenty-six languages – see Wangka Maya Pilbara Aboriginal Centre, <http://www.wangkamaya.org.au>.

4   B. Love, 'Communist Party industrial activity in the post-war years 1945–1953 in Western Australia', *Papers in Labour History*, no. 17, 1996, pp. 19–45; B. Simons, *Communism in Australia: A Supplementary Resource Bibliography, c. 1994–2001*, Australian Society for the Study of Labour History, Sydney, 2002, p. 7 (this publication updated her earlier 1994 bibliography). The Party records are held in Battye Library's Cameron Collection.

5   See, for example: J. Armstrong, 'On the freedom track to Narawunda: the Pilbara Aboriginal pastoral workers' strike, 1946–1998', *Studies in Western Australian History*, no. 22, 2001, pp. 23–40; P. Biskup, *Not Slaves, Not Citizens: The Aboriginal Problem in Western Australia 1898–1954*, UQP, St Lucia, Queensland, 1973; Brown, *The Black Eureka*; L. Davies, 'Protecting natives?: the law and the 1946 Aboriginal pastoral workers' strike', *Papers in Labour History*, 1988, pp. 31–43; D. W. McLeod, *How the West Was Lost: The Native Question in the Development of Western Australia*, D. W. McLeod, Port Hedland, 1984; D. Stuart, *Yandy*, Georgian House, Melbourne, 1959; J. Wilson, 'Authority and leadership in a "new style" Australian Aboriginal community: Pindan, Western Australia', MA Thesis, University of Western Australia, 1961.

6   Regarding legislation pertaining to Aborigines in WA pre-1946, see: Bunbury, *It's Not The Money It's The Land*, pp. 45–9; M. Hess, 'Black and red: the Pilbara pastoral workers' strike, 1946', *Aboriginal History*, vol. 18, no. 1, 1994, pp. 66–70; J. Wilson, 'The Pilbara Aboriginal social movement: an outline of its background and significance', in R. M. & C. H. Berndt, *Aborigines of the West: Their Past and Their Present*, UWA Press, Perth, 1979, pp. 152–5. Other main legislative controls were the *Aborigines Act 1905* and the *Native Administration Act 1936*.

7   Davies, 'Protecting natives?', pp. 32–3.

8   P. A. Smith, 'Station camps: legislation, labour relations and rations on pastoral leases in the Kimberley region, Western Australia', *Aboriginal History*, vol. 24, 2000, p. 80.

9   R. Fellowes Lukis, 'An interview with Robert Fellowes Lukis: Pastoral Industry in the Pilbara and North West', OH262, Battye Library, December 1977, p. 72. Lukis was lessee of Pilbara's White Springs Station (for 18 years) until 1946, before moving to Munda Station.

10   Australia, Senate & House of Representatives, vol. 187, 27 June 1946, p. 1,871. Dorothy Tangney's trip was reported in *Tribune*, 5 July 1946, p. 7.

11   *Tribune*, 24 December 1946, p. 6. The article detailed other Vestey holdings at that time, including 'Australia's largest meat monopoly, W. Angliss and Co...the largest in the British Empire, the Riverstone Meatworks, the Rockhampton Meatworks, the Redbank (Qld) meatworks, a chain of butcher shops and small goods shops, soap works, ice cream works...[and] the Blue Star Shipping Line'.

12   *Tribune*, 24 December 1946, p. 6.

13   N. Hartley, 'The Communist Party in Western Australia: selected transcripts from the seminar, 2001', *Papers in Labour History*, no. 29, 2005, p. 32.

14   Armstrong, 'On the freedom track to Narawunda', pp. 25–6; J. Hardie, *Nor'Westers of the Pilbara Breed*, Shire of Port Hedland, Port Hedland, 1981, p. 175; Fellowes Lukis, 'An interview with Robert Fellowes Lukis', pp. 70–1.

15   State Records Office of WA: 993, 4/42, in R. A. Hall, *The Black Diggers: Aborigines and Torres Strait Islanders in the Second World War*, Allen & Unwin, Sydney, 1989, p. 24.

16   Biskup, *Not Slaves, Not Citizens*, p. 211; B. Bryan, 'The Northern Territory's one big union: the rise and fall of the North Australian Workers' Union, 1911–1972', PhD thesis, NT University, Darwin, 2001, p. 217.

17   J. Read & P. Coppin, *Kangkushot: The Life of Nyamal Lawman Peter Coppin*, Aboriginal Studies Press, Canberra, 1999, p. 54; Hess, 'Black and red', pp. 66–7.

18   Hall, *The Black Diggers*, pp. 127–30. Port Hedland historian Jenny Hardie suggested the number of soldiers who 'took over' the town was actually 200 – *Nor'Westers of the Pilbara Breed*, p. 167.

19   R. M. & C. H. Berndt, *End of an Era: Aboriginal Labour in the Northern Territory*, Australian Institute of Aboriginal Studies, Canberra, 1987, p. xix.

20   Biskup, *Not Slaves, Not Citizens*, p. 204.

21   W. F. Mandle, *Going It Alone: Australia's National Identity in the Twentieth Century*, Penguin, Melbourne, 1978, pp. 174–7; K. Wilson, 'Pindan: a preliminary comment', p. 334.

22   Wilson, 'The Pilbara Aboriginal social movement', p. 155.

23   Biskup, *Not Slaves, Not Citizens*, pp. 209–11.

24   Markus, 'Talka longa mouth', p. 153.

25   Hess, 'Black and red', p. 69.

26   National Archives of Australia [hereafter NAA]: ASIO; A6119/3306, items 2&3, letters from Ridgeway to McLeod, 17 & 24 August 1945.

27   Davies, 'Protecting natives?', p. 36.

28   Brown, *The Black Eureka*, pp. 6, 114.

29   Wilson, 'The Pindan Aboriginal social movement', p. 167.

30   G. McDonald, *The Evidence: Revealing Extracts on Aboriginal 'Land Rights' From Official Communist Documents*, Veritas Publishing Company, Perth, 1983, p. 22.

31   G. Alcorn, *The Struggle of the Pilbara Station Hands for Decent Living Standards and Human Rights*, Max Brown, Sydney, 2002, p. 8 [this is a collection of notes written by Alcorn in 1952].

32   D. W. McLeod, 'Aboriginal enterprises in the Pilbara', *Westerly*, no. 2, 1957, p. 4.

33   Brown, *The Black Eureka*, particularly pp. 10, 96, 107, 122; Mandle, *Going It Alone*, pp. 172–82.

34   Davies, 'Protecting natives?', p. 34.

35   Stuart, *Yandy*.

36   McLeod, 'Aboriginal enterprises in the Pilbara', p. 5.

37   D. McLeod, *An Interview With Don McLeod: Aboriginal Land Rights in the North West*, 15 November 1978, OH331, Battye Library, Perth.

38   Brown, *The Black Eureka*, p. 96; McLeod, *How the West Was Lost*, pp. 40–1.

39   McLeod, in Bunbury, *It's Not The Money It's The Land*, pp. 49, 51.

40   McLeod, *How the West Was Lost*, pp. 40–1; Read & Coppin, *Kangkushot*, p. 55.

41   McLeod, *How the West Was Lost*, p. 41. Nullagine is 300 kilometres south-east of Port Hedland.

42   McLeod, 'Aboriginal enterprises in the Pilbara', pp. 4–7.

43   McLeod, in Bunbury, *It's Not the Money It's the Land*, p. 48.

44　Mandle, *Going It Alone*, p. 176.

45　Hall, *The Black Diggers*, p. 128.

46　Dorothy Hewett, preface in *The Black Eureka*.

47　Read & Coppin, *Kangkushot*, p. 65.

48　NAA: A8911/90, item 87, CIS report re. *Workers Star*, 5 July 1945.

49　Hess, 'Black and red', p. 70.

50　*Workers Star*, 12 April 1946, p. 1; Brown, *The Black Eureka*, pp. 114, 122. CPA membership in 1944 (in WA) was approximately 1,200–1,500 – B. Love, 'Communist Party industrial activity', p. 40.

51　Brown, *The Black Eureka*, p. 124.

52　McLeod, 'Aboriginal enterprises in the Pilbara', pp. 6–7.

53　Hess, 'Black and red', p. 68.

54　Noel Butlin Archives Centre, ANU [hereafter NBAC]: Michael Hess Collection, Z522, Box 1, Commissioner of Native Affairs to Hegney MLA; and Commissioner to Inspector of Natives, 22 August 1945.

55　NBAC: T. M. Wright papers, Z267, Box 8, McLeod to Wise, 30 April 1946.

56　NBAC: Z267, Box 8, McLeod to Wright, 30 April 1946.

57　*Workers Star*, 3 May 1946, p. 6; *Tribune*, 10 May 1946, p. 6.

58　McLeod, *How The West Was Lost*, p. 42.

59　D. McLeod, *Hedland Voices*, Port Hedland Historical Society, 1997, cited in Read & Coppin, *Kangkushot*, p. 67.

60　D. McLeod, *Donald William McLeod 1908–1999*, 24 December 1996, p. 19, OH2739, Battye Library, Perth.

61　McLeod, *How the West Was Lost*, p. 51.

62　D. McLeod, in *How the West Was Lost* [documentary film], 1987.

63　K. Palmer & C. McKenna, *Somewhere Between Black and White: The Story of an Aboriginal Australian*, Macmillan, Melbourne, 1978, pp. 40–3, 60–4.

64　H. Middleton, *But Now We Want The Land Back: A History of the Australian Aboriginal People*, New Age Publishers, Sydney, 1977, p. 96. See also Brown, *The Black Eureka*, p. 116.

65　Love, 'Communist Party industrial activity', p. 38.

66　McLeod, *How the West Was Lost*, p. 44.

67　NBAC: Hess Collection, Z522, Box 1, Bray to O'Neill, 3 May 1946.

68　McLeod, in *How The West Was Lost* [film], 1987.

69　McLeod, *Donald William McLeod 1908–1999*, p. 10.

70　*Tribune*, 13 August 1946, p. 7.

71　*Tribune*, 7 January 1947, p. 7.

72　A. Welker, 'Communism: it's not just a belief, it's a way of life', *Papers in Labour History*, no. 29, 2005, p. 79.

73　D. McLeod, in Hardie, *Nor'Westers of the Pilbara Breed*, p. 184.

74　Hearn & Knowles, *One Big Union*, pp. 203–7.

75　Biskup, *Not Slaves, Not Citizens*, p. 214.

76　Armstrong, 'On the freedom track to Narawunda', p. 30.

77　Molly Williams, in *How The West Was Lost* [film], 1987.

78   Hardie, *Nor'Westers of the Pilbara Breed*, pp. 106–8.

79   J. Williams, *Anger & Love*, Fremantle Arts Centre Press, 1993, pp. 133–4. Throughout *Different White People*, my usage of 'travelling companion' refers to people described elsewhere as 'fellow travellers' – those who do not join the Party, but who support communism overtly or secretly.

80   F. E. [Bert] Vickers, *The Mirage*, Australasian Book Society, Melbourne, 1955. Details about Vickers were sourced from notes located inside the book's cover.

81   E. Conochie, 'The Communist Party in Western Australia: selected transcripts from the seminar, 2001', *Papers in Labour History*, no. 29, 2005, p. 30.

Notes to Chapter Three

1   G. Alcorn, *The Struggle of the Pilbara Station Hands for Decent Living Standards and Human Rights*, Max Brown, Sydney, 2002, p. 15.

2   *Australian Communist*'s first story about 'natives' was published in vol. 1, 25 February 1921, p. 1.

3   *Workers' Weekly*, 1 July 1927, p. 4; 8 September 1933, p. 3; 22 June 1934, p. 4.

4   *Tribune*, 21 May 1946, p. 1; 24 May 1946, p. 3.

5   D. McLeod, *How the West Was Lost* [film], 1987.

6   J. Williams, *Anger & Love*, Fremantle Arts Centre Press, 1993, p. 128.

7   Alcorn, *The Struggle of the Pilbara Station Hands*, p. 15.

8   D. W. McLeod, *How the West Was Lost: The Native Question in the Development of Western Australia*, D. W. McLeod, Port Hedland, 1984, p. 42.

9   L. Davies, 'Protecting natives?: the law and the 1946 Aboriginal pastoral workers' strike', *Papers in Labour History*, 1988, p. 36.

10   M. Brown, *The Black Eureka*, Australasian Book Society, Sydney, 1976, p. 126.

11   J. Armstrong, 'On the freedom track to Narawunda: the Pilbara Aboriginal pastoral workers' strike, 1946–1998', *Studies in Western Australian History*, no. 22, 2001, p. 34. See also M. Hess, 'Black and red: the Pilbara pastoral workers' strike, 1946', *Aboriginal History*, vol. 18, no. 1, 1994', p. 65.

12   N. Hartley, 'The Communist Party in Western Australia: selected transcripts from the seminar, 2001', *Papers in Labour History*, no. 29, 2005, p. 33.

13   *Tribune*, 21 May 1946, p. 1.

14   *Tribune*, 24 May 1946, p. 3. For further details about these arrests, see Hess, 'Black and red', pp. 73–4.

15   K. Palmer & C. McKenna, *Somewhere Between Black and White: The Story of an Aboriginal Australian*, Macmillan, Melbourne, 1978, pp. 81–2; *Tribune*, 24 April 1963, p. 7.

16   *Tribune*, 21 May 1946, p. 1.

17   J. Williams, cited in B. Bunbury, *It's Not the Money It's the Land: Aboriginal Stockmen and the Equal Wages Case*, Fremantle Arts Centre Press, 2002, p. 55.

18   B. Love, 'Communist Party industrial activity in the post-war years 1945–1953 in Western Australia', *Papers in Labour History*, no. 17, 1996, p. 27; S. Macintyre, *Militant: The Life and Times of Paddy Troy*, Allen & Unwin, Sydney, 1984, p. 100.

19   *Workers Star*, 17 May 1946, p. 1 and 24 May 1946, p. 1; *Tribune*, 21 May 1946, p. 1. Wise was WA Premier from July 1945 to April 1947 (and replaced by Liberal Ross McLarty who remained Premier until 1953).

20   *Tribune*, 13 August 1946, p. 7.

21   McLeod, *How The West Was Lost* [film], 1987.

22   *Tribune*, 24 May 1946, p. 3.

23   *Tribune*, 4 June 1946, p. 5.

24   *Tribune*, 4 June 1946, p. 8.

25   *Tribune*, 18 June 1946, p. 3.

26   *Tribune*, 25 June 1946, p. 3.

27   *Workers Star*, 24 May 1946, p. 1; *Tribune*, 14 June 1946, p. 6.

28   Committee for the Defence of Native Rights, 'S.O.S.' flyer advertising 28 May 1946 Perth meeting [written by Katharine Susannah Prichard], in *Katharine Susannah Prichard Papers*, National Library of Australia [hereafter NLA], MS6201 Series 9, Box 14, Folder 5; NBAC: Wright Papers, Z267, Box 8, appeal for donations to CDNR, 8 June 1946; Hess, 'Black and red', p. 73; Brown, *The Black Eureka*, pp. 131–2.

29   Alcorn, *The Struggle of the Pilbara Station Hands*, p. 15.

30   R. Throssell, *Wild Weeds and Wind Flowers*, Angus & Robertson, Sydney, 1990, p. 54.

31   R. Throssell, *Tribute: Selected Stories of Katharine Susannah Prichard*, UQP, Brisbane, 1988, pp. 96–101, 102–19; Throssell, *Wild Weeds and Wind Flowers*, pp. 48–9.

32   Throssell, *Tribute*, pp. xvii, 128–44.

33   Throssell, *Wild Weeds and Wind Flowers*, pp. 232–51.

34   *Workers Star*, 1 November 1946, in NAA: CIS; A6119/4879, item 4, dossier on Jolly, 1947.

35   NAA: CIS; A6119/4879, item 55.

36   *Workers Star*, 31 May 1946, p. 1; *Tribune*, 14 June 1946, p. 6.

37   NBAC: Wright Papers, Z267, Box 8, Wright to McLeod and McLeod to Wright, 10 May & 17 June 1946.

38   NBAC: Wright Papers, Z267, Box 8, Hodge to Wright, 19 June 1946.

39   NBAC: Wright Papers, Z267, Box 8, Hodge and Jolly to Wright, 24 June 1946, and CDNR appeal to World Federation of Trade Unions, 13 June 1946.

40   *Workers Star*, 28 June 1946, p. 1; *Tribune*, 28 June 1946, p. 3. See also *Tribune*, 28 January 1947, p. 5.

41   'Strike of 800 native workers in Western Australia', *The Anti-Slavery Reporter and Aborigines' Friend*, Anti-Slavery and Aborigines' Protection Society, Great Britain, October 1946, p. 63.

42   NBAC: Wright Papers, Z267, Box 8, Bennett to Wright, 19 June 1946.

43   *Workers Star*, 9 August 1946, p. 1.

44   Sam Coppin, in *How The West Was Lost* [film].

45   *Tribune*, 13 August 1946, p. 7; Sam Coppin, in *How The West Was Lost* [film].

46   NBAC: Hess Collection, Z522, Box 1, McLeod to Anderson, 8 August 1946.

47   NBAC: Hess Collection, Z522, Box 1, Anderson to Bray, 13 August 1946.

48   NBAC: Hess Collection, Z522, Box 1, letter from Kalgoorlie and Boulder Section AWU to Coverley, 3 September 1946.

49   McLeod, *How the West Was Lost*, p. 49.

50   B. Love, 'Communist Party industrial activity in the post-war years 1945–1953 in Western Australia', *Papers in Labour History*, no. 17, 1996, pp. 25, 32.

51   *Workers Star*, 16 August 1946, p. 1. Similar article in *Tribune*, 13 August 1946, p. 7.

52   *Workers Star*, 16 August 1946, p. 1. Similar article in *Tribune*, 16 August 1946, p. 3.

53   Alcorn, *The Struggle of the Pilbara Station Hands*, p. 16.

54   *Workers Star*, 16 August 1946, p. 1; *Tribune*, 16 August 1946, p. 3. In one of its very few articles about the walk-offs, the *West Australian* publicised his plight on 14 August 1946, p. 6. Max Brown described Padre Hodge as a 'Christian socialist' in *The Black Eureka*, p. 154.

55   *Tribune*, 28 January 1947, p. 5.

56   NBAC: Wright Papers, Z267, open letter by Hodge, August 1946.

57   Williams, *Anger & Love*, p. 128.

58   *Workers Star*, 16 August 1946, p. 1; *Tribune*, 16 August 1946, p. 3.

59   *Tribune*, 16 August 1946, p. 4.

60   'Strike of 800 native workers in Western Australia', *The Anti-Slavery Reporter and Aborigines' Friend*, p. 63.

61   Williams, *Anger & Love*, p. 128.

62   *Workers Star*, 23 August 1946, p. 6.

63   *Tribune*, 6 September 1946, p. 7.

64   *Tribune*, 24 September 1946, p. 3.

65   ibid. The trek to Marble Bar is no short hike. The distance from Port Hedland to Marble Bar is approximately 200 kilometres, and roads in 1946 were rough and challenging.

66   ibid.

67   Brown, *The Black Eureka*, p. 28.

68   J. Wilson, 'Authority and leadership in a "new style" Australian Aboriginal community' MA Thesis, University of Western Australia, 1961, pp. 104–5.

69   NAA: CIS; A6126/1188, item 150, CIS report, September 1946.

70   NAA: CIS; A6335/17, item 11, Hill to Chifley, 8 October 1946.

71   NAA: CIS; A6335/17, item 12, PM's Department to Attorney General's Department, 21 November 1946.

72   NAA: CIS; A6335/17, item 3, Mills to Attorney-General's Department, 15 November 1946.

73   NAA: CIS; A6335/17, items 4–10, notes of evidence: Needle v. McLeod, 23 August 1946.

74   *Workers Star*, 8 November 1946, p. 5; *Tribune*, 22 November 1946, p. 3.

75   D. Hewett, *Wild Card: An Autobiography 1923–1958*, McPhee Gribble, Melbourne, 1990, p. 123.

76   Hewett, in Bunbury, *It's Not The Money It's The Land*, pp. 51–2.

77   *Workers Star*, 17 January 1947, p. 2. See also *Tribune*, 18 February 1947, p. 6.

78   D. Hewett, 'Clancy *and* Dooley *and* Don McLeod', in *Windmill Country*, Overland (in conjunction with Peter Leyden Publishing House), Melbourne, 1968.

79   Dorothy Hewett's spelling of Pilbara is: 'Pilbarra'.

80   Hewett, *Wild Card*, pp. 124–7.

81   D. McLeod, 'Donald William McLeod 1908–1999', 24 December 1996, p. 16, OH2739, Battye Library.

82   *Tribune*, 6 September 1946, p. 7.

83   Palmer & McKenna, *Somewhere Between Black and White*, pp. 40–3.

84   Macintyre, *Militant*, p. 100.

85   Brown, *The Black Eureka*, p. 6.

86   Alcorn, *The Struggle of the Pilbara Station Hands,* p. 15.

87   *Tribune*, 7 February 1947, p. 6. *Workers Star* reported *West Australian* and *Daily News* failure to report any details of the arrests, trials or sentences – 7 February 1947, p. 5.

88   *Workers Star*, 7 February 1947, p. 5. See also *Tribune*, 7 February 1947, p. 6.

89   *Workers Star*, 28 February 1947, p. 5.

90   *Workers Star*, 14 February 1947, p. 6.

91   *Tribune*, 11 February 1947, p. 7. Brian suggested the NAWU may have been more influential in the stop-work, but that this is questionable – 'The Northern Territory's one big union', pp. 219–20.

92   Australia, Senate & House of Representatives, vol. 192, 9 May 1947, p. 2,209.

93   T. Wright, 'Fight for the Aborigines', report to Communist Party Central Committee, 14–16 February, in *Communist Review*, April 1947, pp. 498–500.

94   *Tribune*, 27 February 1957, p. 8.

95   Hess, 'Black and red', p. 79; A. Markus, 'Talka longa mouth: Aborigines and the labour movement 1890–1970', *Labour History*, no. 35, 1978 [edition titled 'Who are our enemies? Racism and the Australian working class', edited by A. Curthoys & A. Markus], pp. 152–3.

96   *Tribune*, 7 March 1947, p. 6. This High Court case (*Hodge v Needle* [1947] 49 WALR 11) was also reported in *Argus*, 4 March 1947, p. 7.

97   *Workers Star*, 27 June 1947, p. 5.

98   *Tribune*, 11 July 1947, p. 3.

99   R. Fellowes Lukis, *An interview with Robert Fellowes Lukis: Pastoral Industry in the Pilbara and North West*, December 1977, pp. 157–8, OH262, Battye Library, Perth.

100 NBAC: Hess Collection, Z522, Box 1, note by McDonald, 14 April 1947.

101 *Tribune*, 12 August 1947, p. 6.

102 Australia, Senate & House of Representatives, vol. 195, 19 September 1947, p. 99.

103 S. Macintyre, 'The communists in Western Australia', *Papers in Labour History*, no. 29, 2005, p. 6.

104   *Tribune*, 3 January 1948, p. 7.

105   McLeod, *How The West Was Lost*, p. 99.

106   NAA: CIS; A6119/3306, item 5, Robertson to McLeod, 13 April 1948.

107   NAA: CIS; A6126/1188, item 147, dossier on McLeod, 26 August 1948.

108   F. E. A. Bateman, Report on Survey of Native Affairs, presented to both Houses of Parliament [WA] on 4 June 1948, p. 18.

109   ibid.

110   ibid.

111   Bateman Report, p. 19.

112   *Tribune*, 27 April 1949, p. 7.

113   *Tribune*, 14 May 1949, p. 3. See also Biskup, *Not Slaves, Not Citizens*, p. 237.

114   M. Burgmann, 'Dress rehearsal for the Cold War', in A. Curthoys & J. Merritt (eds.), *Australia's First Cold War 1945–1953*, Allen & Unwin, Sydney, 1984, p. 65.

115   *Tribune*, 14 May 1949, p. 6.

116   Alcorn, *The Struggle of the Pilbara Station Hands*, p. 19.

117   *Tribune*, 18 May 1949, p. 4.

118   *Tribune*, 29 October 1949, p. 8.

119   Australia, Senate & House of Representatives, vol. 204, 1 July 1949, p. 1,908.

120   Australia, Senate & House of Representatives, vol. 203, 10 & 17 March 1949, pp. 1,236, 1,609.

121   *Tribune*, 18 May 1949, p. 4. McLeod's letter to MacDonald was published in full.

122   *Tribune*, 29 October 1949, p. 8.

123   NAA: CIS; A6119/39, item 27, file-note on Hurd [date unknown].

124   Love, 'Communist Party industrial activity', p. 26.

125   Joe Lorbach presented compelling evidence of this worker solidarity in '"We are all workers": the 1949 "black ban" by the Seamen's Union to support the Aboriginal Pilbara strike', Honours Thesis, La Trobe University, Melbourne, 2010.

126   NBAC: Hess Collection, Z522, Box 1, Hurd to Middleton, 30 June 1949. *Workers Star* published the Union's resolution on 1 July 1949, p. 8.

127   *Workers Star*, 15 July 1949, p. 6.

128   *Workers Star*, 22 July 1949, p. 6.

129   *Tribune*, 10 August 1949, p. 3.

130   *Tribune*, 24 August 1949, p. 5.

131   McLeod, *How the West Was Lost*, p. 64.

132   *Tribune*, 27 February 1957, p. 8 [reflective article about the walk-offs].

133   *Tribune*, 26 October 1955, p. 7.

134   Alcorn, *The Struggle of the Pilbara Station Hands*, p. 2.

135   McLeod, *How the West Was Lost*, p. 60.

136   *Tribune*, 24 April 1963, p. 7.

137   D. W. McLeod, 'Aboriginal enterprises in the Pilbara', *Westerly*, no. 2, 1957, p. 8.

138   P. Read, 'Aboriginal rights', in H. Radi (ed.), *Jessie Street: Documents and Essays*, Women's Redress Press, Sydney, 1990, p. 259.

139 *Tribune*, 19 June 1957, p. 10; *Seamen's Journal* [Seamen's Union], August 1957, pp. 18–19. Both articles name the directors of Pindan Ltd (established by camp residents) as Ernie Mitchell and Peter Coppin (Aboriginal men), Don McLeod and Elsie Lee. Jessie Street's 'Report on Visit to Pindan Camps' is located in the *Jessie Street Papers* at NLA MS2683, Series 10, Box 28, Folder 16. Street's relationship with the CPA is unclear. Her writing featured regularly in *Tribune* and she often attended Party events. Her political views were certainly left-of-centre.

140 NAA: ASIO; A6119/3306, item 75, file-note on McLeod by Regional Director WA ASIO, 5 September 1962.

Notes to Chapter Four

1 Australia, Senate & House of Representatives, vol. 190, 6 March 1947, p. 435.

2 Doris Blackburn was called 'Mrs Blackburn' in Commonwealth Hansard. Her husband Maurice had also been a parliamentarian, and so she was identified thus. She was the second female House of Representatives member.

3 P. Morton, *Fire Across the Desert: Woomera and the Anglo-Australian Joint Project 1946–1980*, AGPS Press, Canberra, 1989. See also P. Wilson, 'Rockets and Aborigines August 1945–August 1947: a study of the initial plans for the Woomera Rocket Range and of the protest movement which surfaced to challenge its implementation', Honours thesis, La Trobe University, Melbourne, 1980, pp. 1–11.

4 Royal Commission Into British Nuclear Tests in Australia, *Report of the Royal Commission into British Nuclear Tests in Australia Vol. I & II*, Australian Government Publishing Service, Canberra, 1985.

5 Morton, *Fire Across the Desert*, pp. 6–8.

6 Morton, *Fire Across the Desert*, pp. 8–10.

7 See, for example: R. M. & C. H. Berndt, *From Black to White in South Australia*, Cheshire, Melbourne, 1951; Berndt & Berndt, 'A preliminary report of fieldwork in the Ooldea region, western South Australia. Introduction', *Oceania*, vol. 12, no. 4, 1942, pp. 305–30; Berndt & Berndt, *Aboriginal Man in Australia*, Angus & Robertson, Sydney, 1965; N. B. Tindale, *Aboriginal Tribes of Australia: Their Terrain, Environmental Controls, Distribution, Limits, and Proper Names*, ANU Press, Canberra, 1974.

8 Berndt & Berndt, 'A preliminary report of fieldwork in the Ooldea region', p. 310.

9 R. M. Berndt, 'The "Warburton Range" controversy', *Australian Quarterly*, vol. 29, no. 2, 1957, pp. 35–9.

10 Berndt & Berndt, *From Black to White in South Australia*, pp. 22–30.

11 Berndt & Berndt, *From Black to White in South Australia*, pp. 31–45.

12 Tindale, *Aboriginal Tribes of Australia*, p. x.

13 Wilson, 'Rockets and Aborigines', pp. 31–2; Morton, *Fire Across the Desert*, pp. 73–4.

14 *South Australia Parliamentary Debates*, 22 August 1946, p. 299, in Wilson, 'Rockets and Aborigines', p. 33.

15 NAA: Royal Commission into British Nuclear Tests During the 1950s and 1960s; A6456/R087/020, item 119, The Long Range Weapons Project: Statements by the Minister for Defence (The Hon. John Dedman MP) on 22 November 1946 and 10 March 1947. Andrew Spaull's *John Dedman: A Most Unexpected Labor Man* (Hyland House, Melbourne, 1998) is a useful biography about this important figure in the weapons programs.

16 *Advertiser*, 23 November 1946, p. 1.

17 *Advertiser*, 22 November 1946, p. 1.

18 *Tribune*, 22 November 1946, p. 6.

19 C. Rasmussen, *The Lesser Evil? Opposition to War and Fascism in Australia, 1920–1941*, University of Melbourne, Parkville, Victoria, 1992, pp. 40, 42, 114, 125.

20 NAA: CIS; A6122/417, item 6, 'Sane Democracy League Notes March 1939'. See also Rasmussen, *The Lesser Evil?*, pp. 32, 33, 48–9.

21 NAA: Royal Commission into British Nuclear Tests During the 1950s and 1960s; A6456/R087/020, item 67, Australian Committee on Guided Projectiles Report on Welfare of Aborigines Located Within the Range Area, 1 February 1947.

22 Duguid's opposition to the rocket range and passionate advocacy for affected desert peoples is explored by Rani Kerin in *Doctor Do-Good: Charles Duguid and Aboriginal Advancement, 1930s–1970s*, Australian Scholarly Publishing, Melbourne, 2011, pp. 40–66.

23 Australia, Senate & House of Representatives, vol. 190, 1 May 1947, p. 1,827.

24 Australia, Senate & House of Representatives, vol. 190, 1 May 1947, p. 1,830.

25 Australia, Senate & House of Representatives, vol. 190, 1 May 1947, p. 1,832.

26 Australia, Senate & House of Representatives, vol. 190, 1 May 1947, p. 1,844.

27 D. A. Vachon, 'Political consciousness and land rights among the Australian Western Desert people', in E. Leacock & R. Lee (eds.), *Politics and History in Band Societies*, Cambridge University Press, Cambridge, 1982, p. 470.

28 D. Thomson, *The Aborigines and the Rocket Range*, Rocket Range Committee, Melbourne, 1947, p. 2.

29 Thomson, *The Aborigines and the Rocket Range*, p. 4.

30 Australia, Senate & House of Representatives, vol. 190, 7 March 1947, pp. 484–7.

31 Australia, Senate & House of Representatives, vol. 190, 7 March 1947, p. 491.

32 Australia, Senate & House of Representatives, vol. 190, 7 March 1947, p. 492.

33 Australia, Senate & House of Representatives, vol. 190, 7 March 1947, pp. 492–8.

34 Wilson, 'Rockets and Aborigines', pp. 14–15.

35 Wilson, 'Rockets and Aborigines', p. 26.

36 NAA: MP1217, Box 1656, Army Intelligence Report, cited in Morton, *Fire Across the Desert*, p. 72.

37 NAA: Royal Commission into British Nuclear Tests During the 1950s and 1960s; A6456/R087/020, item 33, Military Intelligence report on Rocket Range Protest meeting, 31 March 1947.

38 NAA: Royal Commission into British Nuclear Tests During the 1950s and 1960s; A6456/R087/020, item 39, Green to Chifley, 16 May 1947.

39 C. Duguid, *The Rocket Range, Aborigines and War*, The Rocket Range Committee, Melbourne, 1947, pp. 13–16.

40 Wilson, 'Rockets and Aborigines', pp. 52, 66.

41 Australia, Senate & House of Representatives, vol. 195, 25 November 1947, pp. 2,563, 2,624.

42 *Report of the Royal Commission into British Nuclear Tests in Australia Vol. I*, p. 118.

43 Australia, House of Representatives, vol. 1, 9 September 1953, pp. 7–8.

44 Australia, House of Representatives, vol. 1, 17 September 1953, p. 317.

45 Australia, House of Representatives, vol. 1, 8 October 1953, p. 1,132.

46 Australia, House of Representatives, vol. 1, 14 October 1953, p. 1,342.

47 Australia, House of Representatives, vol. 1, 21 October 1953, p. 1,610.

48 Australia, House of Representatives, vol. 8, 4 October 1955, p. 1,199.

49 Australia, House of Representatives, vol. 8, 4 October 1955, p. 1,201; vol. 9, 7 March 1956, p. 585.

50 Australia, House of Representatives, vol. 9, 6 March 1956, p. 494.

51 Australia, House of Representatives, vol. 12, 11 September 1956, p. 409.

52 *Report of the Royal Commission into British Nuclear Tests in Australia Vol. I*, p. 311.

53 *Report of the Royal Commission into British Nuclear Tests in Australia Vol. I*, pp. 315–16.

54 *Report of the Royal Commission into British Nuclear Tests in Australia Vol. I*, pp. 277, 300–3, 316–18.

55 *Report of the Royal Commission into British Nuclear Tests in Australia Vol. I*, pp. 323–4.

56 Australia, House of Representatives, vol. 16, 2 October 1957, p. 949.

57 *Report of the Royal Commission into British Nuclear Tests in Australia Vol. I*, pp. 372–3.

Notes to Chapter Five

1 *Tribune*, 27 August 1946, p. 3.

2 U. Werneke, 'A lively mind in a frozen body: the history of Rickety Kate – an Australian poet who suffered from rheumatoid arthritis', *Journal of Evidence-Based Complementary & Alternative Medicine*, July 2011, <http://chp.sagepub.com/content/early/2011/07/22/2156587211414425>, accessed 26 October 2011.

3 *Tribune*, 12 November 1946, p. 4.

4 M. A. Filson, 'Where is the dead heart of Australia?', in *Tribune*, 12 November 1946, p. 4.

5 M. A. Filson, *Feet on the Ground*, L. Bassan, Sydney, 2008, p. 12. Details about the poem are included in this autobiographical novel (originally written during the 1940s).

6 Lenore Bassan [Filson's grand-daughter], email communication, 6 November 2011.

7   Donald Long [Filson's great-nephew], via email communication with L. Bassan, 11 December 2011.

8   Bassan, email communication, 6 November 2011.

9   NAA: Australian Security Intelligence Organisation [hereafter ASIO]; A6119/5318, item 17, report: Arthur Cole Filson, 11 August 1950. Lenore Bassan alerted me to this report about her father and grandmother.

10   New Theatre, *The New Years 1932 –: The Plays, People and Events of Six Decades of Sydney's Radical New Theatre*, The Theatre, Sydney, 1992.

11   F. Capp, *Writers Defiled: Security Surveillance of Australian Authors and Intellectuals 1920–1960*, McPhee Gribble, Melbourne, 1993, pp. 155–65.

12   *Tribune*, 21 March 1947, p. 4. *Workers Star* also publicised the Sydney production for its Perth readers on 11 April 1947, p. 2.

13   New Theatre's permission to allow copies of *Rocket Range* and programs and publicity material for the play is gratefully acknowledged. The original documents are housed in the New Theatre Collection at Mitchell Library, MSS 5277, Box 107.

14   'Budgeree' is an Australian pidgin term that usually refers to something that is good or fine.

15   *Sydney Morning Herald*, 15 March 1947, p. 4.

16   T. Irving & R. Cahill, *Radical Sydney: Places, Portraits and Unruly Episodes*, UNSW Press, Sydney, 2010, p. 214.

17   Jim Crawford, 'Land grab background to Rocket Range scheme', *Guardian*, 23 May 1947.

18   NAA: CIS; A6126/1197, item 106, file-note on Crawford (aka John Oakden Potter), 22 April 1948.

19   *Guardian*, 3 October 1947, p. 5.

20   NAA: CIS; A6126/1197, item 98, report about Crawford, 11 January 1950.

21   M. Bucklow, 'Australia's vanishing people', *New Theatre Review*, December 1946, pp. 4, 8.

22   *Tribune*, 5 November 1946, p. 5.

23   B. Smith, *Noel Counihan: Artist and Revolutionary*, OUP, Melbourne, 1993, p. 4.

24   Letters: L. Donald (Communist Party) to Counihan, 12 September 1945, and Donald to Counihan, 19 October 1945, *Noel Counihan Papers*, NLA MS9107, Series 1, Box 1, Folder 1.

25   Smith, *Noel Counihan*, pp. 205–9.

26   *Tribune*, 28 August 1945, p. 6.

27   *Tribune*, 26 November 1946, p. 3.

28   ibid.

29   Letter: Elkin to Beavis, 1 April 1947, Elkin Papers 176/4/2/206, in Gray, *A Cautious Silence*, pp. 211–12.

30   D. McKnight, *Australia's Spies and Their Secrets*, Allen & Unwin, Sydney, 1994, p. 150.

31   P. Deery, 'Scientific freedom and post-war politics: Australia, 1945–1955', *Historical Records of Australian Science*, vol. 13, no. 1, 2000, pp. 1–18.

32   *Sydney Morning Herald*, 20 May 1947, p. 2.

33   *Canberra Times*, 26 June 1947, p. 4.

34   G. Gray, 'Aborigines, Elkin and the guided projectiles project', *Aboriginal History*, vol. 15, 1991, pp. 153–62.

35   L. Sharkey, *Communist Review*, October 1949.

36   A. Robertson, 'CPA in the anti-war movement', *Australian Left Review*, Oct–Nov 1970, p. 41.

37   C. McLean, 'Fear of peace? Australian government responses to the peace movement 1949–1959', MA thesis, Victoria University, 2001, pp. 26–9; M. Saunders & R. Summy, *The Australian Peace Movement: A Short History*, Peace Research Centre, Canberra, 1986, p. 32.

38   Jim Cairns, *Australian Biography*, 22 May 1998, <http://www.australianbiography. gov.au/subjects/cairns/intertext4.html>, accessed 1 August 2011.

39   Australian Peace Council, report, 12 September 1949, <http://www. reasoninrevolt.net.au/pdf/a000707.pdf>, accessed 1 August 2011.

40   NAA: ASIO; A6119/1711, item 16, file-note: Australian Peace Council,10 August 1950.

41   Robertson, 'CPA in the anti-war movement', p. 41.

42   Robertson, 'CPA in the anti-war movement', pp. 42–3.

43   A. Watt, *Rocket Range Threatens Australia*, Australian Communist Party, Adelaide, 1947, pp. 3–8.

44   Watt, *Rocket Range Threatens Australia*, p. 6.

45   Watt, *Rocket Range Threatens Australia*, p. 16.

46   Australia, Senate & House of Representatives, vol. 190, 1 May 1947, p. 1844.

47   NAA: ASIO; A6119/1007, item 207, dossier on Rose, 30 June 1953.

48   NAA: ASIO; A6119/1007, item 16, Alexander to CIS Director, 23 April 1947.

49   NAA: Royal Commission into British Nuclear Tests During the 1950s and 1960s; A6456, R080/020, items 57–67, report by Australian Committee on Guided Projectiles [CIS file].

50   NAA: ASIO; A6119/1007, item 18, Alexander to Director of CIS, 26 June 1947.

51   NAA: ASIO; NAA A6119/1007, item 38, ASIO report about Rose, 27 May 1951.

52   NAA: ASIO; A6119/43, items 125-6, Prichard to Suchkov, 3 October 1942.

53   J. Collins, 'A mate in publishing', in A. Shoemaker (ed.), *Oodgeroo and Her People: Perspectives on Her Life's Work*, UQP, Brisbane, 1994, p. 10. Kath Walker was described as a 'Party member' in *Tribune*, 19 July 1945, p. 4.

54   Australia, Senate & House of Representatives, vol. 191, 13 May 1947, p. 2,219.

55   *Guardian*, 22 November 1946, p. 6.

56   *Sydney Morning Herald*, 13 May 1947, p. 1 (the ACTU position was also reported the same day in a short front-page article in Melbourne's *Argus*).

57   P. Weller & B. Lloyd (eds.), *Federal Executive Minutes 1915–1955: Minutes of the Meetings of the Federal Executive of the Australian Labor Party*, Melbourne University Press, 1978, pp. 347–8.

58   Australia, Senate & House of Representatives, vol. 191, 15 May 1947, p. 2,450.

59 Australia, Senate & House of Representatives, vol. 191, 15 May 1947, pp. 2,456–9.

60 P. Wilson, 'Rockets and Aborigines August 1945–August 1947: a study of the initial plans for the Woomera Rocket Range and of the protest movement which surfaced to challenge its implementation', Honours thesis, La Trobe University, Melbourne, 1980, p. 79.

61 *Tribune*, 16 May 1947, p. 6.

62 ibid.

63 Wilson, 'Rockets and Aborigines', p. 60.

64 *Argus*, 16 May 1947, p. 1.

65 *Tribune*, 16 May 1947, p. 1.

66 *Argus*, 13 May 1947, p. 2

67 Australia, Senate & House of Representatives, vol. 193, 9 October 1947, p. 588.

68 G. McDonald, *The Evidence: Revealing Extracts on Aboriginal 'Land Rights' From Official Communist Documents*, Veritas, Perth, 1983, pp. 25–8.

69 W. G. Smith, 'Communists and the Aborigines', *Social Survey*, vol. 12, no. 8, 1963, p. 230.

70 A. Davidson, *The Communist Party of Australia: A Short History*, Stanford, California, 1969, p. 120.

71 *Tribune*, 17 June 1947, p. 3.

72 Australia, Senate & House of Representatives, vol. 191, 6 June 1947, pp. 3,660, 3,671.

73 *Tribune*, 17 June 1947, p. 3.

74 NAA: Royal Commission into British Nuclear Tests During the 1950s and 1960s; A6456/R087/020, item 88, Rocket Range Protest Committee to Chifley, 15 September 1947.

75 Wilson, 'Rockets and Aborigines', p. 71.

76 *Argus*, 25 August 1947, p. 4.

77 NAA: ASIO; A6119/472, items 42–45, dossier on Fitzpatrick, compiled in 1956.

78 NAA: ASIO; A9108/Roll 17, item 66, ACTU All-Australian Congress in Melbourne 1–5 September 1947.

79 *Tribune*, 11 September 1948, p. 7.

80 This Donald David Thomson is not to be confused with anthropologist Donald Ferguson Thomson (who also attracted ASIO interest, with a small file dedicated to his activities).

81 NAA: CIS; A6119/1800, item 23, Deputy Director to Director of CIS re. Thomson, 14 September 1948.

82 McKnight, *Australia's Spies and Their Secrets*, pp. 7–9.

83 Australia, House of Representatives, vol. 33, 24 October 1961, pp. 2,404–6.

84 Australia, House of Representatives, vol. 33, 24 October 1961, p. 2,410.

Notes to Chapter Six

1 *Tribune*, 16 April 1952, p. 12.

2 NAA: ASIO; A6119/1711, item 103, Lockwood's speech, 15 March 1953.

3   M. Hearn & H. Knowles, *One Big Union: A History of the Australian Workers Union 1886–1994*, Cambridge University Press, Melbourne, 1996, p. 235.

4   NAA; ASIO; A6122/250, item 14, ASIO memorandum, 13 April 1954.

5   P. Debelle, *Red Silk: The Life of Elliott Johnston QC*, Wakefield Press, Adelaide, 2011, pp. 60–1.

6   *Mail*, 14 March 1953, p. 1.

7   NAA: ASIO; A6122/412, items 55–57, report about CPA and front organisations, October 1955.

8   NAA: ASIO; A6122/412, items 51–54.

9   NAA: ASIO; A6122/412, items 49–51.

10   NAA: ASIO; A6122/412, items 47–48.

11   NAA: ASIO; A6112/412, items 232–233, list of Communist front organisations, September 1956 (located in file about New Theatre).

12   *Tribune*, 7 October 1953, p. 1.

13   *Tribune*, 19 October 1955, p. 2.

14   *Report of the Royal Commission into British Nuclear Tests in Australia Vol. I*, pp. 304–5; S. Davenport, P. Johnson & Yuwali, *Cleared Out*, Aboriginal Studies Press, Canberra, 2005, pp. 26–31; L. Dousset, 'Politics and demography in a contact situation: the establishment of the Giles Meteorological Station in the Rawlinson Ranges, West Australia', *Aboriginal History*, vol. 26, 2002, pp. 1–10.

15   Australia, House of Representatives, vol. 11, 5 June 1956, p. 2,735.

16   Australia, House of Representatives, vol. 11, 6 June 1956, p. 2,828.

17   Australia, House of Representatives, vol. 11, 21 June 1956, p. 3,515.

18   Australia, House of Representatives, vol. 12, 4 September 1956, p. 136.

19   *Report of the Royal Commission into British Nuclear Tests in Australia Vol. I*, pp. 308–9.

20   R. Murdoch, 'The facts of the West Australian natives', *Adelaide News*, 1 February 1957, p. 3. Murdoch's trip to this area is further explored shortly.

21   *Tribune*, 23 January 1957, p. 2.

22   For comprehensive description of this first encounter between government officers and tribal Aboriginal women and children, see Davenport, Johnson & Yuwali's *Cleared Out: First Contact in the Western Desert*. Original footage of this first encounter was filmed by Walter MacDougall. *Contact* (2009) is a powerful documentary film presenting MacDougall's remarkable footage.

23   NAA: Royal Commission into British Nuclear Tests During the 1950s and 1960s; A6456/R022/008, item 78, MacDougall to Department of Supply, 16 January 1956.

24   ibid.

25   NAA: Royal Commission into British Nuclear Tests During the 1950s and 1960s; A6456/R022/008, item 144, report by MacDougall (April–July 1956) to Superintendent, Weapons Research Establishment, Woomera, 6 August 1956.

26   NAA: Royal Commission into British Nuclear Tests During the 1950s and 1960s; A6456/R022/008, item 142.

27   W. Grayden, *Adam and Atoms*, Daniels, Perth, 1957.

28 W. L. Grayden, *Report of the Select Committee appointed to inquire into Native Welfare Conditions in the Laverton-Warburton Range Area*, presented to WA Legislative Assembly on 12 December 1956.

29 Australia, House of Representatives, vol.15, 9 May 1957, p. 1,234.

30 ibid.

31 Murdoch, 'The facts on the West Australian natives', p. 3.

32 Australia, House of Representatives, vol.15, 14 May 1957, p. 1,371.

33 Grayden, *Report of the Select Committee appointed to inquire into Native Welfare Conditions in the Laverton-Warburton Range Area.*

34 *Tribune*, 9 January 1957, p. 3; B. Attwood, *Rights for Aborigines*, Allen & Unwin, Sydney, 2003, p. 149.

35 *Tribune*, 16 January 1957, p. 5.

36 *Tribune*, 20 March 1957, p. 3.

37 Murdoch, 'The facts on the West Australian natives', p. 3.

38 D. W. McLeod, *How The West Was Lost: The Native Question in the Development of Western Australia*, D. W. McLeod, Port Hedland, 1984, p. 76. McLeod identified the Murdoch he spoke to as 'Keith', but as Keith Murdoch died in 1952, we can only assume that (in this retrospective 1984 publication) McLeod mistakenly named the company's head (Rupert assumed control of the publishing empire when his father died).

39 *Tribune*, 23 January 1957, p. 2.

40 J. Horner, *Seeking Racial Justice: An Insider's Memoir of the Movement for Aboriginal Advancement, 1938–1978*, Aboriginal Studies Press, Canberra, 2004, p. 24.

41 *Tribune*, 30 January 1957, p. 3.

42 NAA: ASIO; A6119/363, item 162, extract from *No More Hiroshimas*, vol. 4, no. 13, Oct–Nov 1957, p. 4.

43 *Tribune*, 27 March 1957, p. 8.

44 J. Crawford, *Rocket Range* [play-script, 1957 version], New Theatre Collection, MSS 5722, Box 139, Mitchell Library. The play was also presented at Perth's New Theatre in 1950, and advertised in *West Australian*, 21 October 1950, p. 38.

45 *New Theatre Presents...Rocket Range* [advertising flier], MSS 5722, Box 161X, Mitchell Library.

46 M. Arrow, 'The New Theatre', in T. Irving & R. Cahill (eds.), *Radical Sydney: Places, Portraits and Unruly Episodes*, UNSW Press, Sydney, 2010, p. 214.

47 C. Healy, 'Radical theatre: inner city', in R. Evans & C. Ferrier (eds.), *Radical Brisbane: an Unruly History*, Vulgar Press, Melbourne, 2004, p. 188.

48 NAA: ASIO; A6126/1197, item 75, file-note on Crawford [including transcript from *Guardian* 10 December 1953], no date [but indications are that it was written in 1954].

49 NAA: ASIO; A6119/1091, items 3 and 5, file-note, CPA interest in Aborigines, 1957.

50 NAA: ASIO; A6119/3462, item 102, 'An Appeal From Australian Authors and Artists, 1957'. A copy of this petition signed by Kylie Tennant also located in one of her ASIO files, at A6119/283, item 28.

51 *Daily Mirror*, 23 June 1954, p. 2.

52 *Their Darkest Hour* (or '*The Warburton Film*') was filmed in 1956. Speaker notes accompanying the silent film are described as 'Spoken commentary for Warburton Ranges film belonging to the Aboriginal-Australian Fellowship'. Provision of a copy of the film and notes by AIATSIS is gratefully acknowledged.

53 *Tribune*, 3 April 1957, p. 3.

54 Horner, *Seeking Racial Justice*, p. 24.

55 *Tribune*, 3 April 1957, p. 3.

56 Horner, *Seeking Racial Justice*, p. 25.

57 P. F. McGrath & D. Brooks, '*Their Darkest Hour*: the films and photographs of William Grayden and the history of the "Warburton Range controversy" of 1957', *Aboriginal History*, vol. 34, 2010, p. 128.

58 *Tribune*, 1 May 1957, p. 2.

59 NAA: ASIO; A6119/1091, item 2, file-note about NSW Literature, April 1957 [in Doug Nicholls' ASIO file].

60 Horner, *Seeking Racial Justice*, p. 25.

61 Australia, House of Representatives, vol. 17, 26 November 1957, p. 2,501.

62 *Tribune*, 14 May 1957, p. 9; Attwood, *Rights for Aborigines*, p. 150.

63 F. Bandler, *Turning the Tide: A Personal History of the Federal Council for the Advancement of Aborigines and Torres Strait Islanders*, Aboriginal Studies Press, Canberra, 1989, p. 10.

64 NAA: ASIO; A6119/ 2852, item 132, report, 17 March 1959.

65 M. Bauml Duberman, *Paul Robeson*, Bodley Head, London, 1989, pp. 200–2.

66 J. Hocking, *Frank Hardy: Politics Literature Life*, Lothian Books, Melbourne, 2005, p. 136.

67 Duberman, *Paul Robeson*, p. 491.

68 M. Thorpe Clark, *Pastor Doug: The Story of Sir Douglas Nicholls Aboriginal Leader*, Lansdowne Press, Melbourne, 1972, p. 251.

69 Australia, House of Representatives, vol. 43, 1 September 1964, p. 780.

70 Australia, House of Representatives, vol. 43, 1 September 1964, pp. 781, 784.

71 P. Kelly, 'Maralinga (Rainy Land)', *Paul Kelly: Don't Start Me Talking Lyrics 1984–1999*, Allen & Unwin, Sydney, 1999, pp. 36–7.

72 M. Bramwell, 'Paul Kelly and his songs', *Island Magazine*, no. 56, 1993, p. 52.

73 F. Hollows, *Fred Hollows: An Autobiography; With Peter Corris*, Kerr Publishing, Sydney, 1993, pp. 167–8.

74 *Report of the Royal Commission into British Nuclear Tests in Australia Vol. I*, pp. 319–21.

Notes to Chapter Seven

1 *Tribune*, 7 September 1966, p. 1. This front-page story about the Wave Hill walk-off was published two weeks after workers walked away.

2 L. Riddett, 'The strike that became a land rights movement: a southern "do-gooder" reflects on Wattie Creek 1966–74', *Labour History*, no. 72, 1997, p. 54.

3   J. Elton, 'Comrades or competition? Union relations with Aboriginal workers in the South Australian and Northern Territory pastoral industries, 1878–1957', PhD thesis, Flinders University, Adelaide, 2007, pp. 37–44; D. B. Rose, *Hidden Histories: Black Stories From Victoria River Downs, Humbert River and Wave Hill Stations*, Aboriginal Studies Press, Canberra, 1991, p. 11.

4   Elton, 'Comrades or competition?', pp. 44–7.

5   *Communist*, 26 January 1923, p. 1.

6   *Workers' Weekly*, 9 December 1927, p. 3.

7   *Northern Standard*, '"Reds" among the blacks', 5 February 1932, p. 3, in Elton, 'Comrades or competition?', p. 258.

8   M. A. Franklin, *Black and White Australians*, Heinemann Educational Australia, Melbourne, 1976, pp. 120–1.

9   *Workers' Weekly*, 13 April 1928, p. 4.

10   *Workers' Weekly*, 16 May 1930, p. 5.

11   *Workers' Weekly*, 30 May 1930, p. 2.

12   A. McGrath, *Born in the Cattle: Aborigines in Cattle Country*, Allen & Unwin, Sydney, 1987, p. 95.

13   *Workers' Weekly*, 23 November 1928, p. 1.

14   *Workers' Weekly*, 24 September 1931, p. 2.

15   A. McGrath, '"Modern stone-Age slavery": images of Aboriginal labour and sexuality', *Labour History*, no. 69, 1995, pp. 40–4.

16   *Workers' Weekly*, 15 December 1933, p. 5.

17   *Tribune*, 20 December 1946, p. 7.

18   Elton, 'Comrades or competition?', pp. 316–17.

19   *Tribune*, 24 December 1946, p. 6.

20   M. Hokari, 'Cross-culturalizing history: journey to the Gurindji way of historical practice', PhD thesis, Australian National University, Canberra, 2001, p. 257.

21   P. d'Abbs, *The Vestey Story*, Australasian Meat Industry Employees' Union, Victorian Branch, Melbourne, 1970, pp. 8–18. All profits from book sales went to the Gurindji community.

22   NAA (Darwin), C: A1/15, 1938/329, Cook to Administrator, 16 October 1936, in Elton, 'Comrades or Competition?', p. 291.

23   D'Abbs, *The Vestey Story*, pp. 17–18.

24   R. M. & C. H. Berndt, *End of an Era: Aboriginal Labour in the Northern Territory*, Australian Institute of Aboriginal Studies, Canberra, 1987, pp. 270–3.

25   Australia, Senate & House of Representatives, vol. 188, 6 & 7 August 1946, pp. 3,778–9.

26   Australia, Senate & House of Representatives, vol. 198, 16 September 1948, pp. 513–15, and vol. 204, 2 June 1949, p. 477.

27   Australia, Senate & House of Representatives, vol. 204, 17 & 30 June 1949, pp. 1,162, 1,903.

28   Australia, House of Representatives, vol. 3, 7 April 1954, pp. 88–9.

29   Elton, 'Comrades or competition?', pp. 331–4.

30 *Tribune*, 7 December 1950, p. 8; Elton, 'Comrades and competition?', p. 348.

31 Elton, 'Comrades or competition?', p. 351.

32 *Tribune*, 18 January 1951, p. 1.

33 *Tribune*, 1 February 1951, p. 7; 8 February 1951, p. 8; 21 March 1951, p. 8.

34 *Tribune*, 15 February 1951, p. 8.

35 *Tribune*, 22 February 1951, p. 7.

36 Elton, 'Comrades or competition?', pp. 353–6.

37 B. Manning, email communication, 28 May 2010.

38 B. Attwood, *Rights for Aborigines*, Allen & Unwin, Sydney, 2003, pp. 135–44.

39 *Tribune*, 16 November 1955, p. 10.

40 Australia, House of Representatives, vol. 8, 19 October 1955, pp. 1,667–9. The *Herald* article Hasluck referred to was written by Douglas Lockwood on 8 October 1955.

41 Australia, House of Representatives, vol. 14, 9 April 1957, pp. 682–3.

42 Australia, House of Representatives, vol. 30, 20 April 1961, pp. 1,051, 1,055.

43 Australia, House of Representatives, vol. 30, 20 April 1961, p. 1,058.

44 Australia, House of Representatives, vol. 30, 20 April 1961, p. 1,093.

45 Communist Party of Australia, *The People Against Monopoly: 19th Congress of the Communist Party of Australia 1961*, Current Book Distributors, Sydney, 1961, pp. 34, 56.

46 NAA: ASIO; A6122/1527, item 187, CPA, *The Australian Aborigines in the Present World-Wide Struggle for Emancipation of the Colonial Peoples* [1961?].

47 Australia, House of Representatives, vol. 29, 8 December 1960, p. 3,870.

48 Australia, House of Representatives, vol. 35, 2 May 1962, p. 1,898, and vol. 38, 30 April 1963, pp. 875–6.

49 F. Bandler, 'Hey, what about us?', in Bandler & L. Fox (eds.), *The Time Was Ripe: A History of the Aboriginal-Australian Fellowship (1956–69)*, Alternative Publishing Cooperative, Sydney, 1983, p. 107.

50 *Tribune*, 1 August 1962, p. 6.

51 F. Bandler, *Turning the Tide: A Personal History of the Federal Council for the Advancement of Aborigines and Torres Strait Islanders*, Aboriginal Studies Press, Canberra, 1989, p. 9; P. Read, 'Aboriginal rights', in H. Radi (ed.), *Jessie Street: Documents and Essays*, Women's Redress Press, Sydney, 1990, pp. 259–61.

52 S. Taffe, 'The Federal Council for the Advancement of Aborigines and Torres Strait Islanders: the politics of inter-racial coalition in Australia, 1958–1973', PhD thesis, Monash University, Melbourne, 2001, pp. 7–8.

53 FCAA, notes from the launch of the FCAA, Adelaide Conference, February 14–16 1958, at <http://indigenousrights.net.au/files/F2.pdf>, accessed 27 July 2011.

54 *Tribune*, 21 April 1965, pp. 1–2.

55 *Tribune*, 20 April 1966, p. 4.

56 NAA: ASIO; A6119/1064, item 98, report: FCAA National Conference, 21 April 1962.

57 Taffe, 'The Federal Council for the Advancement of Aboriginal and Torres Strait Islanders', p. 107.

58 FCAA, 'Public meeting notice to launch a national petition for a federal referendum deleting two clauses from the Commonwealth Constitution', 6th October 1962, Sydney.

59 'Referendum – the background', *Smoke Signals*, May 1967, pp. 3–9.

60 Australia, House of Representatives, vol. 38, 23 May 1963, pp. 1,795–7.

61 Taffe, 'The Federal Council for the Advancement of Aboriginal and Torres Strait Islanders', pp. 57, 90.

62 ILO, *Conventions and Recommendation*, pp. 902–4.

63 Australia, House of Representatives, vol. 38, 23 May 1963, p. 1,797.

64 Australia, House of Representatives, vol. 41, 8 April 1964, p. 823.

65 A. Markus, 'Talka longa mouth: Aborigines and the labour movement 1890–1970', *Labour History*, no. 35, 1978 [edition titled 'Who are our enemies? Racism and the Australian working class', edited by A. Curthoys & A. Markus], p. 155.

66 *Tribune*, 25 September 1963, p. 3.

67 NAA: ASIO; A6119/2507, items 88 and 93, Case Officer Reports, 8 April & 12 July 1962.

68 B. Brian, 'The Northern Territory's one big union: the rise and fall of the North Australian Workers' Union, 1911–1972', PhD thesis, NT University, Darwin, 2001 pp. 263–6; *Tribune*, 27 January 1965, p. 3. Sydney James Cook was raised by Charles Duguid's family in Adelaide for six years, before being sent (aged 12) to the NT's Roper River mission, where he grew up with Dexter and Davis Daniels – R. Kerin, *Doctor Do-Good: Charles Duguid and Aboriginal Advancement, 1930s–1970s*, Australian Scholarly Publishing, Melbourne, 2011, pp. 89–111.

69 Brian Manning, personal communication, 9 April 2010.

70 NAA: Department of Territories; A452/1961/3211, items 25–70, Spry to Hasluck, 25 November 1962.

71 'New red plot here', *Truth* [Melbourne], 30 March 1963. Source kindly provided by Jenny Hibben.

72 A. Curthoys, *Freedom Ride: A Freedom Rider Remembers*, Allen & Unwin, Sydney, 2002, pp. 63–4.

73 Communist Party of Australia, *Communist Policy on the Aborigines of Australia (Draft for Discussion)*, Central Committee, CPA, Sydney, 1964, pp. 9–10, 13–14, 16.

74 *Tribune*, 12 February 1964, p. 5. The draft Policy had also been analysed in *Communist Review*, December 1963, pp. 406–7.

75 *Tribune*, 18 March 1964, p. 11.

76 *Tribune*, 24 March 1964, p. 7.

77 *Tribune*, 15 January 1964, p. 5 [of 'Supplement for the Student of Politics'].

78 F. Schatten, *Communism in Africa*, Allen & Unwin, London, 1966, pp. 225, 237.

79 W. G. Smith, 'Communists and the Aborigines', *Social Survey*, vol. 12, no. 8, September 1963, pp. 229–32.

80 *Tribune*, 13 January 1965, p. 8.

81 B. Attwood, 'The articulation of "land rights" in Australia: the case of Wave Hill', *Social Analysis*, issue 44, no. 1, 2000, p. 8.

82 Taffe, 'The Federal Council for the Advancement of Aborigines and Torres Strait Islanders', p. 199.

83 FCAATSI Equal Wages for Aborigines Committee, 'The Facts On Wage Discrimination Against Aborigines', at <http://www.indigenousrights.net.au/ images/pictures/i528_m.jpg>, accessed 31 August 2010 (document circulated in 1964). For discussion about this Committee, see Taffe, 'The Federal Council for the Advancement of Aborigines and Torres Strait Islanders', pp. 176–238.

84 Bandler, *Turning the Tide*, p. 131.

85 Bandler, *Turning the Tide*, p. 27.

86 Bandler, *Turning the Tide*, pp. 22–4. In 1967, FCAATSI listed thirteen trade union bodies as affiliates, including Federal Councils of the BWIU, FMWU and Seamen's Union.

87 NAA: ASIO; A6119/2942, item 42, report on FCAA annual conference, 16 April 1965.

88 *Tribune*, 24 February 1965, p. 2.

89 *Tribune*, 20 January 1965, p. 3; 27 January 1965, p. 3.

90 NAA: Attorney General's Department; A432/1965/2127, item 10, Dean to Barnes, 15 March 1965.

91 NAA: Attorney General's Department; A432/1965/2127, item 11, file-note, 15 March 1965.

92 NAA: Attorney General's Department, A432/1965/2127, item 12, file-note, April 1965.

93 *Tribune*, 19 May 1965, p. 1.

94 *Tribune*, 23 June 1965, p. 1; 14 July 1965, p. 11.

95 *Tribune*, 8 September 1965, p. 8.

96 J. H. Kelly, *Human Rights for Aborigines: Pre-Requisite for Northern Development*, Australasian Book Society, Sydney, 1966, pp. 9, 33. The publisher held strong ties to the CPA and unions.

97 *Tribune*, 29 September 1965, p. 8.

98 *Tribune*, 27 October 1965, p. 3.

99 W. E. H. Stanner, 'Industrial justice in the never-never', *Australian Quarterly*, vol. 39, no. 1, March 1967, p. 40. This article provides useful history of NT industrial regulations for Aboriginal workers prior to the Award hearing. It also presents description of the case itself and industrial outcomes.

100 Australia, House of Representatives, vol. 49, 10 December 1965, p. 3,953.

101 *Tribune*, 9 March 1966, p. 2.

102 ibid.

103 Manning, interviewed in Brian's 'The Northern Territory's one big union', p. 267.

104 Justice Richard Kirby, in B. d'Alpuget, *Mediator: a Biography of Sir Richard Kirby*, Melbourne University Press, Melbourne, 1977, p. 180.

105 Stanner, 'Industrial justice in the never-never', pp. 45, 51.

106 Brian, 'The Northern Territory's one big union', p. 267.

107 *Tribune*, 16 March 1966, pp. 5, 10.

108   C. D. Rowley, *The Remote Aborigines*, Penguin, Melbourne, 1972, pp. 220, 224.

109   Australia, House of Representatives, vol. 50, 9 March 1966, pp. 56, 58.

Notes to Chapter Eight

1   F. Hardy, *The Unlucky Australians*, Nelson, Melbourne, 1968, p. 67.

2   *Tribune*, 4 May 1966, p. 1.

3   *Tribune*, 11 May 1966, p. 1.

4   *Tribune*, 18 May 1966, p. 3.

5   *Guardian*, 19 May 1966, p. 1.

6   *Tribune*, 29 June 1966, p. 10.

7   *Guardian*, 7 July 1966, p. 8; 16 July 1966, p. 1.

8   *Tribune*, 27 July 1966, p. 12.

9   ibid. Frank Hardy described the NAWU as a 'Right-wing led Union' that had alienated Aboriginal organiser Dexter Daniels with its lack of support for the Newcastle Waters people. In Hardy's view, that walk-off was ill-planned and should have commenced on bigger stations such as Wave Hill – *The Unlucky Australians*, p. 21 (on p. 54, Hardy also claimed authorship of the *Tribune* story dated 27 July).

10   F. Hardy, 'Strike in the north', *Nation*, 29 October 1966, p. 11.

11   NTCAR, 'Program for Improved Living Standards for Northern Territory Aborigines', at <http:www.indigenousrights.net.au/document.asp?iID=648>, accessed 1 December 2011.

12   NAA: Department of Territories; A452/NT1966/1830, item 64, NTCAR, 'Program for Improved Living Standards For NT Aborigines', 24 July 1966.

13   NAA: Department of Territories; A452/2795, item 85, Hallam to Holt, 20 August 1966.

14   B. Manning, email communication, 9 April 2010.

15   B. Manning, 'A blast from the past: an activist's account of the Wave Hill walk-off', Sixth Vincent Lingiari Memorial Lecture, NT University, 23 August 2002.

16   Manning, 'A blast from the past'.

17   Hardy, *The Unlucky Australians*, p. 40.

18   Hardy, 'Strike in the north', p. 12.

19   M. Rangiari, in M. Hokari, 'Cross-culturalizing history: journey to the Gurindji way of historical practice', PhD thesis, Australian National University, Canberra, 2001, p. 153.

20   This place is referred to as 'Daguragu/Wattie Creek' in this chapter.

21   B. Manning, email communication, 7 April 2010.

22   B. Manning, email communication, 28 May 2010. The 'previous occasion' refers to the 1955 walk-off from Wave Hill, as described earlier.

23   B. Manning, email communication, 7 April 2010.

24   *Tribune*, 31 August 1966, p. 1.

25   B. Manning, email communication, 7 April 2010.

26 *Tribune*, 31 August 1966, p. 12.

27 Hardy, *The Unlucky Australians*, p. 97.

28 ibid.

29 Manning, 'A blast from the past'.

30 Hardy, *The Unlucky Australians*, p. 75.

31 B. Attwood, 'The articulation of "land rights" in Australia: the case of Wave Hill', *Social Analysis*, issue 44, no. 1, 2000, pp. 14–15.

32 NAA: ASIO; A6119/881, item 181, file-note about Holmes, 1961.

33 NAA: ASIO; A6119/2589, items 149 and 150, intercept report, 26 August 1966.

34 ibid.

35 *Australian*, 27 August 1966. Very similar articles were published that day in *Sydney Morning Herald* and *Canberra Times*.

36 *Canberra Times*, 30 August 1966. An article headed 'Pay rise on way for Aboriginal stockmen' was published the same day in the *Australian*.

37 NAA: ASIO; A6119/2589, items 146–7, phone taps between Hardy and Aarons, 26–31 August 1966.

38 NAA: Department of Territories; A452/NT1966/1830, items 96–99, report, Evans to NT Administrator, 31 August 1966.

39 NAA: ASIO; A6119/4938, item 2, report, 31 August 1966.

40 NAA: ASIO; A6119/4938, items 3–4, report, 12 September 1966.

41 Australia, House of Representatives, vol. 52, 1 September 1966, p. 658.

42 Australia, House of Representatives, vol. 52, 1 September 1966, p. 748.

43 NAA: Department of Territories; A452/NT1966/1830, item 106, telegram, ACTU to Department of Territories, 2 September 1966.

44 *Tribune*, 7 September 1966, p. 2.

45 B. Manning, email communication, 28 May 2010.

46 L. Riddett, 'The strike that became a land rights movement: a southern "do-gooder" reflects on Wattie Creek 1966–74', *Labour History*, no. 72, 1997, p. 50.

47 *Tribune*, 7 September 1966, pp. 6–7.

48 *Tribune*, 14 September 1966, pp. 1, 10.

49 Manning, 'A blast from the past'.

50 NAA: ASIO; A6119/2589, item 156, report, telephone taps, Aarons and Seelaf, 19 September 1966.

51 *Northern Territory News*, 23 September 1966, p. 2.

52 *Tribune*, 21 September 1966, p. 1.

53 *Northern Territory News*, 23 September 1966, p. 1.

54 NAA: ASIO; A6119/2589, items 144–5, reports, 15 and 16 September 1966.

55 NAA: ASIO; A6119/2589, item 153, file-note, telephone tap, Walker and ASIO informant, 27 September 1966.

56 B. Manning, email communication, 18 September 2012.

57 NAA: ASIO; A6126/1106, item 5, file-note, 20 January 1967.

58 *Tribune*, 21 September 1966, p. 11.

59 NAA: Attorney General's Department; A432/NT1966/4806, items 8 & 9, Hugel to Holt, 25 January 1967.

60   NAA: Department of Territories; A452/NT1966/1830, items 113 & 120, Warwick Smith to NT Administrator, 15 September 1966.

61   *Tribune*, 28 September 1966, p. 5.

62   B. Brian, 'The Northern Territory's one big union: the rise and fall of the North Australian Workers' Union, 1911–1972', PhD thesis, NT University, Darwin, 2001, p. 227.

63   Australia, House of Representatives, vol. 53, 26 October 1966, p. 2,250.

64   *Tribune*, 12 October 1966, p. 3.

65   H. Middleton, *But Now We Want the Land Back: A History of the Australian Aboriginal People*, New Age Publishers, Sydney, 1977, pp. 113–14.

66   Hardy, *The Unlucky Australians*, pp. 75–6.

67   *Tribune*, 19 October 1966, p. 4.

68   *Tribune*, 17 November 1966, p. 10.

69   *Tribune*, 30 November 1966, p. 10.

70   NAA: ASIO; A6119/2589, item 160, phone-tap report, Marks to Davies, 2 November 1966.

71   Hardy, 'Strike in the north', p. 12.

72   *Northern Territory News*, cited in *Tribune*, 26 October 1966, p. 10.

73   *Tribune*, 9 November 1966, p. 3.

74   Hardy, *The Unlucky Australians*, p. 96.

75   *Tribune*, 17 November 1966, p. 10.

76   NBAC: Assn. of Architects, Engineers, Surveyors and Draughtsmen of Australia, Federal Council, E192/9/4, NTCAR Newsletter, 12 March 1967, p. 1.

77   NAA: ASIO; A6126/1106, item 3, file-note, 11 January 1967.

78   *Tribune*, 25 January 1967, p. 10; NBAC: E192/9/4, NTCAR Newsletter 12 March 1967, p. 1.

79   F. Stevens, *Aborigines in the Northern Territory Cattle Industry*, ANU Press, Canberra, 1974, pp. 3–9.

80   Stevens, *Aborigines in the Northern Territory Cattle Industry*, pp. 159, 164.

81   NAA: ASIO; A6119/3187 Attachment – STEVENS, Francis Seymour [is an attachment to his original ASIO file], 'ASIO and I: Frank Stevens and His ASIO Records', fourth draft of manuscript, 2004.

82   W. Hedley, 'Man to the north', in *Identity*, Realist, Melbourne, 1968 [her first book of poetry]. *Tribune* published the poem on 5 October 1966, p. 5.

Notes to Chapter Nine

1   Minister for Social Services and Aboriginal Affairs William Wentworth MHR, Australia, House of Representatives, vol. 60, 13 August 1968, p. 19.

2   From this point, Wattie Creek is usually referred to as Daguragu.

3   *Tribune*, 19 April 1967, p. 1.

4   NAA: ASIO; A6119/4938, item 7, report about Hardy, 4 April 1967.

5   F. Hardy, *The Unlucky Australians*, Nelson, Melbourne, 1968, pp. 173–4.

6   F. Hardy, 'Strike in the north', *Nation*, 29 October 1966, p. 13.

7   NAA: ASIO; A6119/4938, item 7.

8   Australia, House of Representatives, vol. 53, 27 October 1966, p. 2,359.

9   Petition to Lord Casey, Governor-General of Australia, from the Gurindji Spokesmen, April 1967, at <http://www.indigenousrights.net.au/files/f23.pdf>, accessed 31 August 2012.

10   Australia, House of Representatives, vol. 55, 20 April 1967, pp. 1,475–6.

11   Casey's Response to Gurindji Petition, 20 June 1967, < http://www. indigenousrights.net.au/files/f46.pdf >, accessed 31 August 2012.

12   FCAATSI statement, in *Tribune*, 9 August 1967, p. 4.

13   D. B. Rose, *Hidden Histories: Black Stories From Victoria River Downs, Humbert River and Wave Hill Stations*, Aboriginal Studies Press, Canberra, 1991, p. 227.

14   R. Francis, B. Scates & A. McGrath, 'Broken silences? Labour history and Aboriginal workers', in T. Irving (ed.), *Challenges to Labour History*, UNSW Press, Sydney, 1994, p. 205.

15   B. Attwood, 'The articulation of "land rights" in Australia: the case of Wave Hill', *Social Analysis*, issue 44, no. 1, 2000, p. 9.

16   C. D. Rowley, *The Remote Aborigines*, Penguin, Melbourne, 1972, p. 342.

17   M. Hokari, 'Cross-culturalizing history: journey to the Gurindji way of historical practice', PhD thesis, Australian National University, Canberra, 2001, pp. 129, 133–7. Jimmy Mangayarri also told Hokari that President Kennedy had jetted in to Wave Hill, met with Moray, then pledged US support for the Gurindji campaign – p. 143.

18   Hokari, 'Cross-culturalizing history', pp. 137, 142.

19   Hokari, 'Cross-culturalizing history', p. 149.

20   *Tribune*, 3 May 1967, p. 3.

21   F. Bandler, *Turning the Tide: A Personal History of the Federal Council for the Advancement of Aborigines and Torres Strait Islanders*, Aboriginal Studies Press, Canberra, 1989, pp. 171–3.

22   CPA, *Full Human Rights for Aborigines and Torres Strait Islanders*, D. B. Young, Sydney, 1967; *Tribune*, 19 April 1967, pp. 9–13. This program (adopted at the Party's 21st Congress in 1967) was largely an updated version of the 1964 policy.

23   CPA, *Full Human Rights for Aborigines and Torres Strait Islanders*, p. 17.

24   *Tribune*, 19 April 1967, pp. 15–16.

25   *Tribune*, 21 June 1967, p. 4.

26   B. Manning, in Hardy, *The Unlucky Australians*, pp. 220–1.

27   NAA: ASIO; A6119/4938, item 10, report, 4 June 1967.

28   Australia, House of Representatives, vol. 56, 6 September 1967, pp. 872–3.

29   Australia, House of Representatives, vol. 83, 5 April 1973, p. 1,179.

30   *Tribune*, 26 July 1967, p. 2.

31   *Tribune*, 11 October 1967, p. 4.

32   Hardy, *The Unlucky Australians*, pp. 239–40.

33   D. Daniels, in Hardy, *The Unlucky Australians*, pp. 243–4; *Tribune*, 13 December 1967, p. 1.

34   *Tribune*, 24 April 1968, p. 1.

35   NBAC: E192/9/4, letter, Sadler to NAWU Aboriginal Fund, 10 October 1967.

36   *Tribune*, 15 May 1968, p. 3.

37   *Tribune*, 26 June 1968, p. 3.

38   *Tribune*, 3 July 1968, p. 12.

39   NAA: Department of the Cabinet Office; A5882/CO98 [no item number], Cabinet Submission: NT Land for Gurindji people, 7 May 1968.

40   ibid.

41   NAA: Department of the Cabinet Office; A5882/CO98 [no item number], letters from De Vos to Nixon, 17 and 22 April 1968.

42   *Tribune*, 10 July 1968, p. 12.

43   *Tribune*, 17 July 1968, p. 1.

44   *Tribune*, 21 August 1968, p. 10. An article in the *Australian* (26 July) also identified Gibbs as the very unofficial messenger relaying the government decision.

45   *Age* [editorial], 12 July 1968, p. 2.

46   *Canberra Times*, 12 July 1968, p. 2; *Australian*, 12 July 1968, p. 2; *Sydney Morning Herald*, 12 July 1968, p. 2.

47   NAA: ASIO; A6119/2590, items 141–3, report, 12 July 1968.

48   *Tribune*, 24 July 1968, p. 9.

49   *Tribune*, 31 July 1968, p. 1.

50   *Tribune*, 7 August 1968, p. 6.

51   *Tribune*, 7 August 1968, p. 12; 21 August, p. 10.

52   *Tribune*, 14 August 1968, pp. 1, 4.

53   *Tribune*, 28 August 1968, p. 5.

54   NAA: ASIO; A6119/2590, item 125, report, 12–14 April 1968.

55   *Tribune*, 18 September 1968, p. 3.

56   *Tribune*, 18 December 1968, p. 2.

57   NAA: Department of Territories; A452/1961/3211, items 7–12, report on 1968 FCAATSI Executive [date unknown, but written post-April 1968].

58   *Tribune*, 18 December 1968, p. 2.

59   *Tribune*, 11 March 1970, pp. 10, 12.

60   *Tribune*, 18 March 1970, p. 1.

61   *Tribune*, 1 April 1970, p. 12.

62   *Tribune*, 15 October 1969, p. 3.

63   *Tribune*, 19 November 1969, p. 7.

64   *Tribune*, 8 April 1970, p. 12.

65   NAA: Department of External Affairs; M251/22 Part 2, items 101–10, Anti-Slavery Society report, Jan–Feb 1970.

66   NAA: Department of External Affairs; M4251/22 Part 2, item 100, Montgomery report summary, Jan–Feb 1970.

67   NAA: Department of External Affairs; M4251/22 Part 2, item 166, press release, 23 July 1970.

68   NAA: Department of External Affairs; M4251/22 Part 2, item 169, Wentworth to McMahon, 31 July 1970.

69   NAA: Department of External Affairs; M4251/22 Part 2, item 166, Wentworth to McMahon, 25 September 1970.

70   NAA: Department of the Cabinet Office; A5882/CO98 [no item number], petition, 8 October 1970.

71   NAA: Department of the Cabinet Office; A5882/ CO98 [no item number], Cabinet Submission, 8 October 1970.

72   ibid.

73   NAA: Department of External Affairs; M4251/22 Part 2 [no item number], personal letter, Wentworth to McMahon, 12 October 1970.

74   NAA: Department of External Affairs; M4251/22 Part 2 [no item number], official letter, Wentworth to McMahon, 12 October 1970.

75   Australia, House of Representatives, vol. 71, 18 March 1971, p. 1,125.

76   *Tribune*, 15 July 1970, p. 12.

77   A. Curthoys, *Freedom Ride: A Freedom Rider Remembers*, Allen & Unwin, Sydney, 2002, pp. 306–7.

78   *Tribune*, 22 July 1970, pp. 1, 5.

79   *Tribune*, 29 July 1970, p. 1.

80   *Tribune*, 22 July 1970, p. 5.

81   *Tribune*, 22 July 1970, p. 2.

82   *Tribune*, 11 March 1970, p. 10; 22 July 1970, p. 10.

83   *Tribune*, 5 August 1970, p. 1.

84   *Tribune*, 5 August 1970, p. 12.

85   *Tribune*, 12 August 1970, p. 12.

86   *Tribune*, 26 August 1970, p. 4.

87   *Tribune*, 2 September 1970, pp. 1, 3.

88   L. Riddett, 'The strike that became a land rights movement: a southern "do-gooder" reflects on Wattie Creek 1966–74', *Labour History*, no. 72, 1997, p. 55.

89   *Tribune*, 9 December 1970, p. 2.

90   *Tribune*, 14 October 1970, p. 5.

91   *Tribune*, 5 May 1971, p. 7.

92   *Tribune*, 22 September 1971, p. 7.

93   *Tribune*, 8 December 1971, p. 10.

94   *Tribune*, 8–14 February 1972, p. 3.

95   *Tribune*, 16 June 1971, p. 3.

96   *Tribune*, 17 November 1971, p. 1. The amount raised by the WWF may have been misreported by *Tribune*. Riddett referred to the amount as $17,000, and raised via union levies – 'The strike that became a land rights movement', p. 62.

97   Australia, House of Representatives, vol. 76, 23 February 1972, p. 108.

98   *Tribune*, 23–29 May 1972, p. 5; 4–10 July 1972, p. 6.

99   *Tribune*, 30 May–5 June 1972, p. 5.

100   *Tribune*, 25–31 July 1972, p. 1; 1–7 August 1972, p. 10.

101   *Tribune*, 19–25 September 1972, p. 12; 28 November–4 December 1972, p. 2.

102   Australia, House of Representatives, vol. 76, 23 February 1972, pp. 122–9.

103   Australia, House of Representatives, vol. 76, 23 February 1972, pp. 129, 133.

104   *Tribune*, 19–25 September 1972, p. 6.

105   *Tribune*, 21–27 March 1972, p. 12.

106   *Tribune*, 23–29 May 1972, p. 5.

107   *Tribune*, 16–22 May 1972, p. 11.

108   *Tribune*, 13–19 June 1972, p. 7.

109   *Tribune*, 13–19 June 1972, p. 7.

110   W. E. H. Stanner, 'Industrial justice in the never-never', *The Australian Quarterly*, vol. 39, no. 1, March 1967, p. 51.

111   NAA: Cabinet Office; A5882/CO98 [no item number], Department of Prime Minister and Cabinet, Cabinet briefing paper and recommendation re. Wave Hill and Wattie Creek, 18 August 1972.

112   NAA: Cabinet Office; A5882/CO98 [no item number], Cabinet decision No. 1303 (AA), 24 August 1972.

113   A. Markus, *Australian Race Relations 1788–1993*, Allen & Unwin, Sydney, 1994, p. 183.

114   ACTU Congress, 'Resolution of the 1973 Congress of the Australian Council of Trade Unions in respect to Aborigines', reproduced in H. Middleton's *But Now We Want the Land Back: A History of the Australian Aboriginal People*, New Age Publishers, Sydney, 1977, pp. 178–81.

115   Riddett, 'The strike that became a land rights movement', p. 54.

Notes to Chapter Ten

1   Australia, House of Representatives, vol. 70, 20 October 1970, p. 2,508.

2   *Tribune*, 29 November 1967, p. 5.

3   ibid.

4   *Tribune*, 6 December 1967, p. 8.

5   ibid. Jeffrey's account of this story is also included in Hardy's *The Unlucky Australians*, p. 164.

6   *Tribune*, 13 December 1967, p. 8.

7   ibid.

8   B. Manning, email communication, 1 October 2010.

9   Australia, House of Representatives, vol. 57, 26 October 1967, pp. 2,301, 2,306, 2,316–17. The Jeffrey 'controversy' was reported in the *Australian* and Melbourne's *Herald* on 27 October 1967.

10   T. Egan, *Sitdown Up North*, Kerr Publishing, Sydney, 1997, pp. 262–3.

11   P. Kelly, *Paul Kelly: Don't Start Me Talking, Lyrics 1984–1999*, Allen & Unwin, Sydney, 1999, pp. 107–8.

12   Egan, *Sitdown Up North*, p. 252; T. Egan, *The Aboriginals Songbook*, Greenhouse Publications, Melbourne, 1987, p. 77.

13   Egan, 'Gurindji blues', in *The Aboriginals Songbook*, pp. 78–9. All profits from the song recorded by Egan and Galarrwuy Yunupingu aided the Tent Embassy

a few years later – Egan, *Sitdown Up North*, pp. 252, 262–3. It was also included in the *Builders' Labourers' Song Book*, Widescope, Melbourne, 1975, pp. 12–13.

14   *Tribune*, 14–20 November 1972, p. 7.

15   B. Manning, email communication, 18 September 2012.

16   Australia, House of Representatives, vol. 70, 20 October 1970, p. 2,508.

17   *Tribune*, 29 July 1970, p. 8.

18   NAA: ASIO; A6119/4270, item 66, phone tap transcript, Mounsey and Salmon, 18 August 1970.

19   Egan, 'Gurindji Blues', in *The Aboriginals Songbook*, p. 79.

20   P. Fox, in D'Abbs, *The Vestey Story*, Australasian Meat Industry Employees' Union, Victorian Branch, Melbourne, 1970, pp. 47–50.

21   *Tribune*, 9 December 1970, p. 5.

22   H. Middleton, 'A Marxist at Wattie Creek: fieldwork among Australian Aborigines', in C. Bell & S. Encel (eds.), *Inside the Whale: Ten Personal Accounts of Social Research*, Pergamon Press, Sydney, 1978, p. 239.

23   NAA: Department of the Cabinet Office; A5882/C098, Cabinet Submission: Wattie Creek, 8 October 1970.

24   Middleton, 'Marxist at Wattie Creek', pp. 241, 246.

25   NAA: Attorney General's Department; A432/1969/2615, item 14, Spry to Department of Interior, 3 May 1968.

26   NAA: Attorney General's Department; A432/1969/2615, item 1, Department of Territories to Prime Minister's Department, 10 May 1968.

27   Australia, House of Representatives, vol. 59, 4 June 1968, p. 1,886.

28   L. Riddett, 'The strike that became a land rights movement: a southern "do-gooder" reflects on Wattie Creek 1966–74', *Labour History*, no. 72, 1997, pp. 57, 59.

29   J. Mangayarri, in M. Hokari, 'Cross-culturalizing history: journey to the Gurindji way of historical practice', PhD thesis, Australian National University, Canberra, 2001, p. 93.

30   Rose, *Hidden Histories: Black Stories From Victoria River Downs, Humbert River and Wave Hill Stations*, Aboriginal Studies Press, Canberra, 1991, p. 141.

31   Riddett, 'The strike that became a land rights movement', pp. 59–61.

32   ibid.

33   ibid.

34   NAA: ASIO; A6126/1278, item 13, report, 20 December 1971.

35   NAA: ASIO; A6126/1278, items 7 and 8, 27 May and 19 June 1971.

36   NAA: ASIO; A6126/1278, item 5, file-note, 29 June 1971.

37   Australia, House of Representatives, vol. 75, 9 & 10 December 1971, pp. 4,519–20.

38   ibid.

39   P. Nitschke, interview with the author, 4 August 2011.

40   ibid.

41   F. Hollows, *Fred Hollows: An Autobiography; With Peter Corris*, Kerr Publishing, Sydney, 1993, pp. 87–90.

42   Hollows, *Fred Hollows*, pp. 94, 105–6.

43   *Tribune*, 13 August 1952, pp. 7–8.

44   K. S. Prichard, Endorsement of Frank Hardy for Federal seat of MacKellar, c. 1955, *Katharine Susannah Prichard Papers*, NLA, MS6201, Series 9, Box 14, Folder 4.

45   J. Hocking, *Frank Hardy: Politics, Literature, Life*, Lothian Books, Melbourne, 2005, p. 169.

46   Hocking, *Frank Hardy*, pp. 171–2.

47   *Tribune*, 24 July 1968, pp. 12–13.

48   Hokari, 'Cross-culturalizing history', pp. 128–9.

49   *Tribune*, 5 June 1968, p. 12.

50   Australia, House of Representatives, vol. 59, 28 May 1968, p. 1,609.

51   *Tribune*, 19 June 1968, p. 12.

52   *Tribune*, 26 June 1968, p. 11.

53   ibid.

54   F. Hardy, *Australian Biography* [SBS], July 1993, in Hocking, *Frank Hardy*, p. 172.

55   Hocking, *Frank Hardy*, pp. 173–5.

56   C. Holmes, *One Man's Way*, Penguin, Melbourne, 1986, p. 97.

57   D. Denoon, 'Guilt and the Gurindji', *Meanjin*, vol. 29, issue 2, 1970, pp. 253–65.

58   B. Manning, in B. Brian, 'The Northern Territory's one big union: the rise and fall of the North Australian Workers' Union, 1911–1972', PhD thesis, NT University, Darwin, 2001, p. 267.

59   Hocking, *Frank Hardy*, p. 182.

60   M. Rangiari, in Hocking, *Frank Hardy*, p. 255.

Note to the Conclusion

1   See, for example: B. Attwood, *Rights for Aborigines*, Allen & Unwin, Sydney, 2003; B. Attwood & A. Markus, *Thinking Black: William Cooper and the Australian Aborigines' League*, Aboriginal Studies Press, Canberra, 2004; J. Maynard, *Fight for Liberty and Freedom: The Origins of Australian Aboriginal Activism*, Aboriginal Studies Press, Canberra, 2007.

INDEX

www.ingramcontent.com/pod-product-compliance
Lightning Source LLC
Chambersburg PA
CBHW020332270326
41926CB00007B/150